Dunfermline Athletic On This Day

In this year of distortions, an empty East End Park is seen here through a wide-angle lens. On the cover, the same image has its width constrained.

Dunfermline Athletic On This Day

*David W. Potter
and
Gordon McKenzie*

*with a Foreword by
Duncan Simpson*

Published by:

Kennedy & Boyd
An imprint of Zeticula Ltd
Unit 13
196 Rose Street
Edinburgh
EH2 4AT
Scotland
http://www.kennedyandboyd.co.uk

First published in 2021

Text © David W. Potter and Gordon McKenzie 2021

Cover photograph © Peter Miles 2021
Photograph credits are on page 470. Every effort has been made to contact and credit original photographers. If any have been omitted please get in touch via the publisher. It will be corrected in future editions. Copyright remains in each case with the photographer.

ISBN 978-1-84921-211-3 hardback
ISBN 978-1-84921-210-6 paperback

All rights reserved.   No reproduction, copy or transmission of this publication may be made without prior written permission.

Acknowledgements

A number of people have helped in bringing this book to production. Most notably, various members of Dunfermline Athletic Heritage Trust have provided assistance and access to various items of background material, in particular, Duncan Simpson, Craig Brown and Brian Duncan.

Permission for us to use archive material from the *Dunfermline Press* was organised, and we are grateful to Ross Hart, sports reporter, for arranging this and to Simon Harris, editor, for agreeing to it.

During the Covid-19 pandemic, access to public libraries has been, by necessity, much more limited than normal. However, staff at Fife Cultural Trust, in particular Sara Kelly and Sharron McColl, have been very helpful in allowing access to the large collection of local history available in the beautiful reading room in the recently refurbished Dunfermline library.

Thanks also to David McKenzie for taking me to games when I was wee and therefore passing on the passion for football in general and Dunfermline Athletic in particular, and to those various friends with whom I have watched the Pars at grounds across Scotland. Their memories of certain games, however vague, were helpful in researching content for this book.

Foreword

I am pleased, on behalf of Dunfermline Athletic Heritage Trust, to write some words of introduction to this latest and most welcome addition to the story of Dunfermline Athletic Football Club.

Much more ought to have been written about the Pars rich and proud history, so this book will go some way to correcting the deficit. Its author, David W. Potter, is a renowned writer of Scottish sports books, perhaps most notably *The Encyclopaedia of Scottish Football*. David himself is not a Pars fan but he did call on a fervent Athletic supporter to assist him with the book. Gordon McKenzie is a member of the Dunfermline Athletic Heritage Trust group, and it was at Gordon's request that we got involved in this production.

The Trust was formed in 2014 with the aim of preserving and maintaining the history of the Dunfermline Athletic Football Club, and of promoting a better understanding of it through a wide range of educational activities. One of the ways that this can be achieved is for us to encourage more to be written about the club and David and Gordon have done just that.

The page for each day of the year formula has worked well in some of his earlier books, and the usage of football stories, combined with snippets from whatever happened to be going on in the world at that time, makes for a good and interesting read.

We are delighted to be associated with the publication of this book and we hope that it will provide many hours of pleasure for Pars fans the world over.

Duncan Simpson
Chair, Dunfermline Athletic Heritage Trust
October 2020

Contents

Acknowledgements — v
Foreword — vii
Contents — ix
Illustrations — xi
Introduction by Gordon McKenzie — xiii

July — 1
August — 37
September — 75
October — 115
November — 157
December — 193
January — 229
February — 265
March — 301
April — 339
May — 395
June — 435

Illustration Credits — 470
Index — 475

Norrie McCathie remembered

Illustrations

An empty East End Park is seen here through a wide-angle lens.	*ii*
Norrie McCathie remembered	*x*
An early picture of East End Park	*2*
Dunfermline Athletic in 1907-08.	*4*
Jock Stein	*9*
Bobby Skinner, star of 1925 -1926	*29*
Fixtures for season 1939/40	*38*
Past Players at the Centenary Game in 1985	*47*
Andy Geggan in action against East Stirlingshire in 2013	*65*
Alex Edwards	*67*
A young long-haired Jim Leishman	*76*
Charlie Dickson	*83*
Programme Cover, Fife Select against Sunderland	*87*
Action in the League Cup quarter final against Rangers in 1950	*94*
Dunfermline Athletic, season 1951-1952	*96*
Dunfermline Athletic 1949.	*101*
Kyle Turner has just scored against Partick Thistle in 2019	*103*
Sol Bamba in action against St Mirren in 2006	*106*
Dunfermline Athletic in 1981-1982.	*119*
George Peebles, 1961	*122*
Programme cover, Hibernian v Dunfermline Athletic, 1949	*127*
Willie Callaghan	*145*
Programme cover, Scottish League Cup Final, 1949	*151*
Jimmy Clarkson and George Johnstone, 1949.	*153*
Bert Paton	*163*
John Lunn	*170*
Dunfermline Athletic 1911.	*185*
Jenkins, McCathie and Watson in 1984	*203*
Moffat scores with a header against Ayr United in 2015	*208*
Programme cover, Inter Cities Fairs Cup, 1962	*216*
Programme cover, European Cup-Winners Cup, 1969	*246*
Dunfermline score against Wigtown and Bladnoch	*259*
Scott Wilson scores against Hearts in 2007	*269*
Noel Hunt about to score against Dundee United in 2004	*274*
Clearing the snow at Broadwood	*276*
Roy Barry	*288*
In the last game before the 2020 lockdown	*313*

Andy Wilson	*317*
Programme cover, CIS Insurance Cup Final, 2006	*324*
Dunfermline Athletic at the end of the Great War.	*328*
Harry Melrose has just scored in the Scottish Cup	*335*
Programme cover, Scottish Cup Semi-Final, 1968	*338*
Programme cover, Scottish Cup Semi-Final, 1961	*340*
Roy Barry exchanges pennants with the captain of Slovan Bratislava in 1969	*351*
Dunfermline Athletic Second Division Champions 1925-1926.	*353*
Gary Riddell in action in a game v St Mirren on April 16 1988.	*360*
Harry Melrose in 1961	*365*
Barry Nicholson scores against Inverness in 2004	*366*
Programme cover, Scottish Cup Final, 1961	*369*
Programme cover, Scottish Cup Final, 1965	*373*
Hardie celebrates in 2011 after scoring against Raith Rovers	*374*
Dunfermline score first goal in 1961 Scottish Cup Final replay	*377*
Dave Thomson stooped to score with a header	*379*
Jock Stein congratulates his players in 1961	*380*
Dunfermline Athletic with the Scottish Cup in 1961	*381*
That year they also won the Fife Cup and the Penman Cup	*382*
Programme cover, Scottish Cup Final, 1968	*385*
Glasgow Evening Times reports on two milestones	*386*
George Farm congratulates his players in 1968	*387*
Peter Wilson, manager of Dunfermline in 1938 and 1939	*403*
Andy Rolland scores with a penalty against Falkirk in 1979	*417*
Programme cover, Scottish Cup Final, 2007	*428*
Dunfermline Saturday Press, 1885	*442*
Bert Paton, Manager of the Month	*446*
Gary Riddell	*448*
Dunfermline Athletic in the 1890s	*453*
Lasting memories ... East End Park in more normal times.	*471*
Lasting memories ... Harry Melrose with the Scottish Cup	*473*

Introduction

In the early 1950s, my family's interest in Dunfermline Athletic began. My Grandad, a Sunderland fan who saw his side beat Preston North End at Wembley to win the 1937 FA Cup, moved from the North-East of England to Fife to take work at Rosyth Dockyard. A football fan all his life, it was only a matter of time before he'd take the Pars as his adopted team, the real trigger being a decade later with the famous 1961 cup win. He took my Dad for the first time when Everton were beaten at East End Park and, in passing the bug to my Dad, there was no going back.

I'm unashamedly jealous of them both, and of everyone else who saw the great teams of the 1960s. However, although that famous era will always be huge in the story of the club, that decade forms only one part of the history of Dunfermline Athletic. Whatever age we happen to be, we all have our memories – good, bad and bizarre. And we all have emotions bound up in what happens out on the park in front of us. All clubs have their ups and downs, but as one of those with a higher than average number of promotions and relegations, it could be argued that Dunfermline have had more than most.

When I heard that David was intending to write this book, along similar lines to those he's already done about other clubs, I was very interested and gave some suggestions on things to include. It was a bit of a surprise to then be asked if I'd be interested in writing some sections of it. As I got more into it, I realized that the collection of events in the book is really just a tribute to all those memories and emotions from the past, be they memories of our own or memories of others as they committed them to print in years past. There are mentions of many good days – I'll tell anyone about Marc Millar's penalty against Airdrie in 1996 – but also plenty of horrible ones. Scottish Cup loss to East Stirlingshire in 1984 and the Cowdenbeath play-off – they're both here as well.

Although the bad days are incredibly hard to take at the time, the pain of them dies through time and I surely can't be alone in looking back and smiling at some of them. As a club firmly established in what the legendary Bob Crampsey described as the 'middle order' of Scottish football, it's unlikely the Pars will ever win the league or get very far in Europe. So, we might as well embrace what we have for what it is, and celebrate that ridiculous collection of memories our love of football has given us. Many people who don't like football sneer at those of us who do – let them sneer, I say. Standing in an enclosure at Elgin, under a rickety corrugated iron roof while the rain hammers down on a grim November Scottish Cup Saturday with the side from the higher division away from home – if someone doesn't understand why that can be the most romantic thing in the world, they probably aren't worth listening to.

Maybe you think this is soppy, emotional nonsense? If so, I agree. But, football has always been a vehicle for soppy, emotional nonsense, and is by far the better for it. Dunfermline Athletic is part of that, and while football at East End Park is rarely top standard, the emotions and memories each of us hold most certainly are. Memories not just of the football on the park, but of what else happened and the people around us that day. I have fond memories of a 3-2 defeat at Brechin – a sore last minute loss after being 2-0 up, but I loved the chat and piss-taking with two elderly Brechin fans beside us on the hedge side who insisted on handshakes at the end of the game. I also have good memories of my Grandad being really happy when the Pars team took to the park in red – with his Sunderland sympathies, he always found black and white stripes a bit difficult!

Hopefully this book does justice to some of these, and maybe even reawakens others.

Gordon McKenzie
Dysart
September 2020

July

An early picture of East End Park

July 1 1916

Today is generally believed to have been the worst day in the history of the British Army. It was, of course, the first day of the Battle of the Somme with casualties on an almost unbelievable scale illustrating some astounding incompetence and indifference on the part of the British officers. And the finger must be pointed unwaveringly at Field Marshal Douglas Haig, a man who claimed some tenuous Fife connections.

Typical of the devastating loss of young life was a young man called David Izatt who had played for Dunfermline Athletic as a half back before the war. He enlisted in the Royal Scots just shortly after the war started and was able to play the occasional game in the 1914/15 season when he was still doing his basic training. He was only 24.

He was a local boy who was a plumber by trade and who worked with A. Rolland and Co. His father William Izatt was still alive and lived at 33 Chalmers Street. He is commemorated on the Thiepval Memorial on the Somme.

It is perhaps the most graphic comment on this colossal disaster that although David was certainly killed on that dreadful first day of July, it was nearer the end of the month before relatives could be informed and news released of his death. It had taken so long to find, to disentangle, re-assemble and identify the remains.

David Izatt was the best-known Dunfermline casualty, but he was far from the only man of the town or indeed the only football player to have met his death on this dreadful day.

Dunfermline Athletic in 1907-08. Players: Back row - Herd, Inglis, Spittal, McLaughlan; Front Row - Pithlado, Livingston, Grier, Brown, Anderson, McDougall, Fraser.

July 2 1908

It was not the best of summers for Dunfermline Athletic.

They had been unsuccessful in their attempts to join the Scottish League Second Division – a particularly sore blow because neighbours Raith Rovers and Cowdenbeath were now members, and people asked why a town like Dunfermline did not have a team in this League.

They were forced to play in the Northern League. The problem was that Dunfermline were the furthest south team; every away fixture therefore involved a long and expensive train journey, with no guarantee of any kind of financial windfall in games against Forfar and Aberdeen Reserves.

It was for these reasons that the officials of the club had to announce with regret that they were forced to shelve, for the time being at least, plans for the erection of a grandstand at East End Park. It was just too expensive.

On the other hand, they had secured the services of a goal-scoring forward in Ben Sutherland, from Raith Rovers.

The only way to make any difference to the club's current mediocrity would be to win the Northern League, and possibly enjoy an eye-catching run in the Scottish Qualifying Cup and the Scottish Cup itself. Such things might just make a difference in their future applications to join the Scottish League.

There were also moves afoot to join a Central League, something which might alleviate the travel problems of the club. The uncertainty about the club's position was not really reflected in the town or the country at large, where the Liberals, in power, were introducing with some determination and intelligence some much needed social reforms, including mind-boggling things like free school meals and old age pensions!

July 3 1921

It is reported today that a couple of Dunfermline's Directors are to set out to Middlesbrough, cheque book in hand, determined to do business.

Andy Wilson, of course, is a Middlesbrough player now that Dunfermline are in the official Scottish League Division Two but that does not mean that Dunfermline cannot make a bid to bring him back.

There have also been rumours that Jock (sometimes called Jack) Marshall, a Scottish International full back, was unsettled at Middlesbrough and Dunfermline also intended to make a bid for him.

They certainly needed a full back now that Arthur McInally had gone. But not for the first or last time, it became apparent that Dunfermline simply did not have the money to compete with English teams, and Marshall and Wilson preferred football at the Boro over the joys of the new Scottish Second Division.

Wilson at the moment was in the USA with an unofficial Scottish International team and could only be contacted by cablegram. He was, in addition to other things, a war hero and when he went to Montreal, there were plans to honour him.

Third Lanark meanwhile showed what they thought of this Scottish tour by summoning their players home. It was now July and the players were now under a new contract to Third Lanark who were thus legally entitled to demand that they should do this!

The players needed to rest before the start of the new season which would now also contain automatic relegation and promotion between the First and Second Divisions.

July 4 1924

The AGM of Dunfermline Athletic FC was held last night in the committee room of the St Margaret's Hall. There were causes for concern.

The loss of £207 over the year was a substantial one in 1924, the main reason being that income through the turnstiles had dropped nearly £938.

An early exit in the Scottish Cup at home to Arbroath had been a major cause for earnings being lost. The team had finished seventh in the Scottish League Second Division, which had been a reasonable performance.

What really hurt was that rivals Cowdenbeath, "the Miners" as they called themselves, would be playing in the First Division next year as they had finished second behind St Johnstone.

The people of Dunfermline felt entitled to ask the question why their town, a far larger one than Cowdenbeath, would not be hosting big games against Celtic and Rangers next season whereas Cowdenbeath would.

Raith Rovers had finished fourth in the First Division as well, and to the west, Falkirk, another town of similar size, was doing better than Dunfermline.

All these points were no doubt discussed by the shareholders and supporters at this meeting, but Secretary Willie Knight, the man who ran the playing side of the club, was able to announce that 10 players had been signed for the start of the season – Paterson, Baird, McCleary and Sutton from last year and six new players.

The two retiring Directors, John Fraser and Thomas Burns, indicated their willingness to serve again and were duly re-elected. The start of the season was little more than a month in the future.

July 5 1975

Dunfermline fans were as shocked as anyone when they heard of the road accident involving Jock Stein in the early hours of this Saturday morning.

He had been driving up the M74 when returning from a holiday in Minorca when his Mercedes had been hit by a Peugeot driving on the wrong side of the road.

In the car were also his wife Jeanie, Mr and Mrs Bob Shankly, one time Manager of Dundee and Hibs, and Tony Queen the Bookmaker.

Stein needed an emergency operation at the newly opened Dumfries Hospital, and for several days his life was in danger.

Prayers were said for him in various Churches in Dunfermline the following day, for he was well remembered and loved for his time in Dunfermline from 1960 until 1964.

During this time he had pulled Dunfermline up from being a poorly-supported under-performing club, in perennial danger of relegation, into Scottish Cup winners and one of the leading lights of the game — with not a few fine European performances to their credit as well.

The highlight of course remained the Scottish Cup triumph in 1961, something that was still fondly remembered by everyone old enough. Jock would thankfully recover, but he would be out of the game for the whole of the 1975/76 season; because of this Celtic would struggle, failing to win any of the three Scottish trophies that year.

Stein would come back however, to the great relief of everyone, but those close to him say that he was never quite the same after that accident, even though he later managed Scotland and took them to the World Cup of 1982.

Jock Stein

July 6 1939

One would have to be a supreme optimist in summer 1939 to believe that war was not approaching, for the signs were all over the place with air raid shelters being planned and defences being strengthened at Rosyth dockyard and other places.

The good news about this was that most people now had a job; the horrible days of the economic depression of the early 1930s were over.

However, the general atmosphere, even in the glorious weather, was one of gloomy foreboding, although those who clutched at straws pointed out that a military alliance between Great Britain and the Soviet Union might yet deter Hitler.

Meanwhile there were signs that football would soon be back. 1939 had been good, but not good enough for Dunfermline with the sight of Cowdenbeath winning the Second Division a sore one! The fixtures for 1939/40 were issued today. Dunfermline would open their season with a trip to Stenhousemuir on August 12.

Meanwhile the Board had elected Robert Wylie to be the new Chairman, although there was no change in personnel of the Board. On the playing front, Manager Peter Wilson announced that he is quite happy with the new signings that he had made, except for the inside right position. "I would be glad to hear from any possible candidates" he said with a twinkle in his eye.

A scheme was also announced to find more money for the club with various funds to be opened for supporters and local businesses to contribute. In particular, there was an appeal for a local business to become interested in the building of a new stand.

July 7 1915

Today the officials of Dunfermline Athletic received official intimation of something that they had known or suspected for some time, namely that their ground at East End Park would be required for military purposes.

Under the terms of DORA (Defence of the Realm Act) brought in last year, there was little that the club could do about it other than to make a protest. The military were unlikely to change their mind.

All this meant that if Dunfermline were to continue playing (and that was a big "if"), it would have to be at some other ground. That need not necessarily be an insuperable problem, but it did mean that they would be much diminished in terms of attracting players and supporters.

The other worry of course was the long term damage that might be done to their ground by the soldiers. It was widely believed that the ground might be used to train horses. If this were so, who knows what permanent harm might be done to the turf?

The future of their football club was nevertheless far from the main preoccupation of the Dunfermline population. The war was now nearly a year old, and there was as yet no sign of any breakthrough in Europe.

Hard though the newspapers tried to put a positive spin on it, it was difficult to believe anything other than that the Dardanelles campaign was a colossal disaster. Good news and laughter were hard to find, but at least the cinemas were functioning and Charlie Chaplin was always guaranteed to put a smile on most faces.

July 8 1947

Dunfermline's Manager Willie McAndrew today was happy to announce that he had signed on left winger Davie Kinnear for season 1947-48.

Kinnear was one of the few players who had endeared himself last season, with a run of consistent performances impressing the fans to the surprise of those who felt that the Second World War had finished his career after his halcyon years with Rangers in the 1930s.

McAndrew now felt that he had his squad in place for the new season, and Kinnear would be joining the squad when the training started again in a couple of weeks' time.

Dunfermline had not recovered from the Second World War as well as some other sides, and the supporters were far from happy with the position. Willie McAndrew had only been in position a matter of months, but there were other problems as well, not least those of money but also the fact that as rationing was still in force, it was difficult to buy new strips, for example.

New football boots were almost impossible to come by, so players of all teams would take the field wearing boots that had been well cossetted and looked after for a period of many years!

And yet the situation was improving in some ways. Full employment had more or less been implemented since the end of the war, all the soldiers and sailors were home, and crowds had been high last season. Now everyone, even in the middle of summer, talked about football!

The new season would be an important one for Dunfermline with a return to the First Division an absolute necessity.

July 9 1922

Dunfermline today announced their fixtures for next season, their second season in the revamped post-war Scottish Second Division.

They had not done all that well in the first season, but the fact that it had been won by Alloa, a team not all that far away geographically from Dunfermline and one that had a smaller catchment area than Dunfermline, was a source of some encouragement to the belief that Dunfermline could do it sometime.

The opening three fixtures looked interesting. The first was a trip to Hampden to play Queen's Park, a team who even as early as 1922 were looked upon as being out of kilter with everyone else for staying amateur.

Then the home season opened with the visit of Dumbarton before, in early September, a local derby against Cowdenbeath.

Manager Willie Knight told everyone that he was working hard to sign new players, but everyone knew that there was not a great deal of money forthcoming.

There was total unanimity among the support that what was really lacking at East End Park was the much lamented Andy Wilson, but there was still reflected glory in how well he was continuing to do for Scotland.

The war had now been over for the best part of four years, but times were still hard with unemployment, labour problems and the all-pervasive presence of so many limbless young men who were paying a high price for the so-called victory.

No-one seriously thought that a successful football team at East End Park would in any way alleviate anyone's suffering, but it would certainly be a change! Raith Rovers had finished third in the First Division in 1922 – and that undeniably hurt everyone in Dunfermline.

July 10 1952

The Courier this morning announced that Dunfermline Athletic had made a loss of £1436 over the last financial year.

This was clearly not good news for supporters, and it meant that new Manager Bobby Ancell would not have a great deal of money to bring in new players.

The team had reached fifth place in the Second Division in 1952, by no means a disaster but clearly well below the expectations of supporters, particularly as both Raith Rovers and East Fife were now doing a great deal better and were both respectably placed in the First Division.

The total gate money came to £19,000 but players' wages took about half of that, and there were so many other overheads in terms of rates etc., not to mention the transfer fees for players and money that had to be paid to visiting teams and referees.

Yet, there was still a residue of goodwill towards the team, and it was not all that long ago that they had contested a League Cup final, so it was not all gloom.

Things generally had improved since the War with rationing more or less over, and an air of optimism was widespread with an era of full employment now with us. Houses were being built, and prosperity was in the air – although it had clearly not yet reached East End Park!

The League Cup had been drawn and the Pars were in the same section as Kilmarnock, Arbroath and Alloa with the opening game at Gayfield on August 9.

July 11 1940

The Annual General Meeting of Dunfermline Athletic FC took place tonight where the Chairman announced a loss of £81 for season 1939/40.

In the circumstances, this was by no means surprising; indeed it compared favourably with season 1938/39, when the loss was a great deal more than that.

But the main problem was what was going to happen to the Pars next season. The British Empire was now alone it its stance against Nazi Germany, France having surrendered about three weeks ago, and an invasion was expected any time now.

So, what was going to be the future of Scottish football? The Scottish Football League intended to continue with 16 teams, but they did not include any Fife team or any from north of the river Tay.

It would eventually call itself the Southern League, and would be a success of sorts in the West of Scotland. Dunfermline, like other clubs in the area, did not seem to have anywhere to go.

In time, a League for local teams would be formed, but for the coming season, it was beginning to look as if there would be no Dunfermline Athletic. They did in fact manage to play a few local friendlies, but there was no League or Cup, and the players were at liberty to join other clubs if they wished.

But the AGM tonight finished on a typical 1940 note of defiance, the atmosphere being that the short-term future was far from promising but that there was a determination to get through the crisis – and crisis there was, as the heavily protected Rosyth Dockyard indicated.

July 12 1967

Rumours which had been spreading round all of Fife were confirmed today when it was announced that Manager George Farm was leaving Raith Rovers to take charge of Dunfermline Athletic.

Farm had been chosen from over 30 applicants after Willie Cunningham had said that he wanted a break from football. This was a major blow for Raith Rovers because Farm had just led them to promotion to the First Division, and many of their supporters criticised their Directors for not making more of an effort to keep him.

On the other hand, Dunfermline Athletic were definitely a better option in terms of ambition. Dunfermline had a better ground, a bigger support, more money and crucially greater expectations.

It would indeed turn out to be a smart career move. Farm would lead the Pars to a Scottish Cup success in 1968 followed by a good run in Europe the year after, although he would return to Raith for a less successful spell in the early 1970s.

Farm was famously outspoken and "never took any prisoners". He was also single-minded, dedicated, occasionally brusque and reputedly difficult to get on with, but the Pars directors felt he was worth taking a risk with.

He had been a great goalkeeper in his time, playing for Queen of the South and earning caps for Scotland, but his most famous occasion was the "Stanley Matthews" English Cup final of 1953 when he kept goal for Blackpool as they beat Bolton Wanderers 4-3.

Also at one point in his life he worked as a lighthouse keeper!

July 13 1968

The Dunfermline Press today reported on the fatal accident inquiry that took place following the death of a fan at the last game of the season between Scottish Cup winners Dunfermline and league champions Celtic.

The enquiry ended abruptly following objections by DAFC and the Chief Constable as to the relevance of the evidence being led, with the Sheriff directing the jury to return a formal verdict that death was caused by a fall from a roof that took place outside the boundary of the football ground.

However, the court proceedings prior to this do give an idea of attitudes towards fan safety at the time. The Burgh Engineer told the inquiry that there was no legislation to calculate the safe capacity of a ground and that no license was required from the local council.

Capacity had been estimated by allowing a width of 18 inches per person on each step of terracing which, by modern standards, seems absurdly tight.

Why was this relevant? The man who died so tragically had been climbing out of the ground because it was so cramped that he could not see the pitch.

What is most striking is that from comments made by architects, it is clear that East End Park compared favourably with other grounds: "For the last 10 years, we have carried out a steady programme of investment for spectators and our firm have been impressed by the Club's anxiety for the safety of spectators".

It may have been a game everyone wanted to see and traffic delays meaning many arrived late, but the collapse of crush barriers in the north-east corner seems to show that the area was overcrowded. It is perhaps fortunate that East End Park is not synonymous with a crush that resulted in many deaths.

July 14 2019

Bastille Day (an event in the French Revolution of 1789) is indeed a very early day to start a football season, but this was what Dunfermline did today.

In the Scottish League Cup, at the new St Mirren Park in Paisley, Stevie Crawford's men got proceedings underway with a good 3-2 win over Premiership St Mirren.

The crowd was just over 2,000, the bulk of them being Buddies there to see the first game under the charge of Jim Goodwin who had been appointed manager only two weeks before.

The Irishman had of course played for the Saints and had until recently been the successful manager of Alloa, but today the Pars got the better of him.

In a blistering first half, Dunfermline scored three times with goals from Ryan Dow, Andy Ryan and Tom Beadling. All three goals were the result of some sort of mistake in the St Mirren defence, but credit is due to Dunfermline for being sharp and slick enough to take advantage.

It is often believed that players need some time to adjust to the start of the season, but it was clear that on this occasion, the pre-season had been a success.

But it was only half time, and St Mirren came back into it, scoring twice in two minutes through Cody Cooke and Danny Mullen, to the alarm of the Dunfermline support who had been rather enjoying the game up to that point.

St Mirren now piled on the pressure to get a draw and the penalty shoot-out that it would have brought, but Dunfermline held on, even though in "kitchen sink" time, St Mirren sent their Czech goalkeeper Vaclav Hadky up to try to score a goal from a set piece.

July 15 2017

In a slightly unreal atmosphere at East End Park because of the early start to the season, Dunfermline Athletic today beat Second Division Elgin City 6-0 in the opening game of the Scottish League Cup section before a crowd of 1757.

This had followed a slightly disappointing pre-season, but today the men from Morayshire were put to the sword. This was Elgin's first visit to East End Park since their admission to the SFL in 2000, their only previous visit being for a Scottish Cup tie in 1983 as a Highland League side.

The hero of the hour was undeniably Nicky Clark who scored a hat-trick before half-time then another goal immediately afterwards. His first half hat-trick were all headers and simple ones as well with the Elgin men clearly all at sea. Michael Paton scored another goal in the first half and Callum Smith added the sixth.

Joe Cardle also missed a few chances, and if they had been going flat out, Dunfermline might well have reached double figures. Clearly this result in itself against poor opposition did not mean very much at all, but it did at least build up some confidence for the season ahead.

Qualifying for the League Cup quarter final would mean a lot for the club, but a more difficult assignment now awaited on Tuesday night against East Fife.

Manager Allan Johnston stressed the need not to read too much into one result, but enthused about the quality of the crosses and the form of Nicky Clark. There would certainly be tougher tests to come at East End Park this season.

July 16 2016

Having been promoted in May, there was excitement around East End Park.

Dunfermline tonight opened the 2016/17 season with a competent 3-0 win over Arbroath in the Scottish League Cup. The League Cup, which for a period in the 80s and 90s had drawn large crowds, had suffered a drop in interest in recent years, leading to a new format being trialled this season with the first round played in groups of five teams.

Well-known former player and manager Dick Campbell was in the away dugout tonight, Arbroath being his latest managerial appointment after a long recent spell at Forfar.

Dunfermline's players showed him little sympathy, although as often happens in the first game of the season, it took a long time for the action to start.

Quite a few of the 1,974 crowd on this lovely balmy evening were queuing for their half-time pies when Dunfermline scored first, mainly through a calamitous error from Arbroath's goalkeeper, Robbie Mutch, which left Michael Moffat with the easiest of chances.

The game picked up a little in the second half, but the Pars were always well on top of the League Two side and two further goals were scored by tap-ins from Andy Geggan and Michael Moffat again after some fine build-up play.

Newcomer Kallum Higginbotham came on in the second half and made an impressive debut and, generally speaking, there was little to be unhappy about on this fine, warm night.

Ominously, though, news arrived that Dundee United had thrashed Cowdenbeath 6-1. They would clearly be a difficult team to beat, and there was also Inverness Caledonian Thistle in this group. It was not the easiest of sections, but tonight's performance gave some grounds for hope and optimism.

July 17 2019

Dunfermline tonight dished out a severe thrashing to Albion Rovers in the Scottish League Cup at East End Park.

The score was 6-0 but in fact it should have been a lot more than that. It led Albion Rovers boss Kevin Harper to declare that it was one of the worst humiliations he had suffered in his admittedly brief managerial career; he compared it with several doings he had received as a player, notably one while playing for Hibs against Rangers where the scoreline was similar.

Tonight the wee Rovers were simply swept aside by Steve Crawford's very impressive young side, and the goals came at regular intervals. It was 5-0 at half time but then Albion Rovers, some of whose players gave the impression of never even having met each other before, steadied things a little.

Otherwise, the score may well have been in double figures. As it was, Kyle Turner (twice), Kevin Nisbet (twice) and Aaron Comrie scored in the first half and then Kevin Nisbet notched his hat-trick in the second half.

Both teams had won on the Saturday, in Dunfermline's case a very impressive victory over St Mirren in Paisley, but this time there was absolutely no doubt that the Pars were light years ahead of Albion Rovers.

The crowd was 1693, about average for an early season cup tie at East End Park. The Pars were clearly off to a very good start and the next game was away to Edinburgh City at Ainslie Park.

July 18 1992

Having been relegated in May after a particularly dismal season in the Premier Division, Dunfermline started the new season with a friendly against Brechin City at Glebe Park.

The game itself was of little consequence as a strong side won 5-0 with goals from Eddie Cunnington, Roddy Grant, Scott Leitch and two from George O'Boyle.

More interestingly however, this was the first game the Pars played with the new 'passback' rule in force. Widely considered one of the more successful changes to the Laws of the Game, the new rule banning goalkeepers from handling the ball when kicked to them directly by a team-mate was introduced in summer 1992.

This came about as recent years had seen passing back to the goalkeeper become more and more effective in wasting time and killing games with the 1990 World Cup regarded as the most boring to date, partly due to widespread use of this tactic.

The change would force goalkeepers to control the ball with their feet, something they were quite unaccustomed to at that time, giving completely unpredictable results whenever they had to deal with a pass-back.

Indeed, when speaking about the game that summer day in 1992, City manager John Ritchie put two of the goals down to confusion about the new rule.

Although Roddy Grant scored against Brechin in this game, City would be the last club in the Scottish League he would score against in a competitive game, amusingly completing the set with an own goal while playing for the club several years later!

July 19 1919

"Cowden" writing in the *Dundee Evening Telegraph* is far from happy about the prospects for the resumption of football after the war, particularly as it affects Fife teams.

Last season had been an unofficial season for the war did not finish until November 1918. For the first official season after the war, there was to be no Scottish League Second Division, and although there was to be a First Division of 22 teams, the only Fife team to be included being Raith Rovers.

This was bad enough but "Cowden" is even less happy with Dunfermline who have seceded from the wartime Eastern League and joined a Central League. Indeed, they were one of the main proponents.

Not only that, they have persuaded East Fife to join them but Cowdenbeath and Lochgelly are staying in the Eastern League. The attraction for Dunfermline in the "rebel" or "unofficial" Central League is of course that they can sign players like Andy Wilson even though he is on contract with Middlesbrough.

A disadvantage is that they will miss out on lucrative derby games with the local clubs, and will have to play against teams like Bo'ness, Broxburn and Falkirk Reserves.

This was an issue that would dominate footballing discussions in the first few years after the Great War until the Scottish League in 1921/22 resurrected the Second Division.

To be fair, the Second Division of the Scottish League had not been a great success before the war, suffering mainly from the lack of automatic promotion and relegation.

July 20 1936

On the first day of the Dunfermline Trades holiday, Dunfermline Athletic today resumed training with new Manager David Taylor in charge for the first time.

He was not all that well known and his record as a Manager of St Johnstone between 1924 and 1931 was mediocre. He had played for Rangers thirty years ago and had won English Cup medals with Bradford in 1911 and Burnley in 1914.

He was taking over from Willie Knight in difficult circumstances, for it was no secret that the club were in financial trouble. Dunfermline had now survived two years in Division One (not without the odd moment of glory, either) but financial constraints meant that with the season three weeks away, Mr Taylor had only 14 signed players with no great chance of him being able to add to the squad, other than through Junior or Juvenile ranks.

Indeed, there were only six players at East End Park today – Syme, Bolt, Harrison, McGrogan, McGowan and goalkeeper Farquharson. The other eight who lived in the West of Scotland or Edinburgh were training with other clubs – an odd arrangement in some ways, but it saved paying travelling expenses!

Meanwhile in the outside world, alarming news was being reported from Spain with the term "civil war" freely used in some newspapers. The problem had been brewing for some time, and it seemed to be an uprising of the Spanish Army under General Franco against the Republican Government. It was hoped at this stage that the problem could be confined to Spain, and would not affect the rest of Europe.

July 21 1945

Dunfermline had their first taste of football action (if it could be called that) in the post-war world with a trip to Gayfield in Arbroath for a Five-A-Side tournament and a general sporting afternoon organised by Arbroath Supporters' Club.

Manager Sandy Archibald can hardly have been encouraged by what he saw, for his five men were defeated 5-0 by Dundee in their only game! It was however by no means the strongest five that he could have chosen, for although the European War had now been finished for a couple of months, life was still chaotic and of course the War in the Far East was still going on.

Air raids on Japan were reported to be increasing and an invasion was expected soon. The country was also in limbo, not knowing what Government it would have. Election Day had been July 5 but results would not be declared until July 26 when all the forces' votes would have been brought home and counted.

This year coming up would see the return of the Scottish League First and Second Divisions with the Pars in the 14 team Second Division, but it would still be an unofficial season with no automatic promotion and relegation, no Scottish Cup and no official Internationals.

Yet no-one could mistake or under-estimate the passion for football. In a sense, football had had a good war with supporters impatient for the return of the "real" football as distinct from the wartime football which had attracted loads of interest but had in some ways lacked credibility because of its patchy and unpredictable nature.

It was now time for the proper stuff.

July 22 2018

It is always sad to visit Dens Park, Dundee nowadays.

Dundee remain a classic example of a football club who had their heyday in the 1950s and 1960s but lost it all through improvident stewardship which included the selling of star players a time when they didn't necessarily have to.

Mind you, Dunfermline had their moments of greatness too, and today on this warm Sunday, the two old rivals met in the Scottish League Cup.

Dunfermline had already beaten Peterhead and Dundee had beaten Stirling Albion, but it was Dunfermline who emerged triumphant today with an early goal from Jackson Longridge as he powerfully headed home a Ryan Williamson cross.

That was in the second minute, and if you were late in arriving, you missed all the goals! The rest of the game, although not devoid of some good play, yielded no further goals.

Myles Hippolyte came close once or twice in the first half, but as the second half wore on, it became increasing obvious that the players were not yet up to full fitness and were struggling in the heat.

This was not a great advertisement for summer football, and it is perhaps significant that referee Bobby Madden had no occasion to book anyone, or even to talk sternly to anyone.

516 Pars fans were among the crowd of 2,870, the Dundee fans departing in sadness and wondering when they would ever rise again, but the Pars fans had another win to cheer and a feeling of confidence that they could beat Brechin and Stirling Albion to top the group and qualify for the next round.

July 23 2016

Local rivals they may be, but it is always a pleasure to go to Central Park, Cowdenbeath.

The "Miners" as they used to be called and in later days "Blue Brazil" are a remarkable outfit in an even more remarkable stadium with all its lights, fences, apparent "no go" areas and car tyres designed to protect drivers and spectators from the dangers of Stock Car Racing.

Situated in by no means the most affluent area of Scotland or even of Fife, Cowdenbeath have struggled but have always seemed to survive.

They were struggling today, having experienced a 6-1 hammering from Dundee United a few nights ago while the Pars had been more successful than their local rivals in beating Arbroath.

As Cowdenbeath had been relegated last season to League Two, and the Pars were now two Divisions above them, this looked like it would be the only West Fife derby of the season. 1,481 turned up and they saw a tight and interesting first half which however proved goalless.

Gradually the better-trained Pars began to take control of the game and eventually after a period of pressure, they scored in the 57th minute through Andy Geggan who hit a cracker from the centre of the penalty box into the top right-hand corner.

Ten minutes later Lee Ashcroft scored another past the goalkeeper's left to make it 2-0 and then Geggan added a third near the end. This result was no real surprise, given the relative positions of the teams, but it meant that the Pars were now off to a great start with two wins out of two in their Scottish League Cup section.

July 24 1926

Oh dear! Something that Dunfermline supporters would rather have not known about!

The town was of course in prolonged euphoria about last season's success and was counting the weeks and the days until the start of the season which would see Athletic play at last in the First Division.

This piece of news, however, concerned the hero of the hour, Bobby Skinner, who had scored 53 League goals in 38 games in the triumphant winning of the Scottish League Second Division Championship last year.

Today, however, Robert (sic) Skinner found himself admonished at Glasgow Southern Police Court for an "assault" in the pavilion of Rosebery Park, the home of Shawfield Juniors.

The "assault" had happened during a five-a-side football tournament, and Skinner was a spectator. After one of the games, a "discussion" was taking place about rough play, Skinner foolishly got involved and struck one of the men and "slackened his teeth with the blow". Skinner admitted the assault but claimed that it was in self-defence.

It was clearly one of these "rammies" or "affrays" that one gets a lot of in junior football, and it was difficult to disentangle truth from fiction. The wise Bailie Maguire decided that an admonishment was enough but advised Mr Skinner to curb his temper and reminded him that the SFA were very strict about such things on the field of play.

It was a very minor incident, but enough to show that Skinner like so many great Scottish football players of that era, like Hughie Gallacher and Tommy McInally, had a strong, essentially Scottish, penchant for self-destruction.

Bobby Skinner, star of 1925 -1926

July 25 2011

This was flag day, or rather flag night for Dunfermline, as they were presented before the start with the flag for winning the Scottish League Division One (the second tier) last season.

It was possibly the highlight of the evening, for the first 90 minutes of the season failed to produce a goal for either Dunfermline Athletic or visitors St Mirren.

The game was played on a Monday night for television reasons, and it was presumably television who had a say in the rather strange decision that both the Pars and the Buddies should play in their change strips.

It would surely have been better for the Pars to play in their black and white stripes for this historic occasion. As it was, they played in a yellow colour ("urine yellow" as a fan unkindly put it) and St Mirren wore orange and black vertical stripes.

Dunfermline just did not look like Dunfermline to their fans in the 5,035 crowd, and they had a tough baptism in the Scottish Premier League.

St Mirren had the bulk of the play, forcing Dunfermline on to the back foot for large chunks of the game. Fortunately goalkeeper Paul Gallacher earned his spurs by saving a penalty kick and generally having a great game, while the defence showed a certain ability to stand up to pressure.

Indeed the Pars might just have won the game at the end after a fine move involving Andy Barrowman, but a draw was by no means a disaster. It was however a salutary lesson of just how difficult life was going to be this season in the Scottish Premier League.

July 26 1990

An emotional day for all connected to Dunfermline today.

Jim Leishman, the manager who had brought about the incredible 1980s revival that took the club from bottom half of the Second Division to being survivors in the Premier Division, left the club.

For several days, rumours had been flying around to the effect that Leishman had been sacked and instead offered the job of commercial and public relations manager with no direct football involvement.

At this time, Dunfermline had two co-managers as Leishman shared these duties with the recently promoted Iain Munro. To say that the fans were unimpressed would be a huge understatement, as shown by a demonstration outside a meeting the previous night and a general feeling of astonishment that the club's board would consider sacking Leishman and giving sole charge of football matters to Munro.

In the end, Leishman could not accept the offer to join the board as the club's first executive director and left the club after seven years, saying simply "I want to be a football manager".

Director Blair Morgan explained that the Leishman/Munro partnership had not been working, and the board wanted a way of keeping both at the club. It was not to be, and despite a protest march through the town the following weekend, the excitement of the Leishman era was over more suddenly than anyone could have expected.

Disillusion and anger replaced excitement and enthusiasm, with the Directors considered to have made a serious misjudgement. The future looked uncertain.

July 27 1955

One of the problems about winning promotion is that other teams want your Manager, who has clearly done a good job for you.

In this case, it was full-time Motherwell who fancied Bobby Ancell, and to-day after a day or two of speculation, the former Dundee full back announced that he would like to move to Fir Park.

Dunfermline did not want to stand in his way, but as this was perilously close to the start of the season, they said that they would want him to serve his notice to give them a chance to appoint someone else.

In to-day's *Courier* an advertisement duly appeared for the job.

People questioned whether Ancell was making the right choice in going to Motherwell, a team who would have been relegated this year from Division One if the Leagues had not been restructured so that there would be 18 teams rather than 16.

Motherwell had had a funny few years, winning the Scottish League Cup in 1950/51, the Scottish Cup in 1952, then being relegated in 1953, promoted again in 1954 and finishing second bottom again in 1955.

But they were a richer team than Dunfermline and probably had better players, and Ancell was ambitious.

Dunfermline would eventually get Andy Dickson to take over at East End Park, and he stayed with the club until 1960 with a tolerable degree of success although DAFC remained a yo-yo club until Jock Stein arrived.

Meanwhile the new season was approaching, and part-time Dunfermline, with one or two juniors, were now training at East End Park three nights a week.

July 28 2018

Dunfermline today completed a splendid League Cup qualifying campaign with a 3-1 victory over Stirling Albion at East End Park before 2359 fans in the summer sunshine.

Stirling Albion scored first in the first half but in the second half, Dunfermline scored three times, once through James Vincent and the other two from the wonderfully well-named Myles Hippolyte.

This performance meant that the Pars now had a 100% record in a section which might have caused a few problems as Dundee, Brechin City and Peterhead had all had their moments in the past.

But Dunfermline had beaten them all, their best performance possibly being the 1-0 defeat of Dundee at Dens Park last Sunday. Manager Allan Johnston had every right to feel that his season was off to a good start, and it was an upbeat crowd who walked home that sunny afternoon, revelling in the victory and looking forward to the League campaign.

The first game was against Dundee United in the Championship, and the good news was the Pars had been given a good tie in the knock-out stage of the Scottish League Cup at East End Park against Hearts.

Hearts were a crusty kind of a side, but if the opposition ran at them it was possible they might crumble. A good crowd looked likely, but the main thing was a chance to make it to a quarter final.

The Pars were, after all, the seeded side having won all four group games while Hearts scraped across the line after being deducted two points for fielding an ineligible player.

July 29 2000

Dunfermline today began another season in the SPL.

They had been a yoyo team throughout the 1990s, and there had been a certain amount of political shenanigans in the summer of 2000 from which Dunfermline had been the beneficiary.

The Scottish Premier League was being increased from 10 to 12 teams, and with First Division winners (St Mirren) automatically promoted, the intention had been to hold a three way play-off between the bottom SPL team (Aberdeen) and the 2nd and 3rd placed teams in the First Division (Dunfermline and Falkirk).

But Falkirk were still playing at Brockville, and failed to meet the entry requirement of an all-seated stadium with 10,000 seats. The playoff was therefore unnecessary with Aberdeen staying up and Dunfermline promoted.

The cynics (not all of whom lived in Falkirk) felt that this was an "old pals" act to keep the well supported Dons in the SPL.

However that may be, by sheer chance, Dunfermline and Aberdeen played each other on the opening day at East End Park. It was a fine warm day, with the appearance of a male streaker before half time (which everyone agreed was by no means a pretty sight!).

There was little in the way of good football to enthuse anyone, the highlight being the sending off by referee Stuart Dougal of Derek Young of Aberdeen after a sly kick at Jason Dair. He had in any case already been booked.

All this was before half time, and it was expected that Dunfermline would now make their advantage count, but it didn't happen and the second half was punctuated with a few more bookings, but no goals.

July 30 2011

Dunfermline Athletic and their fans (in reasonable numbers) made history today by paying their first ever visit to a ground called Galabank to play Annan Athletic.

This was for a Scottish League Cup tie and Dunfermline were the first Premier League team to pay a visit to this ground.

It was a longer away trip than most, but the fans were rewarded with a lovely warm sunny day, an interesting trip through some beautiful scenery and a 2-1 victory to put the club into the next round. It was a hard fought game watched by Justice Secretary Kenny MacAskill and some 767 others.

Dunfermline went ahead in the first half with a looping header from Andy Barrowman from a Joe Cardle corner kick.

Annan however did not stay behind for long and in five minutes the much-travelled David Cox equalised with a fine individual effort. (Cox was awarded the Man of the Match for his goal and the rest of his play.)

That was the score at half time. Early in the second half, Andy Kirk headed the Pars back into the lead and that was the way that it stayed until the end of game.

The heat was quite enervating and the pace visibly slackened towards the end of the 90 minutes with Dunfermline and their supporters quite glad to hear the final toot of referee Charlie Richmond's whistle.

Although far from the best game ever seen, it was a nice experience to visit a new ground, and the day was much enjoyed by all. The journey home was a pleasant one.

July 31 2016

Dunfermline's hopes of qualification to the next round of the Scottish League Cup were hanging by the slenderest of threads before they went to Tannadice today, but this Sunday finished it off.

Wins over Arbroath and Cowdenbeath had been encouraging but then the team had horrified their fans by going down 1-5 to Inverness at home. With all other games having been played the day before, both clubs knew that a win would see them advance though a draw would be enough for Dundee Utd.

The Tannadice club had been through a rough time of late following an astonishing sale of players in 2015 and, like Dunfermline, they were no strangers to serious financial problems.

Both teams could have done with a run in the Scottish League Cup. 4,951 turned up this Sunday afternoon, and they saw a good performance from the Pars – at least in the first half.

Rhys McCabe was taken off injured however, and then the Pars had a good penalty claim turned down by referee John McKendrick when Joe Cardle was clearly brought down in the penalty box.

Then just on the half time whistle, Nat Wedderburn headed narrowly over the bar. That was sadly about as good as it got for Dunfermline, for Simon Murray scored with a header early in the second half to put United on top.

Then hard as Dunfermline tried, they could not get back into the game, and in the 83rd minute Scott Fraser killed Dunfermline's fast vanishing hopes with a well-taken free kick. For the Pars supporters, this was not the start to the season that they had been wanting but it was now time to focus on league football once again.

August

FOOTBALL.

DUNFERMLINE ATHLETIC CLUB'S FIXTURES.

The fixtures of Dunfermline Athletic for the ensuing season are as follows:—

Aug. 12—Stenhousemuir	Away.
,, 19—Queen's Park	Home.
,, 26—Leith Athletic	Away.
Sept. 2—Brechin City	Home.
,, 9—East Stirlingshire	Away.
,, 16—Dundee	Home.
,, 23—Edinburgh City	Away.
,, 30—East Fife	Home.
Oct. 7—Dundee United	Away.
,, 14—Forfar Athletic	Home.
,, 21—King's Park	Away.
,, 28—Montrose	Home.
Nov. 4—Raith Rovers	Away.
,, 11—East Fife	Away.
,, 18—Dumbarton	Away.
,, 25—Airdrieonians	Home.
Dec. 2—Leith Athletic	Home.
,, 9—Morton	Away.
,, 16—Montrose	Away.
,, 23—Stenhousemuir	Home.
,, 30—Brechin City	Away.
Jan. 1—Dundee United	Home.
,, 6—Dumbarton	Home.
,, 13—Morton	Home.
,, 23—St Bernard's	Away.
Feb. 3—Raith Rovers	Home.
,, 17—Queen's Park	Away.
Mar. 2—King's Park	Home.
,, 9—Airdrieonians	Away.
,, 16—St Bernard's	Home.
,, 23—East Stirlingshire	Home
,, 30—Dundee	Away
Apr. 6—Forfar Athletic	Away
,, 13—Edinburgh City	Home

Fixtures for season 1939/40

August 1 2015

It is always a good feeling to beat the Blue Brazil of Cowdenbeath.

To do it emphatically 5-1, in the first home game of the season and in glorious weather like today (well, there were a few heavy showers, but this is Scotland!) renders this a very good day indeed.

No-one could deny that the Pars supporters have been through the mill in recent years, but there is reason to believe now, is there not, that the corner may have been turned?

This game attracted a healthy attendance of 2,756 to East End Park and they were rewarded by some very fine football. The amazing thing was that, in spite of 45 minutes of almost incessant Pars pressure, the first half proved goalless.

It was only after the turnaround that the goals began to flow. Faissal El Bakhtaoui scored the first; Shaun Byrne then added another.

Cowdenbeath quickly pulled one back but any chance of a fightback virtually disappeared when goalkeeper Andrews was shown the red card by referee George Salmond (a man who had once been captain of Scotland's cricket team) for bringing down Ryan Wallace.

It may have been a "denying a goal scoring opportunity" red card, but most supporters felt that it was bad enough anyway without that legal technicality.

Cowdenbeath then imploded as Wallace scored the resultant penalty and Byrne and El Bakhtaoui scored a couple more.

After opening with a 4-1 win at Gayfield in the Challenge Cup last week, it was a good start to the season and an indication that more was to come. 2015/16 would be a good season.

August 2 2014

Dunfermline today got their season off to a good start by convincingly beating Annan Athletic 5-1 at East End Park before a fairly sparse crowd of 1544.

The weather was disappointing for August with the permanent threat of rain, but at least there would be a game today .

The season should have started last week but a sudden downpour in the half-hour before kick-off caused the game against Raith Rovers to be postponed – in July!

There was little to be unhappy about on the field as the Pars won convincingly against the men from Dumfriesshire, who had finished second in League Two last season.

Jim Jefferies' men started well in their red strip attacking the Halbeath end of the ground with Faissal El Bakhtaoui looking particularly lively. It was however full-back Alex Whittle who opened the scoring for the Pars with a charge up the wing, a shot and a deflection; it was no more than the Pars deserved.

Before half time, new signing Gregor Buchanan headed a second, and the game was more or less finished at that point. Michael Moffat scored his first competitive goal for the club soon after the restart.

Although Annan pulled one back ten minutes later after some AWOL defending from the Pars, substitute Ryan Wallace shortly restored the three-goal cushion before Lewis Martin added another right on the final whistle.

It was a convincing win, and although one has to allow for the fact that Annan Athletic were anything but top class opposition, there were grounds for optimism that a good season lay ahead.

August 3 2013

It is a shame that East Stirlingshire are no longer with us in the Scottish League.

Sadly they were relegated to the Lowland League in 2016, yet they are a team with a great history, playing in the old First Division (the top tier) of the Scottish League as late as 1964.

They used to play at a ground called Firs Park in Falkirk, but since 2008 they had been sharing with Stenhousemuir at Ochilview. Today at Ochilview, the Pars were playing in a new dazzling light blue away kit and kicked off into the sun and wind, both of which capriciously and disconcertingly came and disappeared at intervals.

Dunfermline won 2-0 with a Ryan Wallace penalty and a late Craig Dargo strike, but this game lives in the memory only because of the sheer awfulness of it.

With neither side really looking coherent, the wind making it difficult to play long passes and a poorly prepared artificial pitch making football on the ground difficult also, it is not surprising that this was not a thriller.

Of far more significance, this was the first game played after the agreement of a CVA (Company Voluntary Arrangement) which would allow the club to exit administration.

It had been a tough few months and the last week had been tense – had the CVA not been agreed, liquidation and the death of the club were likely. Although the financial situation going forward was still fragile, the Pars United group could now go ahead and take over the club, mainly thanks to those who had been owed money agreeing to write off these debts.

August 4 1914

It did not seem to have any great or immediate connection with Dunfermline Athletic at the moment, but what happened tonight changed life forever both in Dunfermline and everywhere else.

The season was not due to begin until Saturday August 15, against Dundee Hibs. This Tuesday night, Dunfermline's players (all of them part-time) were at East End Park for training.

All were totally aware that by 11.00 pm tonight (midnight in Europe) if the Germans did not evacuate Belgium, there would be a war.

Everyone knew that the Germans wouldn't evacuate, and that a state of war would exist tomorrow. It was fair to say that people did not really understand what it would all be about.

Wars had existed before in South Africa, Sudan and Crimea but well away from home, with even the Napoleonic War of a hundred years ago not really impinging too much on the civilian population. But everyone seemed to be concerned about this one, although there was a feeling of excitement as well.

For football players, there might be a chance to play for some of the Army teams if they joined up. Or maybe the navy? Rosyth was not far away, and there might be the opportunity to sail the ocean. But football would surely remain the same, would it not?

The season would still be starting a week come Saturday. It would be the start of Dunfermline's third season in the Scottish Second Division, and, Kaiser or no Kaiser, they really would have to work hard to get the better of last year's winners, local rivals Cowdenbeath.

August 5 2014

The League Challenge Cup does not usually attract very many supporters but there were 4,230 at East End Park tonight. There were two reasons for this.

One was that it was a local derby against Raith Rovers – and there is always a lot of rivalry there. The other was that the Rovers were the current Cup holders, having beaten Rangers in a thrilling final last year at Easter Road which was enjoyed by many fans on TV.

This match had been postponed on the original date ten days ago because of a late downpour. Manager Jim Jefferies had wanted the game to go ahead on the first available date last midweek but had been thwarted. The Police had no officers available due to the Commonwealth Games which were taking place at the same time in Glasgow.

Finally then, this game went ahead tonight and with Dunfermline currently a division below Raith, it was likely to be the only meeting of the sides this season. Rovers started the better but by half-time Dunfermline were on top.

The Pars employed a weird routine when they won a corner kick. Four players formed a circle on the edge of the penalty box and waited until just before the ball was kicked, and they then scattered to look for the ball.

The benefit of this was that it bewildered the defence (and it certainly mystified the crowd), but it was not really effective in scoring a goal!

The only goal came late in the game when Ross Millen's shot from outside the box was just beyond Kevin Cuthbert's reach. It was a narrow but well-deserved victory for Jim Jefferies' men.

August 6 2011

At the start of what would prove to be Dunfermline's only season (in recent years) in the Scottish Premier League, Dunfermline and Inverness Caledonian Thistle served up a 3-3 draw at East End Park.

0-0 draws can sometimes be good games while occasionally a high-scoring draw can be a poor game – this was one of these.

Some felt that the Pars were fortunate to earn a late draw, but having had the better of the game, that was not an opinion shared by those of the Pars persuasion who had stayed to see Martin Hardie's curling stoppage time free kick!

Sadly some fans (as is often the case) had gone away before full time, and this writer is surely not the only person who wonders why people do that when the game is so tight.

It was Andy Kirk who had scored the first two goals for Dunfermline, a crisp finish after some good build up in the 26th minute, and then a header in the 53rd minute after Greg Tansey had equalised for the Highlanders.

At this point Dunfermline looked likely to register a rare win over Inverness, but then goalkeeper Paul Gallacher couldn't hold a fierce drive and Jonny Hayes (later to star with Aberdeen and Celtic) was on hand to bang in the rebound.

Well within the last ten minutes, Greg Tansey headed a third for Inverness, and those of little faith began to disappear, until Martin Hardie, who hadn't in all truth had the best of games so far, proved his value as a free-kick specialist.

It being only the second game of the season, a draw against Inverness was not considered a disaster, though the Highlanders were still proving to be something of a bogey team.

August 7 2004

A new season and a new Manager for the Pars!

Jimmy Calderwood had now gone to Aberdeen after a reasonably successful five years at East End Park, and the mantle had now passed to Davie Hay, who had been Manager at Motherwell, Celtic, St Mirren and Livingston — with varying degrees of success.

He had however enjoyed a certain recent impressive triumph when Livingston won the Scottish League Cup (their first and only major trophy) in the spring of this year.

Today the first visitors of the season were Dundee United on a very warm and pleasant day in front of a large crowd of 6,512. The Pars opened by kicking towards the Halbeath end.

A few words had been said about Dunfermline's plastic pitch, but there did not seem to be any sort of problem, for the standard of play was good.

The first half was closely contested but goalless with, if anything, Dundee United having the better of the exchanges.

Early in the second half, the Pars went ahead after United's defence had failed to deal with a cross from the right and Andy Tod was on the spot to prod the ball home after the ball took a slight bobble which may or may not have been caused by the pitch.

Minutes later, the game might have been all over, but Barry Nicholson blasted the ball over the bar when it looked easier to score. Dunfermline had cause to regret that miss and a few other half chances when Jim McIntyre, who had come on as a substitute, levelled the score after a neat move from Dundee United.

A draw was probably a fair result.

Past Players at the Centenary Game in 1985

August 8 1953

On a roastingly hot day at East End Park, Dunfermline began their season with a good 2-1 win over Arbroath in their sectional game of the Scottish League Cup.

A crowd of about 4,000 were there and they were nursing hopes as they left that there might be an upturn in the fortunes of the Pars after last year's disappointing campaign.

Everything was looking good at the moment with the country still basking in the afterglow of the Coronation in June. The flags were still up in many places and today's good weather only added to the feel-good factor.

The victory was a competent one with goals from McSeveney and Henderson, and the Press gives qualified approval to the players other than young O'Brien on the right wing who was new to the spot and whose "shooting could have been better".

There is an interesting comment from Manager Bobby Ancell in today's programme to the effect that "I am convinced that the drop in the standard of play in Scotland is due to the lack of tolerance in crowds for the better type of football – the studied and intentional play".

It is an odd comment in some ways, but it possibly means that fans now expected to see goals and to be thrilled rather than the more patient build up. But in any case, Dunfermline supporters were now looking forward to a trip to Dumbarton on Wednesday night.

The other team in the section was Forfar Athletic, so confidence in qualification for the quarter finals was now quite high.

August 9 2003

It was the opening day of the season, and the weather was very hot indeed with some reports of the temperature being above 90 degrees.

In the circumstances it was hardly surprising that the game between Dunfermline and Celtic ended in a 0-0 draw. It was not a dull game however, for both teams had chances to score a crucial goal, but Dunfermline's celebrations at the end showed how much this draw meant to the East End side.

That was not surprising, since the last day of the previous season (Dunfermline had lost 6-1 at Ibrox, Rangers winning the title on goal difference ahead of Celtic, by just one goal) had seen the team accused, by Celtic forward Chris Sutton and many Celtic fans, of lying down to Rangers.

That had obviously stung, and there was clearly a real determination to get something from this game.

There were other sideshows going on as well. One was the return of Jim Leishman, not as Manager (as many Pars supporters would have preferred him to be) but in an executive position.

Another was that this was to be the last game played for a while on grass at East End Park, for Dunfermline were to participate in a UEFA trial of new-generation artificial pitches and would become the first senior team in Scotland since Stirling Albion (1987-1992) to play on a non-grass surface.

Artificial surfaces of course remain controversial and this particular one was not destined to remain for very long, but it was a sign of some forward thinking at East End Park. Because of the new pitch being laid, the Pars would not have another home game until the visit of Hibs in mid-September.

August 10 1963

The weather was nothing like suitable for the first day of the football season, but Dunfermline got off to a good start.

A 1-0 win over Airdrie at Broomfield in the first game of the Scottish League Cup section which also contained Dundee and Third Lanark. (Today Dundee beat Third Lanark 2-1 at Cathkin). Dunfermline's goal came from Jim Kerray.

It was actually quite a good game on the lush Broomfield surface with most newspaper reports agreeing that 2-0 or 3-0 for Jock Stein's side would not have been an injustice at that strange little ground with its old pavilion in the corner.

Everyone was reasonably optimistic for the football season, although the Pars were painfully aware that there would be no European campaign this year.

Two other things were dominating conversation in 1963 – one was the Great Train robbery of a few days ago.

The other was the ongoing scandal of Christine Keeler whose "friendship" with John Profumo, the Minister of War, was at the same time as she was equally "friendly" with an attaché at the Soviet Embassy. Poor old Harold McMillan, the Prime Minister, was struggling to cope with it all.

Life was interesting in 1963, the Beatles were in their prime, there had been a great cricketing season with the West Indies in England, but one thing that everyone agreed on as they got into their cars and buses to go back to Dunfermline was that the weather really would have to improve from today's very soggy start to the football season!

August 11 1919

Today was announced the death of Dunfermline's most famous son Andrew Carnegie, multi-millionaire and philanthropist, born in the "auld grey toon" in 1835 but who had made most of his wealth in the USA.

It was probably true to say that opinions in Dunfermline were divided about Carnegie.

On the one hand it was surely good that a man could rise from humble beginnings (although the Carnegie family wasn't in the most abject of poverty, if truth be told) to such dizzy world heights; the man was to be commended for all his philanthropy, which included donating swimming baths, theatres, halls and particularly libraries.

His detractors were not slow, however, to point out the dreadful conditions of poverty in which his workers were forced to live.

They also pointed out that, although he did (laudably) make a few statements against war, he was nevertheless a war profiteer and not only in the Great War which had just ended.

The balance sheet was probably in Carnegie's favour, for there were other grasping capitalists of the time who singularly failed to distribute their largesse as Carnegie had done.

Nevertheless, a lot of Dunfermline Athletic supporters must have wished that he had stayed in Dunfermline for a little longer and watched the birth and growth of Dunfermline Athletic.

A look at the somewhat primitive and decrepit stadium at East End Park as the team prepared for the first official peacetime season would have suggested that a bob or two from Andra's wealth could have been put to good use!

August 12 1970

There was a pop song at the time which contained the lyrics "Now the good times are all gone, and I think I'm moving on".

This seemed more and more to apply to Dunfermline in 1970, and even at this early stage of the season, trouble was brewing. The first game of the season against Rangers at Ibrox was a 4-1 defeat.

That could be forgiven because it was Rangers and it was away from home, but tonight's home defeat 0-2 to Morton, a different matter altogether, left the 4,000 fans full of foreboding for the season ahead.

It had been a summer of discontent as well with one or two players disciplined for failing to turn up for training, several transfer requests submitted and rumours abounding that players were finding it difficult to cope with the dictatorial behaviour of Manager George Farm. Farm was still popular enough with the fans however, for the team had done well enough in the past few years.

Tonight was an unfortunate game with Morton scoring twice in a three-minute spell round about the half hour mark, Hannigan and Copland taking advantage of defensive frailties.

The players were booed as they went off at half time. In the second half they did at least earn the respect of the fans with a spirited display. Sadly, however, it failed to bring any goals in spite of several net-bound shots being cleared off the line.

It was an ominous display of how this season was going to develop, and the visit to Motherwell on Saturday was discussed in hushed terms.

August 13 1958

The Pars, already cock-a-hoop following their opening day 3-1 win over East Fife at Bayview, took things a little further tonight in their first home match of the season.

By smashing Stirling Albion 6-1 they became one of the only five teams in Scotland to win their two opening games of the season.

Still on a high after last season's promotion and the decision taken in the close season to offer several of their players full time terms, there was a clear determination that Dunfermline were going to stay in the First Division this year.

This was still the Scottish League Cup. Brechin City were the other team in the section, but there was to be no stopping the Pars!

Tonight was a case in point, and the fans all left the ground happy. Dickson scored two, Melrose scored two, Harvey scored another and there was an own goal scored by the luckless Beecham who simply could not get out of the way of a cross that he was hoping to clear!

Thus, season 1958/59 was well-launched with the Directors and management giving clear evidence of a desire to stay up and to improve.

1958 had been, so far, a traumatic year for football with the Manchester United air crash in February and then a dreadful, sobering experience of the World Cup finals in Sweden in which a rather serious lesson had been delivered to Scotland, not least in the desirability of having a Manager! But at least things were looking up in Dunfermline!

August 14 1963

Dunfermline disappointed the large crowd that had turned up for the first home game of the season by losing 2-3 to Third Lanark at East End Park in the sectional stage of the Scottish League Cup.

The result was all the more disappointing as the Pars had won the first game of the season at Airdrie on Saturday. It was a travesty of a score line. Dunfermline were on top throughout, but as Manager Stein never tired of telling them, that counted for nothing.

It was goals that were important. Third Lanark had gone ahead in the first half through a goal which had deflected off Willie Callaghan, a lead they held until half-time when Jackie Sinclair equalised.

Then a soft penalty was awarded against goalkeeper Jim Heriot and converted by McMorran; Murray scored a third for the Cathkin side then Dunfermline got a penalty which George Miller put away.

Strive hard though they did, Dunfermline could not grab an equaliser with Third Lanark's central defenders McGillivray and McCormick outstanding.

It was a sore blow for the Pars who now had to travel to Dundee to face the section favourites on Saturday.

It was clear that Dunfermline were in a state of transition as their Cup winning team of two years ago was slowly breaking up and other players were being brought in.

As for tonight's opponents, Third Lanark, it was no secret that they were beginning to struggle financially. The red strips that they wore tonight looked distinctly faded!

August 15 1925

Bright sunny weather today heralded the start of the new football season, and Dunfermline got off to a good start, beating Nithsdale Wanderers of Sanquhar 4-1 at East End Park.

It was the first day of the reign of new Manager Sandy Paterson, and it was also the first day of a new rule. From now on, the offside rule was simplified so that a player was *onside* if there were two opponents between him and the goal line (previously it was three).

The idea was to see more goals being scored, for the authorities felt that there were too many sterile goalless draws and that this was having an adverse effect on attendances. It was a slightly controversial move, by no means agreed with by everyone.

It did not seem to have a great deal of effect on Dunfermline Athletic today for their victory over Nithsdale Wanderers (last year's Division Three champions) was a convincing one with two goals from Skinner, one from Stein and one from McKenzie.

From the way that *The Sunday Post* describes them, all would have been scored under the old system as well. Skinner's two goals and Stein's one came from fine "combined play of the half backs and the forwards" whereas that of McKenzie was a "swerving shot from 25 yards". The significance of this game was that it was a good start to what would turn out to be one of Dunfermline's best seasons.

The crowd was described as "healthy", although no number is given, and they all departed with a confident spring in their step.

August 16 1902

Today saw the opening of the football season, and the start of a new venture for Dunfermline.

Today they played their first ever game in the Northern League, an organisation which consisted of three teams from Aberdeen (Orion, Victoria and a team called Aberdeen), two from Dundee (Wanderers and Lochee), Forfar, Arbroath, Montrose, St Johnstone and two local rivals in Lochgelly and Cowdenbeath.

Dunfermline's first game was a home game against Dundee Wanderers, a now defunct team who played at Clepington Park on more or less the same site as Dundee United's Tannadice is now.

The weather was not all that hospitable at the fairly primitive East End Park slightly to the west of the current ground, but a reasonable crowd turned up to see the game.

They left disappointed with the 3-3 draw, which they felt really should have been a victory — particularly as Dunfermline scored within a minute of the start of the game through Adamson.

But the Dundee side fought well, and by half-time they were actually 3-2 up.

The Dundee Courier is peremptory and dismissive about the second half. It was "dull and uninteresting and resulted in the Fife men equalising" — a method of description which makes one think that the writer had sympathies for the Wanderers.

Nevertheless, it concedes that Dunfermline might well have won, and although the Fife supporters left disappointed, they had every reason to be happy about their team's performance. It was, after all, only the first game of a long season to come.

August 17 1912

Dunfermline Athletic today competed in the Scottish Football League for the first time, opening the season with a match at North End Park, home of Cowdenbeath.

The two sides were already familiar with each other, having met in the Fife Cup final the previous Thursday, but this league opener marked a significant day in the club's history.

League expansion had come about at a good time, with the club in a strong position after the previous season's Qualifying Cup win and were admitted at the same time as Johnstone, a Renfrewshire club, a year after the similarly named St Johnstone of Perth.

Cowdenbeath had made it to the Scottish League before Dunfermline, and so there was great excitement on this August day of 1912 as the local rivals met for the first time at this level before a large crowd.

Athletic captain Ronaldson won the toss but Cowdenbeath started the better side, taking a first half lead. However, a remarkable turnaround took place before half time as a reshuffle of the Athletic forward line brought them back into the game with two goals almost immediately.

Firstly, a Hall shot from 40 yards was somehow diverted into the net, and a minute later Izatt put Dunfermline ahead.

Leading at half-time in their first Scottish League match was a great start, but the match would finish 2-2 after an equaliser by Tracey from a second half corner.

Reports of the game describe Dunfermline goalkeeper Slavin having an impressive game, helping his side to take a point. A new era in the history of Dunfermline Athletic had begun.

August 18 1954

A good 3-1 win this Wednesday night for the Pars against Dundee United pleased their 4,000 fans in the late summer sunshine and sent everyone away optimistic for the new season.

There was a pleasing amount of Dundee United supporters, sometimes difficult to distinguish from the Pars supporters because they all had the same colours.

Just occasionally an older Dundee United supporter could be heard to shout for "the Hibs" – not of course the Edinburgh variety but because Dundee United used to be called Dundee Hibs.

This was the second game of the season, the first game having been a creditable but uninspiring 1-1 draw against Brechin at Glebe Park last Saturday. The other team in the League Cup section was Ayr United and the Pars now awaited them on Saturday with a degree of optimism.

Last year had been another disappointment, but this year it was beginning to look as if Manager Bobby Ancell had at long last assembled a side which might challenge for promotion.

Dundee United, another team with promotion aspirations, took the lead in the first half through a free kick from the edge of the box, scored by Cross whose "shot was as quick as the whistle and left the homesters gasping" as *The Dundee Courier* put it.

But Dunfermline turned it round in the second half, and it was newcomer Duffy who scored within five minutes of the restart.

From then on it was more or less one-way traffic towards Alex Edmiston in the Dundee United goal, and it was to Edmiston's credit that the Pars scored only another two goals, one from Reilly five minutes after Duffy's goal and then a McKinlay header twenty minutes later.

August 19 1903

Tonight, in heavy rain which brought a premature ending to proceedings, the new East End Park was officially opened in a game against Celtic.

The final scored was 5-1 with Jimmy Quinn of Celtic scoring most of the goals, but that was hardly surprising as the Glasgow men were full time professionals.

Dunfermline's President Tom Robertson had dipped into his own (not unsubstantial) pocket to provide new "togs" for the team.

The Dundee Evening Telegraph is impressed with the new pitch slightly to the east of Dunfermline's original ground saying that it is a "vast improvement" on the old ground.

"It is nothing if not commodious… being broader than the general run of provincial enclosures. Although by no means like the proverbial carpet, it played well last night and in the course of time should be one of the best fields belonging to a Northern League club".

The Dunfermline team on this historic occasion was Thomson, Pitblado and Vail; Strang, Anderson and Nicol; Dewar, McLeod, Woods, Clark and Moffat.

About halfway through the second half and in torrential rain, local referee Mr Burns of Dunfermline, in agreement with both teams, called a halt to proceedings, Dunfermline not wishing to damage their new pitch and Celtic not wishing to exhaust their men.

Everyone then adjourned to a local hotel, the health of both clubs was proposed and Celtic's Manager, the ever-genial Willie Maley, was heard to say how delighted he was that the game of football was advancing in Fifeshire.

August 20 1921

History was made today as Dunfermline Athletic played their first ever game in the newly revamped Second Division of the Scottish League.

There had, of course, been a Second Division before, and Dunfermline had been elected in 1912 and played until 1915 when the sheer logistics of playing war-time football on a limited budget led to so many teams being unable to continue.

This was however a new enormous Division of 20 teams, and the first thing that Dunfermline would now have to do was to learn to live without Andy Wilson.

Things would not be so easy, it was said, and so it proved. Today, for example, Dunfermline travelled to Sports Park, Broxburn to play Broxburn United and lost 2-3.

The first half was quiet and uneventful, but then all five goals came in the second half with Sinclair of Dunfermline scoring first and last. There was little wrong with Dunfermline's defence according to most accounts, but their attack lacked punch.

Today, of the 20 teams who played that day, eleven are no longer in existence or have fallen out of the national league – Armadale, Vale of Leven, Bathgate, Broxburn United, Bo'ness, St Bernard's, Johnstone, East Stirlingshire, King's Park, Lochgelly United and Clackmannan.

Dundee Hibs have changed their name to Dundee United, whereas Dunfermline are still plodding on along with Arbroath, St Johnstone, Alloa Athletic, Cowdenbeath, East Fife, Stenhousemuir and Forfar Athletic.

At the end of the season, Alloa would turn out to be the first Second Division Champions.

August 21 1926

A large crowd of apparently well over 10,000 were at East End Park to see Dunfermline's first ever home game in the Scottish First Division.

Promoted from the Second Division last April, this day had been much looked forward to.

Sadly Dunfermline Athletic had already lost twice away from home – a bad blow at Cappielow when they lost 0-3 to Greenock Morton last Saturday, and a slightly more predictable loss to Rangers in midweek at Ibrox.

Today's opponents Hamilton Academical were a team that Dunfermline could be reasonably expected to beat at home if they were to stay in the First Division for more than one season.

Sadly, Bobby Skinner, their star goal scorer, was out. Skinner had of course been the main reason for last season's winning of the Second Division with his 53 goals, but the snag was that the team had come to depend on him too much.

Today was an excellent example of this, for Dunfermline had loads of pressure throughout the game but simply couldn't score.

Hamilton capitalised on virtually the only chance that they had, scoring through Moffat, and then being able to hold out against the Dunfermline attacks which were hysterical and enthusiastic, but lacked the finishing touch.

It was a salutary experience for the Dunfermline side, showing that they really had to have some sort of back up for their one star player. The other point was that there was a wide gulf between the Second Division and the First Division.

However, only three games played – there was still time, but games like Hamilton at home really needed to be won.

August 22 1987

This was the first visit of Celtic on League business to East End Park for well over 12 years, and the ground was filled to capacity.

They saw a great performance by the Pars who just edged to victory over a new-look Celtic; Billy McNeill had now returned as Manager after a four year spell in England as Manager of Manchester City and latterly, Aston Villa.

He had bought a few players like Andy Walker and Billy Stark, and had started the season well.

Dunfermline on the other hand were newly promoted and needed to win as many of their home games as possible if they were going to stay in the Premier League.

It was Dunfermline who scored first through Craig Robertson, Celtic then equalised through an Andy Walker penalty kick after Billy Stark had been blocked in the box, but it was a header from Eric Ferguson that would win the game for the Pars.

The Man of the Match was probably goalkeeper Ian Westwater who had several good saves in the second half when Celtic pressed. It would not have been the biggest injustice in the world if Celtic had equalised but the important thing for Dunfermline was that they hung on to collect two points.

Sadly the two points would not be quite enough to save them at the end of the season (nor would the two points lost here deny Celtic the League title), but at least the Pars were off to a good start.

August 23 1919

Dunfermline Athletic today gave a strange and somewhat depressing performance at East Stirlingshire as they went down 1-2 to the home side at Merchiston Park.

It was all the more disappointing for the crowd, as it contained quite a few who had travelled from Dunfermline, enthused by their new star, Andrew Wilson, who had scored four lovely goals last week against Hearts "A" in the Central League.

A veteran and war hero, Wilson had already played for Scotland in the Victory International in May and was already well known as a goal scorer.

Indeed his goal scoring would continue for both Dunfermline and Scotland, but today he was disappointing.

The Sunday Post contained this rather strange comment on him: "Andrew Wilson gave a fifteen minutes' exhibition of class football, which included some splendid drives. Afterwards he practically retired from the game. He apparently found it difficult to make headway against Stirling (the East Stirlingshire defender) whose height stood him in good stead".

Presumably this means that he had picked up a knock or an injury, but whatever it was, it was a huge disappointment to the Pars supporters who had travelled there in their hundreds. Dow scored Dunfermline's only goal in the first half - "a fluke goal. The wind caught the ball and curled it under (sic) the post at the far corner" says the curmudgeonly *Sunday Post* of a game which was "not overcrowded with thrills".

A feature of the occasion (as would be the case for several years) was the number of disabled war veterans, some of them still wearing their "hospital blue" uniforms, attending the match and admitted free.

August 24 2013

The first league fixture between Dunfermline and Stenhousemuir in more than 25 years produced the most unlikely comeback.

Relegated to the third tier of Scottish football for the first time since the mid-80s, a young Pars side had the better of the first half play but were unable to score and went in 2-0 down at half-time.

Early in the second half it looked all over as the Warriors went 3-0 ahead. A spirited recovery brought the Pars to within a goal at 3-2, but the home side looked to have done enough when they went 4-2 up with little more than 15 minutes to go.

Very few of the Dunfermline fans at Ochilview today will ever have seen anything like the last six minutes; firstly an Allan Smith shot made it 4-3 with six minutes to go, and there were joyful scenes when a Jordan Moore penalty levelled the scores at 4-4 shortly afterwards.

However, that was nothing compared to what would follow with a minute to go as Andy Geggan incredibly put the away side in front. Straight from the restart Stenhousemuir had a very good chance for an equaliser, but it was not to be their day.

You don't see your team win 5-4 very often, and certainly not in circumstances like that.

It would be the first 5-4 Dunfermline win since 1950, a time when higher scoring games were more common – as well as that 5-4 win over Kilmarnock, season 50/51 also saw an 8-0 defeat at Somerset Park and a 7-2 loss to St Johnstone.

Andy Geggan in action against East Stirlingshire in 2013

August 25 1965

Dunfermline began their League campaign well with a fine 3-1 win over Motherwell at Fir Park this Wednesday night in front of a healthy crowd of about 8,000.

However, it was a game that got a bit tough and tasked referee Mr Ian Foote to the utmost. Bookings became frequent in the second half, particularly after an injury to Jim McLean which did not seem to be result of an accident.

Dunfermline's start to the season had not been 100% satisfactory and Saturday had seen a depressing 1-3 defeat to Kilmarnock at East End Park in a League Cup sectional match, but this was the first game in the Scottish League.

The weather was fine, and the fair amount of Dunfermline's travelling support had cause to cheer late in the first half when Alex Ferguson smashed home an Alex Edwards' cross.

All the rest of the scoring action came in the last 15 minutes of the game when Ferguson scored his second goal, then Motherwell came back into the game through a penalty kick scored by McCallum.

Dunfermline however then clinched the game when Ian Hunter ran on to a loose ball inside the penalty area and scored.

For Dunfermline, Pat Delaney and Alex Ferguson were booked, but it was still looked upon by Manager Willie Cunningham as a good result and a good start to the League campaign.

Motherwell were not a bad team and, under the leadership of Bobby Howitt, were the holders of the Summer Cup, a trophy which had been played for in May.

The trophy had suffered from not having Celtic and Rangers among the competitors but Motherwell still had every reason to be proud of their success, and this made Dunfermline's result tonight all the more creditable.

Alex Edwards

August 26 1995

In some ways, this was a tough time to be a Pars fan.

Bert Paton's teams had played exciting football, but the previous two seasons had ended painfully, losing out on the last day in 93/94 to Falkirk, then suffering the same fate in 94/95 behind Raith Rovers.

Three points for a win had been introduced in 1994.

Still with only one promotion place, winning promotion in 95/96 looked a tough one, with a strong Dundee United side clear favourites after their relegation in May.

Having started with a win at Airdrie on the opening day, today saw the first home league game and the Arabs were the visitors.

In a frantic, action-filled game, the Pars would have the better of the first half without managing to score. With Dundee United coming more into it in the second half, it took until the last 20 minutes for the goals to come.

Firstly Stewart Petrie bundled in after Ally Maxwell saved his initial shot, before the moment the game is best remembered for.

Completely losing it, United's Dave Bowman made two ridiculous, dangerous tackles in the space of two seconds, causing absolute fury on the terrace beside him. There was little complaint about the referee's decision to send him off.

A Greg Shaw header then a glorious breakaway finished off by Allan Moore gave a final score of 3-0, and a very happy start to the season. This was the first indication that this was to be a very special season in the history of Dunfermline Athletic.

August 27 1938

After a poor start that had seen a 4-1 defeat at Alloa on the opening day and a scoreless home draw with Airdrieonians, Dunfermline today achieved their first win of the 38/39 season.

Buses had been organised by the supporters' club to take fans to Stirling for this away fixture against King's Park and those returning on them afterwards would surely have been very happy with the 2-1 win.

Matches between the clubs had become known as unpredictable affairs and this was no different. In a tight game between two well matched sides, the home side led early on with a penalty. After 20 minutes, a fine equaliser after good interpassing between Robertson and Redmond had Dunfermline level.

The same pair would later combine for the winner, with Redmond being put through and shooting past the keeper. Although nobody knew it at the time, this was Dunfermline's last trip to Forthbank Park.

The outbreak of war a year later saw the league curtailed in September, and King's Park did not re-start in 1945 when most other clubs did.

Only one bomb was dropped on Stirling during an air attack in 1941, and it was incredibly bad luck for the football club that it fell on their ground and destroyed the stand.

Financial difficulties meant that this was a blow too far, and it was not possible to find the money to allow the club to continue. With a similar history to Dunfermline's this was a sad loss to the game, though Stirling Albion would shortly emerge as a new senior club in Stirling.

Albion's current ground, Forthbank Stadium, is on a different site but close to the original King's Park ground.

August 28 1915

The Second Division of the Scottish League having been suspended because of the War, Dunfermline returned once again to local competition, in this case to what was called the Eastern League.

Today, Dunfermline travelled to Scott's Park, Kirkcaldy, to play Kirkcaldy United with the future of both clubs in a great deal of doubt. Kirkcaldy had been financially struggling even before the war, and Dunfermline's East End Park had been requisitioned by the military, leaving the club homeless and compelled to play on other grounds.

They had applied to play at McKane Park but the rugby and cricket teams had proved awkward so Athletic were urgently looking for somewhere else. Today, however, at Kirkcaldy the heavy rain severely limited the attendance at the somewhat primitive Scott's Park.

Athletic, having lost to Lochgelly United last week, got their first victory of the season with a 3-1 win. Dunfermline had several "guest" players as was permitted under wartime regulations – notably Robertson of Falkirk and Rattray of Raith Rovers, and a few soldiers on leave – and won a hard match, although it was not until the last ten minutes that they managed to assert themselves with goals from Robertson and Brown.

Wartime football was often like that, of course, because players tired easily, having worked a half-shift in the munitions industries in the morning, and of course having little opportunity for training.

Dunfermline would eventually find temporary and not very satisfactory accommodation at Blackburn Park, but poor Kirkcaldy United would disappear at the end of this season, and never return.

August 29 1989

Dunfermline had a tremendous victory this Tuesday night at Easter Road in the quarter final of the Scottish League Cup.

The game was moved to the Tuesday night because Hearts were at home to Celtic on the Wednesday.

The tie went to extra time and kept the creditable crowd of 16,000 on tenterhooks throughout. Ian Paul of *The Glasgow Herald* was of the persuasion that the victory was due to "collective stamina rather than individual inspiration".

Hibs pressed hard and for long periods of the 120 minutes, it was the Easter Road men who were on top.

It was Doug Rougvie (the possessor of a European Cup Winners' Cup medal from his Aberdeen days) who put the Pars ahead with a header from an Abercromby corner after the Hibs defence had looked static as the ball came across.

Then John Collins equalised for Hibs in the second half, but Collins's drive needed the benefit of a deflection off Norrie McCathie.

And so this pulsating match went to extra time. Hibs had the first chance but fluffed it, but Dunfermline's Paul Smith made no such mistake when the ball came to him immediately after a pass from George O'Boyle reached Smith via the leg of John Collins.

Smith was still able to squeeze the ball in from a very narrow angle. Hibs now renewed their pressure, but Dunfermline resisted until at the very end Ross Jack in a breakaway hammered home the goal that had all the Dunfermline supporters going mad with joy.

Many freely admitted to being weak-kneed after such a great game of football and such a triumphant outcome.

August 30 1919

As happened two weeks ago, the man who made all the difference to Dunfermline today in the Central League was Andy Wilson of Middlesbrough.

The question of how long Dunfermline would be able to hold on to him was asked again in the Press after the 2-1 victory at Brockville over Falkirk Reserves.

Although Reserves teams were often good – and Falkirk's men here put up a good show, they were indeed the Reserves, frequently referred to contemptuously as the "ham an' eggers".

The nickname came from the fact that they weren't always professionals, but they did get their tea which was often ham and eggs, a treat in 1919 Britain, where *The Sunday Post* warned that bread would be dearer tomorrow, and tried, unconvincingly, to blame it all on "more Hun treachery".

The real worry as far as Wilson was concerned was not that Middlesbrough would claim him back but rather that Wilson himself might tire of playing against some poor teams in the Central League when he could be facing more demanding opposition in England.

In addition, how would the Scotland Selectors react to all this?

But Dunfermline now had four points from three games (two points for a win) and were looked upon as potential Central League winners along with Alloa and St Bernard's.

There was little doubt that football was off to a flying start in the first official peace time season.

The admission charge had been raised to 1 shilling, something that had caused a little resentment in certain areas with a few threats of boycott by some supporters, but it hadn't come to much. Men were just glad to be home again and enjoying football.

August 31 1957

Dunfermline had bad luck today when they failed to qualify for the quarter finals of the League Cup.

They had to beat Brechin at East End Park and duly did so, but not by enough goals. The 3-1 score-line was insufficient.

What really killed the Pars was the goal scored by McRae of Brechin, for the goal average system was "goals for" divided by "goals against" which means that the goals against were more important.

McWilliam, Duthie with a penalty kick and Colville scored for Dunfermline with all the goals coming in the second half, but it was to no avail.

Another goal for the Pars would have done the trick and ensured qualification. Brechin, Dunfermline and Ayr United all finished with 7 points from 6 games in what was a very tight section but Dunfermline could hardly complain for earlier lapses (1-4 at Ayr United and 1-2 at Brechin City) and a home draw with Cowdenbeath were what sealed their fate.

Brechin's qualification meant that they now played Hamilton, whom they defeated to reach the semi-final and a money spinning tie against Rangers.

Rangers themselves qualified in a similar scenario to Brechin, for Raith Rovers were simply not able to score enough goals on the last day either.

Tonight was a significant one in Scottish social history for this was the night in which Scottish Television was launched. Dunfermline was just in the area to be able to receive reasonably good quality pictures and sound, and although the reception was not as good as that of BBC, it was good enough and there was now a choice of viewing.

September

A young long-haired Jim Leishman

September 1 1973

It was to be hoped that last year's sojourn in the Second Division was just a temporary blip, but the first game of the League season could hardly have been more difficult – the visit of Celtic, League winners for the last eight years!

However, it was often said that Celtic could be quite vulnerable early in the season and maybe this was a good time to get them.

The Pars had suffered hard luck in the League Cup section, losing out narrowly to St Mirren, and hopes were high that they would at least give a good account of themselves this season.

It was a strange day – very sunny and warm but also with frequent blasts of wind, and today was quite a funny sort of game. Celtic scored in the 20th minute but could not add to their lead, nor could Dunfermline equalise.

It was a good game, however, with loads of good football and Dunfermline at last got their reward in the 80th minute when Mackie equalised.

Sadly level terms did not last long for Paul Wilson headed Celtic in front almost immediately and then poor Jim Leishman conceded an own goal more or less at the end.

Jackie Sinclair then pulled one back for Dunfermline, but there was not even time for the ball to be centred after that, and 2-3 was the result.

Jock Stein, a man who clearly still had some sympathy for the first team that he ever managed, admitted that a draw would have been a fairer result. There were some encouraging signs for the season ahead.

September 2 1939

This was a truly remarkable day in world history.

Football continued nevertheless; Dunfermline continued their early season good form with a 5-2 win over Brechin City at East End Park in front of a crowd of about 1,000 people – a slightly disappointing attendance, perhaps, on a fine, warm, possibly even a little sultry and oppressive day.

In every sense of the word, it was believed that thunderstorms could happen at any time.

Yesterday the German Army had invaded Poland under the specious pretext of wanting a "corridor" to East Prussia and a claim on the city of Danzig. It was however nothing other than international thuggery and Britain and France who had guaranteed the security of Poland were preparing an ultimatum telling Germany to get out or face war.

Frankly, war was inevitable, and the teams ran out today with the House of Commons in emergency session.

Black and Johnston (described as "a grand entertainer" by *The Sunday Post*) each scored two goals, and Murray one after Brechin had pulled a couple back, but welcome as the points might have been, the future was a foreboding one.

Some spectators had come in to the game with their gas mask (conventional wisdom seemed to decree that Dunfermline, an industrial town close to Rosyth Naval Base would be bombed first by the Luftwaffe which had flattened Guernica in Spain).

The National Anthem was played before the game and sung vigorously, and everyone was aware of all the disabled supporters, still not even middle-aged let alone old, who were watching the game from their wheelchairs, victims of an earlier, horrible conflict. Some wept at the end of the game.

September 3 1966

A good day for Dunfermline.

They qualified for the quarter finals of the Scottish League Cup by beating Falkirk 2-1 at Brockville before a large crowd of nearly 10,000 containing many busloads from Dunfermline.

It had been a very close section involving Dunfermline, Falkirk, Motherwell and Partick Thistle; Dunfermline travelled the short distance to Falkirk aware that even a win today would not necessarily guarantee qualification, depending on the result from Firhill.

If Motherwell had won, it would have gone to the quirks of goal average, but in the event, Thistle held Motherwell to a 0-0 draw, and Dunfermline's 2-1 win was enough.

But they did it the hard way. Scott scored for the Bairns in the third minute of the game, and for the remainder of the first half, Falkirk were quite clearly the better team, playing their first really good game of the season.

In the second half Dunfermline fought back, scoring first after about ten minutes through Hugh Robertson after the Falkirk defence had failed to clear a Tommy Callaghan cross, then George Fleming had a fairly easy tap-in to put Dunfermline ahead.

There now followed a nervous half-hour to the final whistle with no-one really knowing for certain what was going on at Firhill either, although the 0-0 half-time score had been encouraging.

Mr Small's full-time whistle brought a little relief (for Falkirk had been fighting hard and the game had become rather feisty) and then a loudspeaker announcement confirmed that the Firhill game had ended 0-0, and that the Pars were therefore in the League Cup quarter finals.

September 4 1915

East End Park had been requisitioned for war purposes.

Dunfermline played their first home game of the season (they had already played two away games) at Blackburn Park, Rumblingwell.

This was in the Eastern League, and it was a very convincing 7-1 victory over Leith.

One year and a month into the war, there was a certain credibility problem about this game. Personnel had changed drastically, the ground was a different one and this was a new competition called the Eastern League.

The encouraging thing was that a good crowd turned up to see the game, some of them soldiers in uniform home on leave with one or two of them seen to be suffering from minor wounds.

Dunfermline probably benefited from the amount of military and naval personnel and munitions workers in the area, and as regulations for "guesting" were not particularly strict, many strangers featured in the Dunfermline team which gave the fans a great deal of entertainment.

Leith actually scored first, but that was only a temporary set-back, and there were "goals galore" in the second half with Robertson of Falkirk and Rhind of Queen's Park doing particularly well for Dunfermline Athletic.

Everyone knew that next week's team would be totally different – but that was war-time football! The "close football down" lobby had now been silenced for a while, and there was a growing realisation that war-time football, even with all its limitations, was nevertheless good for morale in these desperately awful times.

There was no obvious sign of any early resolution to the war.

September 5 1931

Dunfermline today lost 1-2 to Alloa Athletic.

It was, by all accounts, a dreadful game in which Alloa were twice down to 10 men but Dunfermline, in front of a sparse and disillusioned crowd, were unable to take any advantage of the opportunity.

Alloa scored in the first minute, then increased their lead; although Young pulled one back for the Pars, the game finished to a few boos and what is worse, the silence of apathy.

The day was hot and sultry, and the pitch was bumpy but that was no great excuse. But Dunfermline's defeat was hardly the major talking point of the weekend.

Evening papers carried the story of John Thomson of Celtic being carried off with a head injury at Ibrox. "Jock" was well known to many people in Dunfermline, having played for Auchterderran School, Bowhill Rovers and Wellesley Juniors before signing for Celtic in 1926.

Rumours spread that the injury was serious, but it was the Sunday papers the following day that confirmed that he had died of a depressed fracture of the skull in the Victoria Hospital, Glasgow.

Dunfermline Athletic and their fans were well represented at the funeral which took place the following Wednesday at Bowhill Cemetery, Cardenden.

John had won two Scottish Cup medals with Celtic in 1927 and 1931, and had now played four times for Scotland, including a fine performance in the game at Hampden last March when he kept a clean sheet.

Scotland won 2-0, and he had been introduced to the then Labour Prime Minister Ramsay MacDonald – both men quite clearly in awe of each other.

John was mourned in Dunfermline as much as anywhere else.

September 6 1958

Games played in extreme weather conditions often live long in the memory, and that will surely be the case for those who turned up at East End Park for this derby fixture against Raith Rovers.

As *The Dunfermline Press* somewhat romantically put it,

> 'The fact that twenty-two players, a referee, two linesmen and five thousand brave-hearted spectators considered play possible at all is testimony to the magic "pull" of football'.

It might be said that conditions were a wee bit on the wet side. After two pitch inspections, legendary referee Tom Wharton decided to start the game and soon afterwards awarded the visitors a penalty for handball.

With the kick converted, the weather became even worse with lightning cracking overhead, thunder rocking the ground and rain so heavy that visibility was restricted.

It must have been bad, as the referee took the players off for 15 minutes. Upon resumption, play was twice stopped to inspect the ever-increasing puddle at the South-East corner of the ground, but on both occasions referee Wharton decided to play on.

With players on both sides slipping and sliding all over the place, a Charlie Dickson header levelled the scores. However, almost immediately after the restart, the game had run its course and was abandoned.

The *Press* report notes "Next minute Mr Wharton splashed about in the pool and inspected the lines. Then he waved the players off for good and the game was abandoned".

Bearing in mind that this was the 1950s when games were often played on pitches that would never pass inspections today, conditions must have been really ridiculous.

The mental image of 'Tiny' Wharton and his massive frame splashing around in something resembling a duck pond before deciding the pitch wasn't playable is one that must surely bring a smile to the faces of many football fans.

Charlie Dickson

September 7 1935

While the world laughed and scoffed at the idea of Mussolini's Italy possibly invading Abyssinia (tanks and aeroplanes against barefooted warriors with spears!) Dunfermline travelled to Kilmarnock with a new and unknown goalkeeper called William Wilson.

He had played for Newcastle United in the year that they won the English League in 1927, but had most recently played for Duns and possibly feeling that his career was heading to a conclusion.

Dunfermline however had surprised him by offering him terms. Today at Kilmarnock, he showed the world that he was by no means past his best, saving a sadly outplayed Dunfermline time and time again and earning them an unlikely 2-1 victory.

He was beaten only the once, and that was by an unstoppable shot three minutes after the interval. Before that, Syme had scored for Dunfermline against the run of play in the first half, and then seven minutes from time, McGowan scored the winner for the Pars.

Rugby Park was a ground that Dunfermline tended to do well at – they had won there last season as well – and this result was a boost to the small band of Dunfermline supporters who had travelled all the way to the west coast.

Everyone knew that life would be hard for Manager Willie Knight's side this year, but this result early in the season gave them a boost, and with a goalkeeper like Willie Wilson on board, there was little to be afraid of.

But there was more to be afraid of in the International situation. A month later, Mussolini did indeed invade Abyssinia with the League of Nations unable to intervene, and Hitler kept making bellicose noises.

September 8 1962

It was derby day and sunny at East End Park, as Raith Rovers came to town.

They had already met twice this season in the Scottish League Cup section, and both games had been draws in a section won comfortably by Kilmarnock.

That had been a disappointing start to the season, but the general consensus was that Dunfermline were playing better than Raith Rovers.

Not even the most absurd of optimists, however, could have predicted what would happen here today. Dunfermline simply took Raith apart and beat them 6-0 – and it could have been an awful lot more.

Raith were handicapped by a bad injury to their veteran Andy Leigh, the only man left of their famous half-back line of Young, McNaught and Leigh, but that is their only excuse.

George Peebles and Charlie Dickson had scored two each before half time, and the 4-0 score line when shown on the other half-time scoreboards cause a few ripples of comment.

At half-time, Jock Stein urged no easing off, and another two goals were added, one from Alex Edwards and a penalty from George Peebles. Raith Rovers hit the bar at one point, but that was the closest they came. Dunfermline were now top of the First Division.

That didn't last long, although the Pars finished respectably, whereas Raith Rovers were relegated at the end of the season. Raith had been in the First Division since 1949, had enjoyed many glory days, but had now simply run out of steam with all their good players having aged simultaneously.

It was almost as if they were handing over the Fife First Division ticket to the Pars.

September 9 1967

Disaster struck the Fife coalfields today when fire broke out at the Michael Colliery in East Wemyss, claiming the lives of 9 men.

This was the largest pit in Scotland at the time, employing more than 2,000 people. The devastating effects were felt all through the Wemyss villages but also in mining communities across Fife.

The fire caused the permanent closure of the mine and only half of the workforce returned to mining elsewhere. As a fundraiser for the disaster fund, a benefit match was held at East End Park on Monday September 25 1967 between a Fife Select and a visiting Sunderland side.

The Fife eleven contained a balance of players from the four Fife senior clubs and in sombre circumstances, they won 4-2 with goals from Alex Edwards (Dunfermline), Ian Porterfield (Raith Rovers), George Dewar (East Fife), and Andy Rolland (Cowdenbeath). Roy Barry and Willie Callaghan were the other Pars representatives with George Farm also being manager for the evening while Fifers Jim Baxter and George Kinnell both featured for the Rokerites.

Andy Rolland would later play an important role for Dunfermline, notably scoring a vital penalty against Falkirk on the last day of 78/79 to win promotion ahead of the Brockville side.

Ian Porterfield would shortly move to Sunderland, where he would famously score the winning goal for the second division side in the 1973 FA Cup Final against Don Revie's Leeds United.

In this game, however, it was Alex Edwards who stood out, scoring once to equalise before brilliantly setting up goals for Porterfield and Dewar with outstanding wing play.

The 6,000 crowd contained some representatives of English clubs, but the majority were Fifers paying their respects to nine of their own who had died in terrible circumstances.

Programme Cover for Fife Select v Sunderland. Note the misprint concerning the date. The game was actually played on Monday September 25 1967

September 10 1985

Tonight Jock Stein, the Manager of Scotland, collapsed and died.

It was more or less at the full-time whistle of the World Cup Qualifying match at Ninian Park, Cardiff, in which Scotland had earned a play-off place for the 1986 World Cup.

This was of course terrible news for all football, but nowhere more so than in Dunfermline; it had been with Dunfermline that he had first learned how to manage a football team.

He did so with conspicuous success, leading the Pars to a promised land, beyond the wildest dreams of any supporter who had watched the team in that mediocre decade of the 1950s, of trophies and playing in Europe.

He was Manager from 1960 until 1964, arriving from his post as Reserve Team Coach at Celtic Park to, in the first instance, save the Pars from relegation. (He did this by beating Celtic in his first game, incidentally!)

Then against all the odds, he took the Pars to their first ever Scottish Cup final where they beat Celtic on that never to be forgotten night of April 26 1961.

From then on, Dunfermline Athletic were on the map! He never won any other honour with the Pars, but there were several great adventures in Europe.

When he departed in 1964 (to the distress of all his many fans) he left a legacy of success and, more importantly, expectation of success in the minds of all supporters.

He always retained a great affection for the club that gave him his first real chance, and although he was always likely to be linked in people's minds to Celtic for his European Cup triumph and their nine League titles in a row, he will never be forgotten in Dunfermline.

September 11 2004

Dunfermline may have been the Scottish Cup runners-up last year, but this season had not got off to the best of starts for new manager David Hay and his men.

Dunfermline went in to to-day's home fixture with Motherwell without a win to their credit, and only one point from the opening day draw with Dundee United.

Although the defeats had been narrow, the recent spell of poor form had also included the extremely painful late loss to Icelandic team Hafnarfjordur in the UEFA Cup.

To-day however with Scott Wilson and Barry Nicholson returned from injury, things looked a lot better and in 9 minutes Dunfermline went ahead when veteran goalkeeper Gordon Marshall blocked a shot from Darren Young and Craig Brewster was there to score with the rebound.

The 4438 crowd reacted well to this rare event and, for a while after that, everyone enjoyed the pleasant autumn sunshine with the Pars holding the lead. Indeed, Billy Mehmet really should have scored once and possibly twice to put Dunfermline further ahead, but half-time came with everyone happy.

But it is a truism that a 1-0 lead is not enough, and hard though Dunfermline tried, they could not get the goal which would give them a cushion. The inevitable happened.

Motherwell, a reasonable side under Terry Butcher, came more into the game. Their equaliser however was stunning and unexpected, and came from Australian Scott McDonald who volleyed home from at least 30 yards when the ball broke to him unexpectedly.

The fans were naturally stunned and shattered. The outburst of booing and at the full-time whistle was perhaps hard on the Pars players who had been the better side, but it was indicative of a club now seriously struggling at the bottom of the league after a period of comparative success.

September 12 1961

History was made tonight at East End Park when Dunfermline Athletic played their first ever game in Europe.

This was the European Cup Winners' Cup and the game was against the Irish team St Patrick's Athletic of Dublin.

The team won 4-1 with goals from Charlie Dickson, Harry Melrose, George Peebles and Tommy McDonald as against one goal (admittedly a very good one) from O'Rourke of the Irish side.

Thus Dunfermline were able to look forward to their return leg in Dublin in a fortnight's time with a degree of confidence. The crowd was about 12,000 but it was not a great game with Dunfermline finding the close marking tactics of the Irishmen difficult to deal with.

The Glasgow Herald is patronising and damns the Pars with faint praise, describing the Irish part-timers as "little better than a good Scottish Second Division side" (a description that not all that long ago would have been appropriate for Dunfermline themselves!), but the main thing was that the team won comfortably enough.

The predominant emotion of the Dunfermline crowd was one of awe and even a little disbelief that their team was playing in Europe.

It looked as if it were going to be the way of the future but a glance at the old grandstand would have convinced anyone, had they not realised it already, that the ground was as yet far from adequate for even the visit of the bigger teams in the Scottish First Division, let alone the possible arrival of great European teams.

Next year however there would be a new stand, and the future was bright. But more mundane matters awaited – a trip to Kirkcaldy to meet Raith Rovers on Saturday!

September 13 1997

This was a rather disappointing day for Bertie Paton's Pars as they went down 2-5 to Hibs at Easter Road.

It was actually described, prematurely, as a "top of the table" clash. Both teams had already this season beaten Celtic and the Pars had also beaten Hearts twice (in league and Scottish League Cup).

Today, however, they went down rather badly to Hibs. Dunfermline's best opportunity came in the period immediately after they went ahead. Marc Millar scored with a neatly taken penalty after Andy Tod had been brought down by the goalkeeper, but then hit the post a few minutes later and soon after that, Allan Moore missed another chance.

It could have been 3-0, but in fact it was only 1-0, and this Hibs team who had many fine players on view took full advantage of this situation with the maverick Chick Charnley outstanding.

By the time substitute Stewart Petrie scored the second goal for Dunfermline, Hibs had scored five and Dunfermline, although never totally overwhelmed, had been crushed by some fine Hibs play which was not, however, anything like as good as *The Edinburgh Evening News* would have had us believe.

No-one at this stage would have believed that Hibs would be the team relegated at the end of the season. Dunfermline, for their part, were destined to finish third from the bottom, something that supporters found acceptable.

They had a terrible run in midwinter, but picked up enough draws and registered the occasional win (including Hibs when they came to East End Park in November) to ensure safety.

September 14 1963

Dunfermline and Hearts both preserved their unbeaten League records today in a 2-2 draw at East End Park before an attendance of more than 10,000 with the maroon and white colours of Hearts prominent in the crowd.

Both teams had already won twice in the League and the standard of play lived up to the billing, but it was Hearts who looked the livelier team at the start of the game.

Yet they had a lucky escape when Chris Shevlane had to clear a George Peebles shot off the line with Cruickshank beaten, and then immediately after that, Hearts ran up the field and Norrie Davidson scored from a Willie Wallace cross. When Johnny Hamilton then scored with a penalty correctly awarded by veteran Dundee referee Bert Crockatt, the 2-0 score line was hard on the Pars, but before half time they were level, both goals scored by George Miller.

The second half was a little quieter with no further scoring, but that did not mean that it was a poor game. Dunfermline pressed more than Hearts did, but they could not get the ball past the excellent Jim Cruickshank in the Hearts goal.

Full time came with the score still 2-2, and Managers Tommy Walker and Jock Stein were both full of enthusiasm about the play of their sides.

In the meantime on the broader scene, speculation continued as to the future of the government of Harold McMillan, now fatally stricken by the Profumo scandal, and not destined to last very much longer.

September 15 1951

One of the greatest days in Dunfermline's history, today in front of a 20,000 all ticket crowd at East End Park (which looked dangerously over-populated in places), Dunfermline (still in Division "B") beat Rangers for the first time ever.

It was the most animated anyone could remember the town being for many years with thousands of Rangers supporters arriving from early in the morning.

This was the first leg of the Scottish League Cup quarter final (a competition in which the Pars tended to do rather well in those days) and Dunfermline won 1-0 through a Gerry Mayes goal in the second half when he beat Willie Woodburn and squeezed a ball past Bobby Brown in the goal.

It would have to be said that Rangers piled on the pressure but generally failed to get the better of centre half Jimmy Clarkson, and in particular the bald head of goalkeeper John Moodie who had joined the club recently on a free transfer from Cowdenbeath.

Nevertheless, the ageing Bill Struth, the Manager of Rangers, was reluctantly compelled to admit that the better team won. "They scored and we didn't!" he snapped ungraciously at a journalist.

The only fly in the ointment as far as the Dunfermline supporters were concerned was that the game was not yet over, for the second leg had yet to come at Ibrox on Wednesday evening.

Nevertheless, many Dunfermline supporters were now intending to be on the special train that was leaving Dunfermline Upper Station at 3.04 pm on Wednesday afternoon to go to Ibrox to see the second leg.

Action in the League Cup quarter final against Rangers in 1951

September 16 1953

7,000 people were at East End Park to see "B" Division Dunfermline exit the Scottish League Cup to their old rivals East Fife.

It was in fact the second leg of the quarter final, and the tie seemed to have been put out of Dunfermline's reach in the first leg at Methil on Saturday when East Fife won 6-2.

But the optimists always reckoned that an early goal might work wonders, and lo and behold, that was exactly what happened – but at the wrong end! It was Charlie Fleming who scored for East Fife, and he was merely picking up where he left off on Saturday.

Dunfermline were always particularly vexed about Fleming for he came from Blairhall, just a few miles away, and it was often felt that he had slipped through the net.

He was certainly doing the business for East Fife, and he scored another two before half time to record his hat-trick for the night, eight goals for the tie, and to make the aggregate scored 9-2 for East Fife.

To their credit however, the Pars fought back and scored though a Henderson volley and a Clarkson header, to make the final aggregate score 9-4 and earn a degree of respect.

Dunfermline's primitive stand tonight contained quite a few Managers and representatives of English clubs, all here to have a look at "Legs" or "Cannonball" Fleming. It was only a matter of time before East Fife would pick up a fat transfer fee for Charlie, but not before they won the Scottish League Cup again this season.

Dunfermline Athletic, season 1951-1952

September 17 1927

Having just escaped relegation by the skin of their teeth last season, Dunfermline were off to a dreadful start this season with five defeats in a row, two of them real hammerings from Motherwell and Hearts.

Today Celtic appeared at East End Park, and it would have been a very brave Dunfermline man who would have predicted anything out of this game, for Celtic were the Scottish Cup holders and contained some great players like Jimmy McGrory and Tommy McInally.

A large crowd duly appeared with loads of Glasgow accents and green favours among them. It was Dunfermline however who were off to the brighter start and, in the 25th minute, after both sides had missed chances, it was Bobby Skinner who put Dunfermline ahead in a goalmouth scrimmage.

Not that it lasted long, however, for a couple of minutes later the much under-rated but always consistent Adam McLean scored for Celtic with a drive from "about 40 yards out" according to *The Sunday Post* (it was possibly a little less than that, one feels) to make the score 1-1.

Celtic then besieged the Dunfermline goal for more or less the rest of the game, but goalkeeper Harris had a good day, some Celtic players, McGrory in particular, had an off day, and the Pars defence held out heroically.

In fact, they could have won the game near the end but for some fine goalkeeping from a young Fifer called John Thomson, well known to many Dunfermline supporters in the crowd.

Both teams were given a big hand at the end for such a good performance, but Dunfermline's supporters were happier than those of Celtic.

September 18 1948

Dunfermline's Scottish League Cup section this year consisted of three Fife teams and Stirling Albion.

It promised to be tight. Last week Dunfermline and Raith Rovers had played a thrilling 3-3 draw and today Dunfermline travelled to Central Park, Cowdenbeath to win 2-0.

A crowd of 9,000 was an excellent attendance and indicative of the boom in the area in this post-war era when every scrap of coal was needed for post-war recovery (and no-one complained about the use of fossil fuels!)

The victory was not as clear cut as it sounded, for the teams were very equal until Hamilton, the left back of Cowdenbeath, was injured and had to play on the left wing (substitutes were still the best part of 20 years away) thereby giving Dunfermline a definite advantage.

Yet they could not capitalise, for they kept frittering away their chances while Moodie in the Cowdenbeath goal gave an inspired performance.

The game looked as if it were heading for a goalless draw until a slip by Shankland allowed Cannon to run on and score. Dunfermline were now well on top and late in the game a handling offence led to a penalty kick, and McDonald put it away to give the Pars a 2-0 victory.

Joy was however mitigated when the radio announced the scarcely believable Stirling Albion 1 Raith Rovers 7 in the other game in that section. Dunfermline were due to visit Kirkcaldy next Saturday and it was clear that they would have to watch Willie Penman, who scored six goals today.

September 19 1951

Those who feel that referees favour Rangers had grist for their mill in the events at Ibrox this Wednesday evening, and in particular the performance of referee Mr Main of Glasgow was questioned.

This was the second leg of the Scottish League Cup quarter final when Dunfermline went down 1-3 to Rangers.

The game had a tea-time kick-off, for floodlights had not yet arrived in Scottish football.

In the a crowd of 44,000 Dunfermline supporters were clearly in a minority but by no means an insignificant one.

Dunfermline were one up from the first leg and Rangers, grimly desperate to atone for their poor performance at East End Park, went on to the attack and very soon Willie Findlay had scored twice.

Tommy Wright pulled one back, and then Dunfermline were awarded a penalty kick. This was the big chance to go ahead again, but Jimmy Clarkson shot too close to goalkeeper Bobby Brown. The opportunity had gone, to the immense disappointment and distress of the Dunfermline fans.

But then came the moment that Pars fans found hard to accept. A hard shot from Findlay was saved by goalkeeper Moodie, but he was then shoulder charged (still legal in 1951) by Gardiner of Rangers and suddenly Mr Main gave a goal.

Jack Harkness of *The Courier* — goalkeeper of the Wembley Wizards in 1928 — was appalled and says quite directly "it certainly did not look over the line to me".

In addition, a good looking goal from Gerry Mayes was chalked off, so the Pars and their fans had every reason to be unhappy as the left Ibrox that night. When Dundee beat Rangers in the final, no-one in Dunfermline burst into tears.

September 20 1949

In one of the few highlights of the sadly under-performing history of Dunfermline Athletic, this Tuesday night draw earned the Pars a place in the Scottish League Cup semi-final.

Because Rangers were coming to Cowdenbeath on Wednesday, Dunfermline and Airdrie opted to play the second leg of their quarter-final tie early. On the Tuesday, a day before all the other ties being played, they reaped their reward in the shape of a large crowd of 10,000 and loads of attention in the Press. Because of early darkness in September, the game had to kick off at 5.45 pm.

Dunfermline were 4-3 up from the first leg played at Broomfield on Saturday and tonight's game, despite finishing goalless, was no less exciting and hard-fought.

This result of course suited the Pars, who were cheered off the park by their fans at the end.

The Courier singles out centre half Willie Kelly and goalkeeper George Johnstone for praise in keeping Airdrie at bay, but the rest of the team, inspired by Jimmy Clarkson, deserved credit as well.

Near the end, after a few close things at either end, Airdrie almost took the game to extra time as a Murray header hit the bar, the ball rebounded to Seawright who fired in a fierce shot which was well saved by George Johnstone.

Minutes after that, referee Mr Watt of Edinburgh blew for full time, and the Pars were in the semi-final with the luxury now of sitting back to see who would join them.

Hibs v Partick, Forfar v East Fife and, the game that the Dunfermline players would attend, Cowdenbeath v Rangers were all due to be played tomorrow.

Dunfermline Athletic 1949. Back Row - Kirk, McCall, Johnstone, Clarkson, White, McLean; Front Row - Mayes, Cannon, Henderson, Wright, Smith.

September 21 2019

It was with a huge sigh of relief throughout the "auld grey toon" that Dunfermline Athletic notched up their first League victory of the season.

The start to the league season had been abysmal (by no means the first time in history that one could say that!) with two draws and three losses, and questions had been asked of Stevie Crawford as manager.

This recent run of results had come after a less than impressive finish to the previous season. Today's victory was over a club in even more dire straits than the Pars were – Partick Thistle, currently managerless, having sacked Gary Caldwell in midweek.

It was almost like waking up in hospital, and then seeing that one of your enemies was in the next bed! The talk in the Boardroom was about poor performances, lack of money, players that didn't always do as well as they were capable of, and the lack of people coming through the turnstiles.

The crowd was a desperately awful 2,820 (and even that looked an exaggeration at a desolate Firhill on a fine autumn afternoon) but they saw a very good performance from Dunfermline with goals from Kevin Nisbet, Ryan Dow and Kyle Turner.

2-0 up at half-time, a third goal early in the second half killed the game and allowed the Pars to sit deep, defending comfortably.

As it was still early in the season, a win makes a huge difference to one's League position, and Dunfermline were now fourth from the bottom. Form improved a bit after this win, but mid-table was as good as it ever got in this slightly odd, ultimately curtailed season.

Kyle Turner has just scored against Partick Thistle in 2019

September 22 2015

The Pars exited the Scottish League Cup tonight, losing 1-3 to Dundee United at Tannadice after extra time.

Considering that Dundee United were two Divisions above them, it was not a bad performance.

Both Manager Allan Johnston and the travelling fans in the 5174 crowd pronounced themselves happy with what they had seen, if disappointed not to be going any further in the competition.

Dunfermline had beaten United's rivals Dundee in the previous round, and tonight when they scored first, it looked as if a "Tayside double" was on the cards.

The goal was a strange one, scored by Michael Paton after he picked up a pass from Joe Cardle and shot, to his own obvious disappointment, more or less straight at the goalkeeper. Sadly for the goalkeeper, he allowed the ball to squirm through his arms into the net.

It was then that ex-Dunfermline man Callum Morris headed an equaliser for United not long before half-time.

The second half was reasonably even with chances for both teams and El Bakhtaoui in particular having bad luck for the Pars near the end. But to extra time it went, and it was then that the slightly slicker home side got the two goals that settled the tie.

They were scored by Scott Fraser and Blair Spittal. Jackie McNamara, now Manager of Dundee United, was very fulsome in the praise of the team that he used to play for, and the hope was expressed that the Pars should continue their early season form and earn a deserved promotion into the Championship.

September 23 2006

It would be a fair comment that the Pars needed this victory over St Mirren!

Apart from their narrow win over Kilmarnock a fortnight ago, they had been winless in the League and on the Wednesday night previously, they had, without disgracing themselves, gone out of the Scottish League Cup.

Manager Leishman rang the changes, but the 4,914 crowd were distinctly unimpressed by what they saw in the first half.

Fortunately, in the words of the biggest cliché of them all, it was a "game of two halves" (a phrase used by Jim Leishman himself) and the turnaround in the second half was very impressive.

John Sutton had put St Mirren ahead in the first half, but it was the lack of fight from the Pars that had angered the crowd.

In the second half, it was as if Manager Leishman had substituted every single man, and the effect was immediate with the Pars now attacking the Norrie McCathie Stand end of the ground.

Darren Young, hitherto lethargic and anonymous, scored straight from the restart by feeding Jim Hamilton on the right and then hammering home the return.

Those who had spent too long in the queue for half-time refreshments missed that one; the winning goal also came suddenly when the St Mirren goalkeeper threw the ball out to Stevie Crawford who promptly hammered the ball home.

St Mirren now fought hard for an equaliser, but none came. It is to be hoped that Dunfermline supporters enjoyed this victory, for there were not destined to be an awful lot more of them this season!

Sol Bamba in action against StMirren in 2006

September 24 1991

After a penalty shoot-out in a game that was always more than just a little contentious, tonight at Tynecastle Dunfermline reached the final of the Scottish League Cup.

Airdrie were the opponents, a team who had already defeated Aberdeen and Celtic, a tough team who were admired, but never loved, for what they were doing in Lanarkshire.

Their persecution complex was given a major boost tonight by a refereeing decision by David Syme which was controversial to say the least.

Airdrie had scored first through Owen Coyle and for most of the game seemed to be in command against a determined Dunfermline side who picked up no fewer than three yellow cards.

The game seemed to be fizzling out when a huge punt from goalkeeper Andy Rhodes reached the edge of the penalty area and looked to hit Airdrie defender Jimmy Sandison on the chest.

Referee Syme saw it differently, though, and awarded a penalty kick, ignoring all Airdrie protests. Derek McWilliams duly obliged and the game went to extra time with Airdrie still muttering.

They possibly allowed things to upset them too much, however, for they could still have won the game, never more so than when Kirkwood hit the post late in the extra time period. And so to penalties. It was a very parallel contest. Both sides scored, both sides missed, both sides missed again, both sides scored again.

Then John Watson, a one-time Pars hero but now with Airdrie, missed; his friend Norrie McCathie scored — to give Dunfermline a place in the final against the winners of tomorrow night's Hibs v Rangers match.

One would have thought that Airdrie were the only team ever to have had a dodgy penalty kick awarded against them the way that they went on about Mr Syme, whose hand they refused to shake on any subsequent occasion in which they were officiated by him!

September 25 1915

The Battle of Loos started today.

It was possibly the worst so far in the war and included chemical warfare deployed by the British (affecting also their own men when the wind changed!).

Like so many battles in the Great War, it could only be described as a stalemate.

Unaware of such momentous things happening in France (although there had been much talk of an imminent "push") Dunfermline today played St Bernard's of Edinburgh at Blackburn Park (East End Park having been requisitioned by the military) in what was called the Eastern League.

The Scottish League Second Division had functioned last season, but had been stopped because of travel difficulties and because so many clubs were finding it difficult to field a team.

However, an Eastern League of 12 local teams had replaced the Second Division. Certainly no-one would have complained about any lack of entertainment today, for Dunfermline won 5-4, although the standard of defending by both teams led spectators to presume that some of the players might have struggled to get a place in a team in more normal circumstances!

Jimmy Robertson, who had once played for Falkirk before the war, winning a Scottish Cup medal in 1913, was a "guest" player for Dunfermline (such things were allowed under war time regulations).

He scored four times in a game where Dunfermline were 5-2 up before St Bernard's pulled two back to make it 5-4. The referee's final whistle was greeted with a huge cheer by the small but enthusiastic crowd.

September 26 1925

Dunfermline continued their impressive start to the season with a good 5-0 win over Clyde.

"Grenadier" of *The Courier* is convinced that Dunfermline will occupy an "exalted position" in the League at the end of the season, and this result put them in second place behind Third Lanark, whom Dunfermline were due to visit at the end of next month.

Today before a good crowd on a good day, the Athletic simply swept their opponents aside with Bobby Skinner once again convincing the crowd that he was something special.

But for Fraser in the Clyde goal, the tally would have been a great deal more, and it was late in the game before Skinner got himself on the scoresheet.

The first goal was a somewhat fortuitous own goal, then Sutton and Low scored fine goals before Skinner brought the house down with a couple of great individual goals – the first a charge up the field, the second more like "a slalom in ski sport", as he evaded several defenders before crashing the ball home.

Centre half Clark was also praised by the Press, and goalkeeper Muir had a couple of great saves but was an "interested spectator" most of the time.

August had been a little uncertain but form in September made them out to be real promotion candidates. Dunfermline had never been in the top flight before, and this seemed to be their best opportunity for a while.

It was also felt that Dunfermline were benefiting more than most teams from the change to the offside law (intended to allow more goals to be scored) though it certainly helped to have a man who could indeed score goals!

September 27 1930

The economic depression was at its height (or should one say its depth?) when Stenhousemuir came to East End Park today.

Often looked upon as the poorest supported club in Scotland, Stenny nevertheless had managed to keep going through the late 1920s when so many other teams were falling by the wayside.

They had started the season particularly badly however, and today did not make things any better for them when they went down 11-2 to Dunfermline, a score that stays as a record to this day as far as Dunfermline were concerned.

Dunfermline were off to a reasonable start to the season, and at half-time they were 4-2 up. Even the six goals and the generally entertaining game did not keep everyone happy though, for as *The Courier* concedes, Stenhousemuir were, at this stage, every bit as good as Dunfermline.

Goalkeeper Couper and left back Frame were singled out for preventing Stenhousemuir from being in the lead at half-time.

New manager Willie Knight must have said something to Athletic at half time, and another seven goals were added without reply to make it a baker's dozen aggregate of goals.

Rarity, Sclater, Paterson and McAndrew were the goal scorers before half time, and then in the second half, Leggat, Hamilton, Leggat, Sclater, two from Paterson and finally a penalty kick from Hamilton sent the home fans home happy.

Since then high scoring days from the Pars have been something of a collector's item, although the ten scored on the last day of the 1959 season to save them from relegation come close.

September 28 1983

"They couldnae even beat Forfar!" had often been the moan of Dunfermline supporters in times gone by when things were bad.

This remark, patronising and insulting to the good men of Station Park, had come true before, but never more emphatically than on this mild Wednesday night at East End Park.

Only 856 people (and a lot of them were from Forfar!) turned up to see a 2-1 win for the Loons which should in fact have been a lot more.

Paul Donnelly scored for the Pars, but Jim Liddle and Ray Farningham scored for Forfar. Forfar, slicker, more determined and faster to the ball were now clear at the top of the League (and they would win it in April) under the managership of Doug Houston, whereas Dunfermline were struggling near the bottom.

It was now becoming increasing clear that Manager Tam Forsyth was not really cut out for the job, and his days were numbered. It was an odd experience to leave a stadium which had obviously been built for better days.

On the car radio going home, Scottish teams like Rangers, Celtic, Dundee United and Aberdeen were all doing well in Europe.

Dunfermline, who had once beaten Everton, Valencia and West Bromwich Albion, were struggling in the Second Division, their result not even mentioned until the round up near the end.

Yes indeed, changed days! But it wouldn't always be like that. Someone mentioned that they thought Jim Leishman might make a good Manager.

September 29 1962

Today Jock Stein's side travelled to Shawfield to play Clyde.

Shawfield always was a strange stadium, purpose-built for greyhound racing rather than football, and was never the best place to watch a game because the greyhound track created an artificial distance between spectator and player.

Likewise, Clyde were a strange team.

Possibly too geographically close to Celtic to ever command a huge Glasgow support, nevertheless they were always a team which seemed to attract good players.

They had a chequered history, having won the Scottish Cup in 1955, been relegated in 1956, been promoted back up again in 1957, and won the Cup again in 1958!

Their yoyo existence continued and last year they had won the Second Division championship.

Today before a crowd of about 5,000 they started off playing the better football. It was somewhat against the run of play that Dunfermline took the lead from a shot by Alex Edwards in the 19th minute. George Peebles had made some ground then passed to Edwards who kept the ball on the grass as he beat goalkeeper McCulloch.

Dunfermline now took charge of the game, and with a bit of luck they might have scored a few minutes later and then George Peebles hit the post with a penalty awarded by referee Tom Wharton for handball.

Dunfermline's strong defence, with McLean and Fraser outstanding, were always able to prevent Clyde from scoring. The wonder was that the Pars did not add to their lead, but a 1-0 win at Shawfield, a ground at which many a Pars team struggled before and since, was a very good result.

September 30 1905

Scott's Park, Pathhead, Kirkcaldy was the scene today of one of the best achievements of Dunfermline Athletic in their 20-year existence.

Thanks to their victory in the replay of their Second Round Scottish Qualifying Cup game against Kirkcaldy United, the Athletic had now qualified for a place in the Scottish Cup proper after the New Year.

Normally, a team had to play in three rounds, but Dunfermline were one of the lucky teams to be given a bye.

In the meantime, the Scottish Qualifying Cup campaign would of course continue, and a trip to either Ayr Academicals or Beith was the destination for Dunfermline.

Today's game was played in splendid weather although there was a strong wind, and the receipts were £58 plus a "tidy sum" from the grandstand.

No indication of how many people were actually there, but if everyone paid a "siccy" (six pence in old money) that would suggest that there were well over 2,000 spectators.

They saw a good even game, possibly even better than last week's draw, but this time, it was Dunfermline who got the only goal of the game when Douglas "rushed in with the ball at his feet and beat Young from close quarters".

Against that, Kirkcaldy felt that the ball was heading towards the goal at one point until Pitblado punched the ball clear, unseen by referee Mr Neilson of Thornliebank.

Dunfermline supporters who made up a good percentage of the crowd were delighted with their team today. It is always good to beat a team from Kirkcaldy!

October

October 1 1955

Today Dunfermline recorded their first League win of the season at Annfield, the ground of Stirling Albion.

This was of course Dunfermline's first season back in Division One since before the Second World War and no-one had said that it was going to be easy.

Today's game at Stirling was one of these games that Andy Dickson's men simply had to win, if they were to entertain any realistic hope of avoiding relegation, already being mentioned among the more pessimistic fans.

Not only did they win this game, but their victory today was the springboard to a very good October which saw them up near the top of the First Division!

Not that it lasted long, of course, but it gave the fans something to cheer about. Stirling Albion were only a decade old, having emerged after the war to take the place of King's Park, the previous Stirling club.

Last year, by rights, they should have been relegated but because the First Division was being increased from 16 teams to 18, the bottom two teams of Motherwell and Stirling Albion were allowed to remain.

The crowd was about 5,000 on a reasonable day, and it was the Pars who scored first, Miller heading home an Anderson corner kick.

Stirling however equalised before half time, and for a long time in the second half, it was difficult to see any winner in this game, until with fifteen minutes left, a through pass from Peebles found Reilly who ran on and scored.

Dunfermline then managed to hold out in the face of some hysterical pressure from the home side.

October 2 1971

Dunfermline today travelled to Aberdeen.

Against a very good Aberdeen side, with a healthy crowd of 14,855 inside Pittodrie, the Pars lost 2-0.

Dunfermline were very much a team in decline (they had been lucky to avoid relegation last season and would be less lucky this season).

Aberdeen, on the other hand, were a team very much on the up, so much so that they were threatening to replace the currently dysfunctional Rangers side as the main threat to Celtic. Aberdeen had won the Scottish Cup in 1970 and had run Celtic close last season.

As a result of today's game, the Dons were now top of the League as both Celtic and Rangers went down, to St Johnstone and Hearts respectively.

It was Joey Harper who scored first today from the penalty spot after Fraser had brought down Miller, and then Stevie Murray added a second.

Dunfermline Manager Alec Wright brought on Joe McBride as substitute in the second half but even his experience and proven goalscoring ability availed naught.

This well-drilled Aberdeen defence all understood each other and could play the offside trap to perfection.

Dunfermline's best players were Ernie McGarr in the goal and John Cushley at centre half. This defeat, albeit predictable, was depressing for Dunfermline fans (who had travelled north in reasonable numbers).

Although it was as yet a little early in the season to talk about relegation, only one victory in five League games after an appalling Scottish League Cup campaign was a cause for concern nonetheless.

Dunfermline Athletic in 1981-82. Back Row - B Dall, Harris, Henderson, Tait, Blackie, Scullion, S Dall, Wilcox, McGovern, Stewart, Thomson; Middle Row - Johnson, Stewart, Mercer, Leishman, Morrison, Young, Whyte, Robertson, Jenkins, Salton, Forrest, Thomson; Front Row - Nelson, Hegarty, Donnelly, Dunlop, Brown, Hamill, Hutt, Bowie, P Stanton (Manager); Insets K Thomson, McNaughton

October 3 1981

It didn't seem all that long ago since these two, Kilmarnock and Dunfermline Athletic, were playing in Europe and challenging for the old First Division League title.

Nowadays they were in the second tier, confusingly called the First Division when there was in fact a Premier League above them.

On this dull day, Dunfermline travelled through to Rugby Park, Kilmarnock and possibly even surprised themselves with a 1-0 victory over the home side.

Managed now by Pat Stanton, one of Scottish football's best-ever players (certainly one of the best ever to come from Hibs) but arguably without the managerial skills required for the job, the Pars had made a reasonable start to the League campaign.

Today Grant Jenkins put them ahead on the half-hour mark with a shot from the edge of the box. Soon after that, Sandy McNaughton might have made it 2-0 but his header was just over the bar.

The 0-1 score line however was a little tough on Kilmarnock who had enjoyed enough of the play to score but had been denied by Dunfermline's rugged defending. The same was true throughout the second half, but Dunfermline held on to retain their lead.

This result meant that both Kilmarnock and Dunfermline were on ten points from nine games, still some five behind League leaders Motherwell, who had recently appointed David Hay as their Manager.

The rest of this season was a little frustrating for Dunfermline, who never really recovered from a lengthy lay-off because of bad weather in midwinter, and they finished in the lower half of the League – something that the fans did not relish in the slightest!

October 4 1902

At North End Park, Cowdenbeath, Dunfermline brought off a surprise today by beating "the Miners" 2-1 in a Northern League match, with *The Courier* predicting that Dunfermline will this year create a few surprises.

Their previous form, it would have to be said, provided no such encouragement, but today was a different matter altogether for the game was won with "good all round play".

In defence, goalkeeper Thomson was singled out for praise as were the two full backs, Strang and Pitblado.

Beveridge scored two minutes after the start, another goal was ruled out by referee Urquhart, and only nervousness in front of goal prevented Dunfermline from going in a far healthier margin ahead.

In the second half Wilson equalised for Cowdenbeath, although it looked to most people that he was offside.

That refereeing error, if indeed it was one, was cancelled out when Dunfermline were awarded a penalty kick for handling; it looked to the reporter of *The Courier* that it was accidental. However that may be, Pitblado had no hesitation in scoring from the spot.

Dunfermline were considered well worth their victory over Cowdenbeath, who were, of course, an older team (formed in 1881) than Dunfermline were and better established in Scottish football.

It was a great triumph in a local derby. The game was attended by some soldiers, home on deserved leave after the end of the Boer War earlier this year. They were admitted free and clearly enjoyed the attention and the ability they had to entertain the spectators near them with stories (no doubt embellished and exaggerated) about what the war was like.

George Peebles, 1961

October 5 1963

Jock Stein's men fought back well today to consolidate their place near the top of the First Division table with a 2-2 draw at Celtic Park.

Mind you, the way Celtic had been going of late made one feel slightly disappointed that the Pars hadn't come away with a win. Celtic were a team on their knees. They had already lost three times to Rangers since the start of the season, and frankly had not a clue how to deal with the psychological trauma of it all.

It was one of those days when Jock Stein must have looked at the Celtic management… and wondered. The Pars on the other hand, after a disappointing League Cup campaign, had rallied and were undefeated so far in the League.

The weather was pleasant enough, but the Celtic crowd were slow to turn up – a protest against their team's awful performances, and the Pars fans were able to make themselves heard.

It was Celtic, in spite of having both Billy McNeill and Frank Haffey out with flu, who were the better team in the early stages and Bobby Murdoch put them ahead at half time.

When Frank Brogan put Celtic further ahead, things looked grim for the Pars, but this team knew enough about the game to rescue themselves from this tricky situation and first it was Jim Kerray who picked up a through ball from Harry Melrose to crash it past John Fallon.

The second goal was a brilliant header from George Peebles from an Alex Edwards corner kick.

The dispirited Celts were now there for the taking, but Pars lost Jim Kerray, carried off injured, and were not quite able to force a win.

October 6 1962

Top of the table Hearts came to East End Park today.

The kick-off had to be delayed for about 15 minutes to allow the huge maroon-clad contingent of Hearts supporters in the 20,000 crowd to get in.

This was a rare phenomenon indeed, but it did give everyone the opportunity to admire the new stand which had been functioning for a couple or months now.

Even the Hearts fans had to admit that it looked good, contrasting it with their own stand which had seen better days. Hearts were on the crest of a wave at the moment with a 100% record in the League, and on Wednesday night they were due to play in the League Cup semi-final against St Johnstone.

It was the precocious but unstable Willie Hamilton (later to go on to Hibs and to become Jock Stein's greatest player for that club) who made the first goal slipping the ball to Danny Paton to put Hearts ahead.

Then after the Pars had equalised through Alec Smith, Hearts went ahead again from the penalty spot, Willie Wallace (also to become a great player for Jock Stein in the future) converting after Willie Hamilton had been fouled.

In a torrid but all-action second half, Dunfermline equalised — also through the penalty spot — after Harry Melrose had been brought down by Roy Barry; Willie Cunningham did the needful.

The game was not without its controversy and several other penalties might well have been awarded, but everyone agreed that it had been a great game of football with 2-2 a fair result.

October 7 1967

Dunfermline's start to the season had been anything but impressive so far.

Today however they recorded a good away win at Pittodrie, always a place from where it is difficult to pick up points.

Eddie Turnbull's team had reached the final of the Scottish Cup last season and were now showing signs of further improvement.

The Pars on the other hand had not all immediately taken to George Farm whose brusque and occasionally dictatorial manner possibly caused a certain amount of insecurity.

A crowd of about 10,000 saw a good game in which Pat Gardner scored the only goal, a fine effort scored from a Robertson knock-down.

Gardner had of course come to the Pars from Raith Rovers soon after Farm arrived, and he was soon to become an all-time Pars great.

Aberdeen fought back in the second half, but their cause was not helped when Jimmy Wilson was sent off for a spot of retaliation after he had been niggled by a few Pars players.

Pars finished on top and returned south with two points in their pockets and a smile on their faces. It was a bad day for players being sent off, because in England in a game between Manchester United and Arsenal, two Scottish Internationalists, Denis Law and Ian Ure picked a fight with each other and were invited by the referee to depart the scene.

It may have been an old score from a Scotland trip together, or they might just have been over-motivated by their respective Managers. But that was of little concern to the triumphant Dunfermline supporters.

October 8 1949

31,633 were at Tynecastle today to see Dunfermline Athletic beat Hibs to reach their first ever national Cup final.

This was the Scottish League Cup, now in its fourth year and already well established as a major tournament.

It was confidently expected that the two form teams of the era, namely Rangers and Hibs, would reach the final but in fact it would be the Fife duo of Dunfermline and East Fife who would battle it out in three weeks' time.

The Sunday Post has a very enthusiastic reporter of this game who calls himself "The Traveller". "It was an ex-Hib who hammered the Hibs" he trumpets with a reference to Gerry Mayes.

He was carried off at the end by the referee and a team mate for he had collapsed with cramp while defending desperately.

The Pars had one advantage in that Gordon Smith, Hibs' right winger, arguably the best player of the era;. Called the "Gay Gordon" not in any reference to his private life but more in a tribute to the way he could dance through defences, he was out injured and replaced by a man called McDonald who "is full of promise but still a bit short of being a Gordon Smith."

Dunfermline were well supported, with the trains all crowded to Haymarket Station where they disgorged in their thousands for the short walk up to Tynecastle Park.

A semi-final was rare territory for the Pars in 1949, but those who wore the black and white were shocked when Hibs took the lead with a Lawrie Reilly goal in the early stages of the match.

But today was all about Gerry Mayes, a man who had been free-transferred twice in his career, once by Hibs and once by St Johnstone.

He had been picked up by Dunfermline's Webber Lees and was doing a good job for the Second Division side. Today proved the old adage that "ilka doggie has his day" and Gerry scored twice to give the Pars a thoroughly deserved place in the League Cup final.

His equaliser was a glorious diving header from a Smith cross in which he was "horizontal" as he headed home. It was 1-1 at half-time, but as the second half went on, it began to seem inevitable that the full-time training of the First Division side would tell, until, that is, Mayes scored a remarkable goal.

He chased a long ball along with Hibs defender Davie Shaw, and it began to appear that the ball was running out of play with Shaw "shepherding" the ball over the line, until Mayes stuck out a foot and diverted the ball past Tommy Younger into the Hibs net. "The Traveller" tells us that up in the stand behind him "Fifers danced a Highland fling".

The remaining 14 minutes saw Dunfermline having to defend desperately with even Mayes back to help out, but they managed to hold out and returned home to a heroes' reception.

"And," concludes The Traveller "just in case you think they were lucky, let me tell you that Dunfermline were the better team from start to finish. They played almost all the football. They took only two of half a dozen fine chances".

Most of the Dunfermline supporters arriving home that day would have been surprised when they heard the news from Hampden that their opponents in the League Cup final would be East Fife, for whom Charlie Fleming had scored an extra time goal.

The day was however a tragic one for the men from Methil for their esteemed and much loved Chairman John McArthur collapsed and died in the Directors' Box. He had a heart condition and was at this game defying Doctor's orders.

October 9 1965

Only 8,000 turned up at East End Park in fine autumn weather to see what was, arguably, the most attractive game of the day.

It was between two teams who had started the season well – Dunfermline and Dundee United.

This history of these two teams had been remarkably parallel over the past decade. Under-performing outfits in the Second Division for a spell, then they both built a new stand to replace the previous grizzly horrors, and made steady progress in the early 1960s.

Jerry Kerr's outfit had brought a few Scandinavian players to the club and they had a deserved reputation of being hard to beat, particularly at home, and they were gradually ousting out Dundee FC as the top team on Tayside.

Today they played very well to beat the Pars, and Dunfermline had no complaints at all. The first goal was a penalty sunk by Lennart Wing after Willie Callaghan had needlessly handled in the box.

Then, of all people, their rugged left back Jimmy Briggs added a second in a goalmouth scramble before Hugh Robertson pulled one back for the Pars.

The early stages of the second half were Dunfermline's best period of the game, but the game turned when Dundee United scored a third with an all Scandinavian affair – Orjan Persson slipping the ball through to Finn Dossing. Dunfermline appealed for offside but the referee was adamant, and the goal stood.

Then Jimmy Briggs scored his second goal of the game before Alex Smith scored a late consolation goal for the Pars. A 2-4 defeat at home was a sore dunt, but there was little doubt that the better team won.

October 10 1914

Dunfermline's form had not been too good of late.

It was all the more rewarding to see them register a 3-0 victory over Abercorn (a now defunct Paisley team) in the Scottish Second Division today.

Hall scored two for Dunfermline, and Whitelaw one, and it was generally regarded to have been a good and entertaining performance from the East End Park side.

The good people of Dunfermline (and everywhere else for that matter) needed something to cheer them up, for today was the first really bad day in the War.

It was the day that Antwerp fell to the Germans. Antwerp, a strategically important inland port, had been under siege for a couple of weeks, and while much as the British Press talked about heroic resistance and how evil the Germans were, no amount of sugar coating could hide the fact that this was in fact a colossal military disaster, and that Belgium would soon be lost to the Germans.

All this intensified the recruiting drives (there was a speech delivered at half-time at East End Park, talking about "duty" and how much everyone enjoyed life in the army) but they still did not impress everyone.

More people in Dunfermline were badly affected by the story of Lance Corporal Alexander Milne who was married one Wednesday, enlisted the following Wednesday and about ten days later was wounded in the spine at the Battle of the Marne and died in hospital at St Nazaire in France.

The need to have something to counteract such horrors was why football, in spite of many attempts to stop it, remained so important to the civilian population.

October 11 1958

Bottom of the table Dunfermline travelled to-day to meet Kilmarnock, who hadn't started the season all that well either.

The weather was OK, but the crowd was a very poor one, perhaps symptomatic of the age in which one lived in that football clubs could no longer take it for granted that a large crowd would turn up.

The crowd seemed about 3,000 at the start and the atmosphere was non-existent with the sound of players shouting to one another and of dogs barking in the background outside the ground.

The Evening Times tries its best to say something nice about the game, but at half-time with the score apparently immovable at 0-0, it says "Although the football was sometimes neat, it was very far short of being a hair raising first half".

However, things took a turn for the better when Jimmy Watson scored from a George Peebles free kick to the delight of the very small band of travelling Dunfermline supporters.

This was in the 60th minute but then disaster struck veteran Harry Colville. He had played so well against young Joe McBride who had always looked as if he were the most likely of the Kilmarnock players to equalise.

On this occasion however, Colville got in the way of a Muir drive and the ball was deflected into the net.

The 1-1 result was not a disaster, but it was a disappointment after the Pars had been ahead for so long, and the hard facts were that seven League games had been played and Dunfermline had won only one, against Falkirk.

October 12 1985

Meadowbank Thistle were today's visitors to East End Park.

They were not a team that the Pars had met very often, tending to be in different divisions.

They are now of course better known as Livingston, having started life as Ferranti Thistle, but since 1974 they had played at the Meadowbank Stadium in Edinburgh.

Today's crowd of 2,612 was astonishingly large for Division Two (the third tier of three in 1985) and proved what we had always said, namely that Dunfermline were far too big a club for the Second Division.

Meadowbank, not entirely without supporters themselves, seemed to relish playing in front of a large crowd and a good game was enjoyed by all.

Pars supporters would have been a little disappointed, one feels, to have only drawn to a goal scored in the second half by Darren Jackson, a man who would make his name with many clubs.

This had equalised a goal scored by Stuart Morrison in the first half.

Dunfermline stayed second in the table behind Queen of the South but, generally speaking, Pars supporters were happy with their team so far this season with men like John Watson and Grant Jenkins among the goals.

It was a strange season, however, with the country still coming to terms with the death of Jock Stein a month ago in Cardiff and mourned in Dunfermline as much as anywhere, while Scotland were still not sure whether or not they would be playing in the Mexico World Cup of 1986.

A play-off with the winners of the Oceania/Israel section was beckoning. It would in fact be Australia.

October 13 1964

European football returned to East End Park this Tuesday night.

Dunfermline Athletic beat the Swedish side Orgryte 4-2 in front of 8,000 fans.

It was not however all plain sailing for the Pars because two defensive errors meant that the half-time score was 2-2. It was only in the second half that they began to assert themselves as the Swedish part-timers began to tire.

This game may well have been significant in the career of one of the Swedish players, Orjan Persson, who made no bones about the fact that he definitely wanted a transfer to a full-time team, and would not mind playing in Scotland.

Dundee United were in fact watching him that night and would have been impressed by the first goal in which he ran more than 40 yards through a static Dunfermline defence to put the ball past Jim Herriot.

(Jim Herriot was the inspiration for the pen name James Herriot, the pseudonymous writer of *All Creatures Great and Small*. James Wright, the actual author, saw the name in a team line at some point and thought it was perfect for his character.)

McLaughlin and Sinclair scored for the Pars before half time, although Simonsson had scored for the Swedes as well. In the second half it was the same two players who scored again.

Dunfermline finished this game well on top, although certain reservations were expressed about whether a two goal lead was enough for Willie Cunningham's men.

The Swedes had looked good, but quite a few Dunfermline fans began to visit that fairly new phenomenon of the 1960s, the travel agent, to see whether a trip to Sweden was a realistic possibility.

Above all, there was a feeling of relief that at least the Pars were back playing in Europe again. Having not qualified last year, the season had certainly lacked something.

October 14 1922

A touch of heroism was seen here in Dunfermline's unfortunate defeat to St Bernard's at Logie Green in the Scottish League Second Division.

The Athletic goal was scored by outside right Brown who had only just returned to the field of play with what looked like a dislocated arm.

He played on, even after scoring the goal, with his arm hanging uselessly by his side. Even the St Bernard's supporters in the 5,000 crowd gave him a round of applause for that.

It was of no avail, for the Edinburgh side equalised and then won the game after Dunfermline's forwards had repeatedly failed to find a way through the St Bernard's defence.

St Bernard's were a team based in the Stockbridge area of the capital, and so proud were they of their local identity that they insisted that every player who played for them must live within the boundaries of the village of Stockbridge, even though the "village" no longer existed, having been long ago absorbed in Edinburgh.

Both teams were in the middle of the Second Division, and now Dunfermline looked as if they were going nowhere.

The "roaring twenties" had not yet arrived at East End Park, and most Dunfermline supporters agreed that their team was hard-working and honest, but lacking in any kind of sparkle.

With Willie Knight now in charge as Manager, improvements were possible.

Meanwhile, the newspapers were full of speculation about the date of the General Election with the imminent collapse of Lloyd George's war-time coalition.

October 15 1997

Dunfermline put up fierce resistance tonight at Ibrox in the Scottish League Cup semi-final against Celtic, but eventually were beaten 1-0.

The weather was unpleasant and the crowd was a slightly disappointing one of 27,796, but the Pars supporters who had travelled through to occupy the Copland Road end of the ground had every reason to be pleased with their team.

Both teams gave their all in what was a typical Scottish cup-tie of the best order. Half time saw no scoring although Ian Westwater of Dunfermline had been the busier goalkeeper.

Celtic went ahead in the 70th minute when a lay-off from Henrik Larsson to Craig Burley caught the Pars' defence by surprise and Burley hammered home.

Celtic looked now as if they would be able to hold out to reach their first League Cup final since their Raith Rovers disaster of three years ago, but late in the game saw the moment that almost earned Dunfermline what would have been a not undeserved period of extra time.

The grey-haired Hamish French (who was a veteran certainly but not as old as he looked!) hammered in a shot from outside the box which was only seen at the last minute by Jonathan Gould in the Celtic goal.

The Pars fans were already rising to acclaim it as an equaliser, but it was not to be.

Both teams left the field to a standing ovation with Celtic's Manager Wim Jansen paying magnanimous tribute to the Dunfermline team while Bertie Paton was philosophical about his team's bad luck.

Celtic would go on to win the League Cup that season, beating Dundee United 3-0 in the final, but for Dunfermline it was a frustrating night.

October 16 1954

This day saw a serious blow to Dunfermline's promotion hopes when they lost 1-2 to Third Lanark at Cathkin Park.

Third Lanark, sadly no longer with us, were a strong team in 1954 with a good support and their stay in the Second Division was looked upon as a temporary phenomenon.

Nevertheless, it had been Dunfermline who were off to a better start and today's reverse was considered to be a serious blow.

Managed by Bobby Ancell, the Pars had suffered a defeat at Cowdenbeath (always a difficult one to take) but had beaten Ayr United and Brechin City in recent weeks and drawn with Arbroath.

Today's domestic football was overshadowed by the International going on in Wales, and a disturbing new phenomenon, the portable radio, (called by some people a Portobello!) had made its appearance.

It gave spectators the good news that Scotland beat Wales 1-0 with the goal coming from Paddy Buckley of Aberdeen.

It was less good news for Pars fans at Cathkin (a fair amount of them had made the trip) for Dick scored for Thirds late in the first half, and then after George O'Brien had equalised for the Pars from an Anderson cross, Thirds notched the winner late in the game, the score coming from a young fair haired chap called Ally MacLeod.

This man would earn a name for himself as a Manager of Ayr United and then Aberdeen in the 1970s before becoming Manager of Scotland and tragically coming to spectacular grief in Argentina in 1978.

October 17 1925

Today Dunfermline made the short trip to Recreation Park, Alloa to play against a team who were seldom out of the news in the 1920s.

Alloa had been the first winners of the new re-constituted Division Two in season 1921/22, but may well have wished that they hadn't, for they came straight back down again but had made steady progress on the road to recovery in 1924 and 1925.

They were off to a bad start this season, though, but today's game was a highly entertaining one.

Alloa opened the scoring when Scoular headed home a lovely corner kick from Deuchars, but Dunfermline equalised soon after, and it was the man of the moment Bobby Skinner who scored the goal.

He picked up a loose ball in the centre circle and ran towards the goal showing devastating ball control and when goalkeeper Hughes came out, he lifted the ball on to his own head and nodded it into the empty net.

It was a marvellous piece of skill, much applauded by the Dunfermline fans, who now began to realise that they had a goal scoring genius of the type they had not seen since Andy Wilson in the days of the immediate aftermath of the Great War.

Skinner had been with the club for almost a year now, and this season he would score 53 goals in 38 League games, not all of them as good as this one was, but each one very valuable. There was no further scoring in this match, although both teams had a few chances.

October 18 1924

After some mediocre form, Dunfermline suddenly came good today and surprised and delighted their supporters with a 4-1 win at home over Arbroath.

The attendance was not great, although there were a few supporters from Arbroath. It was Jimmy Dickson, one of last year's signings of Willie Knight who came good today with a hat-trick, his first two goals coming from crosses from the right and his third being scored in a melée.

The fourth goal was scored by a man called Marshall, who had recently been signed from Falkirk.

Arbroath's solitary counter came from what looked like an offside position, according to the writer of *The Sunday Post,* who thought that Arbroath were very disappointing.

It is to be hoped that this result would do something to keep the Dunfermline fans quiet, for there had been all sorts of moanings heard, not least because Cowdenbeath and Raith Rovers were both doing better than Dunfermline were.

Certainly, second from bottom of the Second Division table was an unacceptable place for Dunfermline to be. The best team in Scotland at the moment continued to be Airdrie who had won the Scottish Cup last year and were currently top of the First Division.

These matches were played out with the General Election campaign in the background. The first Labour Government of Ramsay MacDonald had come to an end – it was a minority one in any case – and Willie Watson was putting himself forward again for re-election in Dunfermline.

The general consensus was that Watson would win again on October 29, but whether Labour would increase their majority was another matter.

October 19 1985

Today saw a visit to Firs Park, Falkirk, the home of East Stirlingshire, one of the great survivors of Scottish football.

Founded as early as 1881, they even played in the old Scottish First Division as recently as 1963/64, but you wouldn't have thought that at their desolate little ground today.

They are one of the teams that one had to give credit to because of the enthusiasm of just a few people to keep the club going when many others would have folded.

Today's crowd of 1,100 (about 60% of whom seemed to have made the short trip from Dunfermline) was their biggest of the League season so far, and the game was somewhat one-sided.

Not that any of the Pars fans were complaining, for they saw their team consolidating their promotion challenge with a 4-0 victory over the Shire. Grant Jenkins scored twice, and Stuart Morrison and John Watson once each with Trevor Smith missing a first half penalty into the bargain!

It was an extremely confident and comfortable victory for the Pars which strengthened their League position, but today, Pars supporters were in the unusual position of supporting Raith Rovers!

Raith were at home to Queen of the South who were still topping the table, and a win for the Kirkcaldy men would have seen Pars take over at the top. Alas! Queen of the South won 1-0, scoring through a fellow called Dick.

Pars supporters commented uncharitably that it was Raith Rovers who were the real dicks!

October 20 1962

A surprising and disappointing defeat for the Pars today at Firhill, the home of Partick Thistle.

In certain circumstances (a win for the Pars and a defeat for Hearts) Dunfermline might have been top of Division One tonight. Then again Partick Thistle were always known as the "Old Unpredictables" especially at their home ground which was, not without cause, called "Firhill for thrills".

The attendance was surprisingly small on this dreich but dry day in which Partick Thistle were two goals up before half-time, both coming from Gordon Whitelaw.

The first was very much against the run of play and followed a prolonged game of "head tennis" before the ball broke to Whitelaw. Thistle seemed to gain confidence after this, and Whitelaw's second goal was a beautifully controlled drive after an error in the Pars defence.

The Pars rallied in the second half and Alex Smith pulled one back with a header, following a corner kick from George Peebles, but otherwise goalkeepers George Niven and Jim Herriot were in superb form. Although both teams missed chances, there was no further scoring.

It was a disappointment for the club, but the supporters were cheered up by the news that Scotland had beaten Wales 3-2 in Cardiff that day.

Mind you, they would not have been human if they hadn't been just a little concerned about the build-up of tension in the Caribbean Sea after the Americans had found that the Russians had some missiles there pointing towards the United States!

It was what became known as the Cuban Missile Crisis.

October 21 1961

East End Park today hosted the match of the day as table-topping Dundee came to town.

Rather to their own surprise, one felt, Bob Shankly's side had taken the country by storm with some fine performances, and today they brought a large crowd of dark blue and white clad Dundonians (the biggest Dundee crowd that anyone could remember coming to East End Park) to watch them.

Among the normal banter, there were still a few disparaging comments about the old stand, but that would not last much longer.

Jock Stein's men went ahead with a penalty kick sunk by Ron Mailer after George Peebles had been brought down

For a long time it looked as if the Pars were about to inflict on Dundee their second defeat of the season, but with Gordon Smith on the right playing absolutely superbly, Dundee equalised half way through the second half with a shot from an acute angle by Alan Cousin, a man whose day job was a teacher of Classics at Alloa Academy.

The game then see-sawed from end to end, but it was Dundee who got the winner within the last ten minutes through Alan Cousin again.

A late furious Dunfermline rally failed to produce an equaliser, and Dundee edged home. It was in fact a very good day for the Dee because Celtic lost to Hearts and Rangers could only draw with Motherwell.

For the Pars fans, even though disappointed at their team's narrow defeat, it was a great consolation to feel that they were part of the big time.

October 22 2011

This was a grim relegation battle at Inverness.

October is possibly too early to be talking about "relegation" but the descent of the Pars had been quite alarming.

A good start to the Premier League season with wins over St Johnstone and Dundee United had been followed by six defeats and one draw, and today they faced the long journey up the A9 to meet Terry Butcher's Inverness, who were now bottom.

Dunfermline's last goal had been scored a month ago, and today they did not look like getting one either until a late Liam Buchanan penalty saved the day for the Pars.

They had been trailing to a Gregory Tade first half goal; hard though they fought, they did not, in the opinion of the 3,421 crowd and the travelling support, look as if they were going to get back into the game.

Manager Jim McIntyre expressed satisfaction in his team's "resolve", but there did seem to be a distinct lack of talent in the team. Not for the first time in the life of Dunfermline Athletic, people remarked on the huge gap that existed between Divisions.

The team who had done so well to earn promotion last year were clearly struggling this year. Not only was the standard a great deal higher – that was to be expected – it was also a different game, so that they were compelled to play with a draw, like this one, being looked upon as a good result.

It was no great secret either that Dunfermline Athletic, like quite a few other clubs, were in financial trouble.

October 23 1909

Today Dunfermline "pursued their conquering career" by beating Hearts of Beath 5-2 in what was called the Wemyss League, a competition between Fife teams played when there was no Central League or Scottish Qualifying Cup fixture.

Some games were played in the Qualifying Cup today and *The Courier* notes solemnly that Morton, Elgin and Forfar had all "passed away" i.e. they had been knocked out.

But Dunfermline had a "tough nut to crack" today in Hearts of Beath, even though they were always the better team. Not for the first nor last time were complaints registered about the "deplorable state" of the pitch at East End Park, and the game was in any case played with all the brutal ferocity that one would expect of a Fife derby.

Three penalties were awarded and there was also a nasty clash of heads which saw Harvey of Dunfermline and Denholm of Beath carried off.

Harvey was able to resume after treatment but was "nervous because of his injury" which possibly means he was still a little dazed. Wyllie and Hay each scored twice, but there is no mention of who scored the fifth goal.

Rather surprisingly to modern readers, the game finished ten minutes early because of darkness. It is surprising on two grounds – one that there was no apparent protest about this from the defeated side or an attempt to rearrange the fixture, and the other was why they did not "wise up" to this in the first place by starting the game a little earlier?

October 24 1964

Dunfermline continued their good early season form with another impressive win, this time 2-0 over the under-performing Aberdeen side at East End Park.

It was a fine mellow autumn afternoon for the 8,000 crowd and they saw Willie Cunningham's side, without being outstanding, nevertheless do enough to get the better of the Dons whose supporters, there in surprisingly large numbers, left East End Park shaking their heads at the ineptitude of their team.

Aberdeen fans have a reputation of being unhappy, miserable, torn-faced people, and today they had cause to behave like that.

Dunfermline opened the scoring after John McCormick (who had recently joined the Dons from Third Lanark) was short on a pass back and Alex Ferguson pounced, beat Tubby Ogston in the goal and squared the ball to John McLaughlin to finish it off.

The other goal was even more comical and disastrous from Aberdeen's point of view when one Aberdeen defender and two Dunfermline forwards went up for the same ball. It was Aberdeen's Jimmy Hogg who got there first, but it was he who headed the ball into his own net!

In between times, Aberdeen had made several good chances, most of them created by Charlie Cooke, the one player of genuine class in the Aberdeen line up, but had spurned them all.

The game had been watched by a delegation from Wolverhampton Wanderers who declined to say who was attracting their attention. It may have been Charlie Cooke, but it could also have been quite a few of the Dunfermline players – George Miller, Alex Smith or Harry Melrose perhaps, who all turned in impressive performances.

Willie Callaghan

October 25 1969

Table topping Dunfermline went down badly 0-2 at Ibrox today in a game in which everyone felt that they should have performed better.

Rangers were not doing as well as their fans wanted them to in 1969. Fingers were being pointed at Manager David White. His position was constantly being undermined by Willie Waddell, in the *Scottish Daily Express,* for the fairly obvious reason that Waddell wanted the job himself!

Rangers' problem was that Celtic continued to dominate, and at the start of the season, in sheer desperation, they had brought back Jim Baxter. But this was no "slim Jim". He was clearly overweight and his heart was not really in the game anymore.

He was dropped for the visit of the Pars, and this was looked upon as a shock, but Rangers scored early in the game through Andy Penman and then in the second half through Kaj Johansen.

Dunfermline's performance was a great disappointment to their sizeable travelling support especially after so many good games of late. The game was a bad-tempered affair with loads of unnecessary fouls, and perhaps Dunfermline allowed themselves to be influenced by that.

The Glasgow Herald says that the only good players were Bent Martin, Willie Callaghan and ex-Ranger Doug Baillie, and words like "unacceptable" were frequently used.

There was no reason why a highly skilled and professional team like Dunfermline should allow themselves to be intimidated by the large crowd, who themselves were not all that happy today either when they heard that Celtic had beaten St Johnstone 1-0 to win this year's Scottish League Cup.

October 26 1889

Today Dunfermline Athletic sustained their biggest ever defeat when they went down 1-11 to Hibernian at Easter Road in a Scottish Cup 3rd Round replay, in front of 2,000 spectators..

This game was a surprise for the first game at Dunfermline last week resulted in a 4-4 draw.

The Fifeshire Journal published a lengthy report:

The Hibernians won the toss, and Anderson started play. Dunfermline immediately made tracks for their opponents' goal; but the home backs safely returned the ball, and the right wing had a good run down the field, the ball ultimately going by. The Hibernians again showed fine play, and the whole front rank took part in a beautiful piece of passing, from which a corner ensued. Nothing in the way of scoring resulted from this. The home team at this point were doing all the pressing; but, although their play was very carefully judged, it was eleven minutes after the start before James Quigley scored. The Fife men gave a poor display, and failed to hold their opponents, who scored again by James McGhee. A minute afterwards McMahon received a pass from Smith, and dodging round an opponent, the great centre again beat Cree. This seemed to waken up the Athletics, who, getting up the field, had a throw-in close up to the goal, from which they managed to score. The home team now had another try; but Cree punched out, and McLeod had a good run up the right for Fife, the Hibernian defence being rather severely taxed, but ultimately averting danger. The home team again showed their fondness for Cree, who saved a splendid shot from James McGhee, and another from Flannigan. The Hibernians however, would give him no rest, and he had again to fist out; but after a time he was again beaten by Coyle. Smith scored another, the game standing five to one in the Hibernians' favour at half-time. The Hibernians started play in the second half, and in half a minute had a corner. The ball was placed wide, but it was scrimmaged in; and, after some exciting work, James McGhee scored a sixth goal. The Athletics made several attempts to break away, but the efforts of their forwards were very spasmodic, and the home backs easily held them in check. Getting up again, the green Jerseys were again successful, Smith putting on a seventh for them. The Hibernians now had a desperate scrimmage round the Fife goal, but the ball was fouled by them almost on the goal line, and they were forced to retire. It was only for a moment, however, and after Cree had saved several times. Smith scored an eighth goal with a splendid long shot The Fifers now had a run; but after getting a corner, they were forced to retire; and the Hibernians getting up the field once more, James McGhee scored a ninth. In two minutes more McMahon scored a tenth goal, amid laughter. An eleventh followed, and the game ended :- Hibernians, 11 goals; Dunfermline Athletic, 1 goal.

So what had happened since the original game last week? The answer of course can probably be found in the somewhat chaotic arrangements of both teams who tended to have a different set of players available for selection on any given week.

Hibernian had been around since 1874, proud winners of the Scottish Cup in 1887.

In 1889 they were the undisputed representatives of the Irish community in Edinburgh to the extent of insisting that all their players must be of Irish descent and must be practising Roman Catholics.

This policy, unbelievable to 21st century eyes, was admirable in the context of 1889, because the Edinburgh Irish, poor and oppressed, needed a rallying call if they were not to be seduced by less respectable organisations like the Fenians.

In the long run however, this policy did not really do Hibernian any good for a rival organisation, based in Glasgow and called the Celtic, had arisen.

They were better organised than Hibernian, were not shy of pinching Hibs players like Willie Groves and Sandy McMahon — and they made it clear that they were open to Protestants as well.

Nevertheless, Hibs were far too good for Dunfermline to-day, and one wonders whether one of the spectators that day was a young man called James Connolly, a Hibs supporter from Edinburgh who in later years would become one of the leaders of the Irish rebellion of 1916.

For Dunfermline it was a shocker.

October 27 1991

The Pars biggest occasion for well over 20 years was a disappointment to the travelling Pars fans and the others in the town who were watching on TV.

It was one of those days when no cars were seen in Dunfermline after mid-morning when they had all headed westwards.

This was the Scottish League Cup final against Hibs at Hampden, and most Pars supporters had given their team a chance, but not a great deal more than that.

The path to the final had not been uneventful. Manager Iain Munro had been sacked and replaced by Jocky Scott.

The final had been reached after the team had received a distinctly dubious penalty kick in the semi-final against an Airdrie side who failed to see the funny side of it all!

Hibs had beaten Rangers in the semi-final and were considered the favourites. They had their own agenda as well for they had just fended off the infamous takeover bid by Wallace Mercer of Hearts.

Hibs duly won 2-0 and frankly outplayed Dunfermline for most of the game, particularly in the second half when Tommy McIntyre scored a penalty. Keith Wright clinched the game and Dunfermline had no real answer to Micky Weir, the man who always looked as if his shirt was too big for him.

It was a great moment for Hibs – their first trophy since 1972 – but a sad day for Dunfermline who never really got going.

A slight sweetener however was the 40,377 crowd and the live TV fee which was a certain boost to the coffers.

October 28 1961

A huge fire at the Metropole Theatre in Stockwell Street, Glasgow, was seen all over the city.

It meant that the Celtic v Dunfermline game today had to be delayed by a few minutes to allow the crowd in on time.

A little over a mile away at Hampden, a crowd of 88,535 were at the Scottish League Cup final between Hearts and Rangers, and it would be fair to say that the streets were congested today.

Dunfermline arrived on a high after their success against Vardar of Yugoslavia in midweek, and this was Dunfermline's first meeting with Celtic since last season's Scottish Cup final in April.

Before the start, Jock Stein was seen to be in long, earnest conversation with his ex-boss Jimmy McGrory, both men clearly in awe of the other.

Celtic certainly started off the better team and were well worth their early lead through Bobby Carroll, with the Pars defence clearly discovering that Celtic were a tougher proposition that the Yugoslav amateurs that they had faced on Wednesday night.

Nevertheless, to the delight of the small band of Dunfermline supporters, by half time they were level thanks to Tommy McDonald after a prolonged bettering of the Celtic goal.

The second half was a fine contest but Bobby Carroll got the winner for Celtic to a loud roar. A minute later there was another loud roar – but no-one had scored, at least not at Celtic Park!

The new phenomenon of the age, the transistor radio had informed Celtic Park that Hearts had been awarded a penalty. Another minute after that, yet another loud roar announced that Hearts had equalised, and that the League Cup final was going to extra time.

OFFICIAL PROGRAMME

SCOTTISH FOOTBALL LEAGUE CUP 1946

3D

SCOTTISH LEAGUE CUP

EAST FIFE versus **DUNFERMLINE**

FINAL
HAMPDEN PARK
SATURDAY
OCTOBER 29th, 1949

October 29 1949

East Fife recorded their second success in the Scottish League Cup when they beat Dunfermline Athletic 3-0 at Hampden Park before a somewhat disappointing crowd of 39,744.

Dunfermline Athletic were still in Division "B" at this time, and a certain amount of support had been expressed by the neutrals for them.

Today saw East Fife take control at an early stage, score three goals in the first quarter of the game and then await the final whistle.

They were well on top with the Pars never really in the game apart from a rare attack when Clarkson hit the post.

East Fife's goals were scored by Charlie Fleming pushing home a Davie Duncan cross, Davie Duncan himself hammering home another cross from right winger Bobby Black, and then with the game less than a quarter over, Henry Morris scoring a third after a good through ball from the same Bobby Black.

East Fife were wearing a new strip of old gold-and-black collars and cuffs (looking not unlike Wolverhampton Wanderers), and Dunfermline wore black and white hoops.

The teams were East Fife: McGarrity, Laird and Stewart; Philp, Finlay and Aitken; Black, Fleming, Morris, Brown and Duncan. Dunfermline Athletic: Johnstone, Kirk and McLean; McCall, Clarkson and Whyte; Mayes, Cannon, Henderson, McGairy and Smith. Referee: W Webb, Glasgow.

The Courier reports rather improbably that "hosts" of representatives from English clubs like Manchester City, Newcastle United and Burnley were there, virtually cheque book in hand to persuade Scot Symon to part with his men.

This was unlikely, but it was certainly true that East Fife contained quite a few players who would fit in rather well at a richer team than East Fife.

October 29 1949

Jimmy Clarkson (5) and George Johnstone (goalkeeper) in the League Cup Final of 1949.

October 30 1993

Dunfermline continued their fine form with a 4-0 defeat of Brechin City before 3195 fans at East End Park.

This meant that they had played 5 games in October, against Dumbarton, Falkirk, St Mirren and Stirling Albion and now Brechin.

They had won them all, scored 14 goals and conceded two.

In fact their last dropped point had come as long ago as September 25 when they drew with Ayr United.

Bertie Paton's men had now clearly recovered from their awful start to the season, and this was League winning form.

But this was a strange season in the First Division (the second tier). The League structure was to be changed (not for the first nor last time) at the whim of legislators and to the confusion and frustration of the fans.

The Premier League was going down from 12 teams to 10, meaning that 3 teams would be relegated and that only 1 team would be promoted. Promotion was clearly to be the aim of Dunfermline but they would have to win the League to do so.

Today was a bit of a mismatch against a brave Brechin City who were clearly punching away above their weight in this Division (even though they had defeated the Pars at Glebe Park earlier in the season).

Goals from Laing, Sinclair, Smith and McCathie were more than enough to beat the part-timers.

This result lifted the Pars to fourth in the Division (such had been their horrible start to the season that they still had a long way to go to reach the top) but the "in phrase" at the moment was "upwardly mobile".

October 31 1962

The world was still very much holding its breath over the Cuban Missile Crisis, although the worst seemed to have passed.

Everton, sometimes called the "Bank of England club" because of their perceived ability to buy players, came to East End Park to defend the narrow 1-0 lead that they held from Goodison Park last week.

This was the competition then known as the Inter Cities Fairs Cup, which in time became the UEFA Cup, and then the Europa League.

The packed East End Park looked a treat that night with the sparkling new stand and the ground having a trim and neat appearance. Frankly it was light years away from the poverty of the past, and tonight the team gave their supporters a night to remember.

First George Miller equalised from 20 yards, and then with time running out Willie Cunningham released Harry Melrose to score the winner as time was running out.

This result was much welcomed throughout Scotland (and even in England, for not everyone like the arrogant "toffees") but it was overshadowed a little.

Dundee had a fine win over Sporting Lisbon at Dens Park, and at White Hart Lane Spurs beat Rangers 5-2 – a result that did not seem to cause as many tears as one would have supposed!

There was also the ongoing international situation, but this game must go down as one of Jock Stein's best ever results — with a team which cost only a fraction of his opponents' budget. And yet it is sad when we think of Dundee and Dunfermline today – changed days indeed!

November

November 1 1902

Recreation Grounds, Perth, the home of St Johnstone, was the scene of a rather serious disruption to the hopes of Dunfermline winning the Northern League.

They had joined the Northern League this season in a competition which extended as far north as Aberdeen. Today was a comparatively easy trip because Perth had a good railway station, and Dunfermline even managed to take some supporters with them.

The team had been playing well, but today they came down with a rather large bump as they lost 1-4 to the Perth men. *The Courier* however (perhaps because it does not want to alienate its readers in either Perth or Dunfermline) says that although the Saints did not win "by a fluke", it would be "hardly fair to the (sic) Dunfermline to say that the difference in the score was representative in the difference in the play".

Indeed, at the start they looked likely winners "so brisk and business-like was their method of manipulating the leather".

St Johnstone scored a couple of goals before half time before Lawrie pulled one back from the right wing, the "strongest division of the Fifers team".

In the second half, St Johnstone took control and turned in their best performance of the season to win 4-1. This disappointing result meant that Dunfermline were now in third position in the League behind Dundee A (the Dens Park second XI) and Victoria United, a team from Aberdeen, who were currently thinking about amalgamating with another two Aberdeen teams to form a larger team with a view to competing in the Scottish League.

November 2 1974

In this very exciting League where the top ten will be creamed off to join next season's Premier Division, George Miller's team did enough to convince their doubters that they might yet be one of the lucky ten with a good 2-1 victory over Motherwell at Fir Park.

Any away win is a good one, of course, but this one was especially rewarding as Motherwell were one of the teams that might reasonably have been rated as one of Dunfermline's potential rivals for a top ten spot.

The crowd was a poor one of 3,500, and the home support were shocked when Dunfermline went into a 2-0 lead in the first half, with goals coming from Forrest and Watson.

Motherwell then got a penalty in the second half which Goldthorpe converted. There were one or two other times when Motherwell came close but the Pars held out for a good victory.

These were difficult times when inflation showed every sign of getting totally out of control, and people honestly asked the question whether it was possible to govern Britain, such was the industrial chaos that enveloped the nation.

The miners were now settled, but bus drivers, dustbin men and teachers were all still causing problems for the Labour Government of Harold Wilson which had emerged as a minority government in February and which had now won a narrow majority in the October election.

Meanwhile questions were also being asked about the future of football. Today's low attendance was not an isolated phenomenon, and it was becoming clear that supporters were not so keen on the sub-standard facilities at most grounds.

November 3 2007

This one can only really be described as a hammering.

The 0-4 defeat to Livingston at East End Park was about as depressing as it can get.

It followed on the heels of a home 0-5 defeat two weeks ago to Hamilton (admittedly a very good team) and then another reverse at Stirling Albion last week.

The team was now eighth in the First Division, and quite a few of the 3,473 crowd gave every impression that they had suffered enough and would not be back for more as they left the ground in dribs and drabs throughout the second half.

The dull November day, not particularly cold but drab and early dark, reflected the mood.

It was not as if Dunfermline did not have good players – Scott Wilson, Danny Murphy, Stevie Crawford, Stephen Glass and Mark Burchill had all proved themselves elsewhere, but perhaps they were all getting old at the same time.

Certainly today they had no real answer to a Livingston team for whom Steven Craig scored twice on either side of half-time, one with a powerful header and the other after some shocking defensive play in the Dunfermline penalty box.

It is often said that a goal before half time is a great psychological benefit, and that one after the break is even more so, and certainly today, the spirit disappeared from the Pars side who accepted far too early that they were defeated.

A man with a wonderful name, Mark Tinkler, then added a third for Livi and the game was over long before Jason Kennedy scored a screamer in the last minute to make it four.

So once more, it was time for the proverbial "long, hard look at themselves" for the players. One occasionally wondered whether they were quite as "hurt" as they claimed to be, or as the fans certainly were. The "no' comin' back" cry was certainly heard long and loud today.

Manager Stephen Kenny's days were now numbered.

November 4 1961

Annfield, the home of Stirling Albion, was the destination for Dunfermline and their supporters today.

They travelled the short distance to Stirling to take on the team that was happy to describe itself as the "yo-yo" team of Scottish football team; they moved up and down between the two divisions.

That description might well have been applied to Dunfermline themselves as well, and Jock Stein was very aware that, Scottish Cup winners or not, their start to the League fixtures this year had been none too impressive.

This was why today's victory was an important one, but it was also thrilling with the Pars edging home through the odd goal in five on a crisp and pleasant autumn day.

In spite of Cammie Fraser being off with a facial injury, it was Charlie Dickson who put the Pars ahead late in the first half.

In the second half, Stirling Albion fought back and scored through Kilgannon and Lawlor. Kilgannon's goal was a thing of exquisite beauty from the edge of the penalty box, but Lawlor's came from the penalty spot after Willie Cunningham had foolishly handled.

It looked as if Dunfermline were heading for another defeat, but 15 minutes from time Alex Smith equalised after a Dickson cross had been fisted out to his feet.

It was all action stuff now and a winner might have come at either end, but it was Alex Smith who scored again to give Dunfermline a hard earned victory.

You had to be sorry for Stirling Albion, though, and they were fated to be relegated at the end of the season.

Bert Paton

November 5 1966

Clyde were no bad side in 1966.

Today's 4-0 win at East End Park was all the more satisfying because of the quality of the opposition and the quality of the goals, which earned predictable headlines about "fireworks" in the Sunday papers.

There were two downsides however – one was the attendance which was disappointingly low at about 6,000; the other was a bad injury to Tommy Callaghan, who had to be carried off with what looked like a broken leg in the 71st minute.

In the previous midweek the Pars had gone out of Europe narrowly on away goals to Dinamo Zagreb, but any fear that there might be a hangover after this was quickly dispelled.

Dunfermline had got off to a reasonable (but no more than that) start in the League and were generally reckoned to be a hard nut to crack at East End Park, and so it proved today as they scored two goals in each half to beat the Shawfield men.

George Fleming scored the first when he received an inch perfect pass from Alex Edwards, beat a defender and crashed home a wonderful goal. Before half time Bertie Paton had scored another with a lively header from a cross by Willie Callaghan.

In the second half Fleming scored again this time as he ran across the field and then crashed the ball home via the bar, before Alex Ferguson scored late in the game.

The result moved Dunfermline into sixth place in the League, but the really sad part of today was the injury to Tommy Callaghan.

November 6 1971

Dunfermline's poor season continued today with a 2-0 defeat at Easter Road, Edinburgh to a strong Hibs side.

Dunfermline had beaten Airdrie last week (admittedly rather narrowly) and hopes were expressed that this could have been the start of a revival.

Hibs away from home is never an easy fixture and before a crowd of about 9,000, Dunfermline fought well but lost two goals at the wrong time.

The first came on the half hour mark and was a glorious drive from Pat Stanton after a free kick from Hamilton landed at his feet and he hammered the ball home from a distance.

After that Dunfermline pressed with Jim Gillespie in particular looking sharp, but they never found the finishing touch, and after that, the ascendancy passed to Hibs who scored again in the second half, this time from a header by Arthur Duncan from a cross by O'Rourke.

Dunfermline kept battling, but as is the way with teams going through a bad spell, they never had any luck and Hibs finished winners.

It was round about now that the "r" word for relegation began to be heard with increasing frequency.

There had been a narrow escape last season, and things looked as if they would be tight this season again, but the optimistic members of the support still felt that things were going to be all right.

What was clear however was that the great days of the 1960s had gone, perhaps never to return.

Alec Wright was clearly not a Manager in the mould of Jock Stein or George Farm.

November 7 1936

The weather was foul, and Dunfermline today lost six goals, but Monday's *Courier* is not in the slightest bit depressed about them!

The game was played at Cathkin in Glasgow, and the 6-3 score line in favour of Third Lanark is described as "daylight robbery".

This was by no means an appropriate piece of imagery for the game was played in unrelenting gloom, and indeed was lucky to finish as what light there was deteriorated badly.

Dunfermline's fault lay in their lack of shooting ability, according to the reporter, but this seems to be an odd criticism of a team which scored three goals away from home!

On the other hand, the loss of six goals seemed to be a far more serious matter of concern for the Dunfermline supporters.

Goalkeeper Hugh Farquharson is exonerated from blame. "Often brilliant, always safe" he was not to blame for any of the six goals.

Dunfermline's three goals all came from close range, John Reid, Willie Chalmers and Bob McGowan being the scorers.

The reporter remains adamant that there is no cause for despair, but Dunfermline are third bottom and getting very close to the relegation zone.

The news from the outside world is dominated by the Battle of Madrid in Spain where Franco's Moors are reported to have entered the north west of the city but are encountering fierce resistance.

The gossip columns, who clearly know a lot more than they are allowed to say, keep hinting about King Edward VIII and some American lady.

November 8 1989

With a third of the season played, this game between Motherwell and newly-promoted Dunfermline at Fir Park took place amid somewhat improbable circumstances – the winner would go top of the Premier Division.

This game was played on a Wednesday night, brought forward to give Motherwell's Davie Cooper the best chance possible of being fit for Scotland's vital World Cup qualifier against France next week.

That was just a distraction to Athletic manager Jim Leishman however, who confidently pointed out before the game that his side were in great form with 11 points from 14 and unbeaten in 7 games.

As it turned out, neither side managed to get the win, but the Pars went top of the league regardless, edging ahead of Rangers on goals scored.

For much of the game it looked that this game would end in disappointment as an early Nick Cusack goal gave the home side a lead they would hold until late in the game.

A scrappy game would see Motherwell defending their lead comfortably with little threat of an equaliser, until with two minutes to go Doug Rougvie crossed from the left, George O'Boyle flicked on, and Ross Jack knocked in the equaliser that would put Dunfermline top.

Manager Jim Leishman said after the game that he wasn't really that bothered about the league position, but the wild celebrations of the large away support suggested they saw it differently.

The crowd for this? Over 9,000, for a midweek game between Motherwell and Dunfermline in the first half of the season.

November 9 1935

It was widely believed in Dunfermline that Monday's *Courier* would arrive in Dunfermline all draped in black following Dunfermline's fine 3-2 victory in the rain at Dens Park today.

Dunfermline often played well against Dundee, and this was certainly one of their better performances.

Dunfermline's star man was inside forward Alec Thomson from Buckhaven and one time of Celtic for whom he was a legend.

His ability had not entirely disappeared, as he showed at Dens Park today. He scored one goal and created another for young Campbell.

The other goal came from Bob McGowan after a free-kick that *The Courier* disputes (but then again, *The Courier* would, wouldn't it?).

The game finished in the dark of a dull November afternoon with the crowd struggling to see what was going on at the far end, and with the few Dunfermline supporters afraid that the game would have to be abandoned.

But 3-2 it was, and for all the moaning of the Dundee Press, it was a good win for the Pars. This result moved Dunfermline up to a very respectable ninth in the First Division, a state of affairs that Manager Willie Knight pronounced himself to be very happy about!

Meanwhile Great Britain was preparing for a General Election on Thursday (the National Government would retain power, although Labour would make a few gains).

The world stood back and watched what could only really be described as some sort of International rape as Mussolini's Italy simply invaded Abyssinia, (using tanks against spears!) and the League of Nations, already discredited, sat back and did nothing!

November 10 1956

It was now clear that the British Prime Minister Sir Anthony Eden had made a huge mistake.

In allying himself with France and Israel to invade Egypt to seize the Suez Canal, he had alienated the United Nations together with the USA and the USSR.

In addition, he had not been supported 100% by the British public.

But the issue was still being argued about as 6,000 fans made their way to East End Park to see the Pars take on Queen of the South.

They saw a great game between two teams currently in the top half of the First Division, and the Pars emerged narrow winners by 4 goals to three.

It was 1-1 at half-time this dull November day, the Pars goal having been scored by George O'Brien. Dunfermline had quite clearly been the better side however and in a purple patch in the middle of the second half, they scored three goals in quick succession through O'Brien (again), George Peebles and Alex Anderson to make the score 4-1.

However the Doonhamers were no bad side and fought back, taking advantage of an injury to Harry Colville — who was therefore slower and less mobile — to score twice.

That made the score 4-3 and made Dunfermline sweat for their victory. It was a well fought victory, and at this stage of the season, no-one ever mentioned the "r" word for relegation – it was too early and in any case the Pars were more than holding their own.

After the New Year, it would be a different matter altogether.

John Lunn

November 11 1974

Football, often portrayed as a nasty, grasping, money-grubbing business (not without cause on occasion) can sometimes show itself at its best.

This is what happened here at East End Park this Monday night.

Dunfermline arranged a testimonial game for John Lunn who had played for Dunfermline in the 1960s but had tragically died of leukaemia aged only 27 in December last year. 11,054 turned up to pay their respects and to allow a large cheque to be presented to John's family.

This was a game between a Dunfermline team with Alex Edwards now of Hibs and Donald Ford of Hearts as guests against a Celtic-Rangers select which also included Denis Law, now officially retired from football, but still a great Scottish personality.

Helping to organise things was Jock Stein, who, of course, had signed John Lunn as a teenager in 1963, and he was visibly upset about John's tragic death.

The whole occasion was of course very light-hearted after due respects had been paid to Lunn with Billy McNeill, John Greig and Kenny Dalglish all taking part in the fun.

The game ended 3-3, but then the game went to penalty kicks and Dunfermline won 4-3; the man who missed the penalty for the Select was Dixie Deans, who only two weeks previously had scored a hat-trick to win the Scottish League Cup final for Celtic.

Dixie had of course on a far more serious occasion missed a penalty in a shoot-out to deprive Celtic of a place in the European Cup final of 1972. This time he was a lot less bothered about it!

The general fun of the occasion did not in any way diminish the respect in which John Lunn continued to be held.

November 12 1921

Dunfermline's disappointing form in their first season in the Scottish League Second Division continued in a poor game at East End Park, but this time at least they won, beating the Renfrewshire team Johnstone 2-0.

It was their first win for over a month but *The Courier* quotes a "rabid" (sic) supporter who said philosophically that we had been playing well of late but getting nothing in return.

Both goals were scored in the early period of the game by Hugh Strachan, his second one being a great goal in which he beat three men before firing home.

After that, there was little in the way of good football – but it did mean two points for the team, with centre half Bob Mercer the star of the game. The League table that night did not make for great reading but at least Dunfermline were now only fourth bottom.

The problem was, as everyone knew, that Dunfermline were missing the goal scoring talents of Andrew Wilson. Today he scored for Middlesbrough in their 2-0 defeat of Manchester United at Ayresome Park, and he would still be in contention to play for Scotland when the International season came round again.

For Dunfermline however, the future did not look good and they were affected, as indeed were all the smaller teams by the general economic situation of the country.

The end of the war in 1918 had not made the country "fit for heroes to live in" as strikes, poverty, violence and crime all abounded in the land.

November 13 1954

It was a typical November day – wet, dull and unpleasant at East End Park today as Dunfermline beat Dundee United 3-1.

Both of these teams could realistically have been described as promotion hopefuls but it hadn't looked like that so far this season.

There was always the feeling with Dunfermline that they were not all that far away and that today's 3-1 win might just be the start of something.

For Dundee United, it seemed that they were destined always to be the poor relations of Dundee, a team who had twice won the Scottish League Cup in recent years.

A cruel joke used to go round Dundee that United "weren't in the same street" as Dundee. In fact, they were, of course, geographically speaking, but in playing terms, they were poles apart.

Today it was Jimmy Miller who opened the scoring for Dunfermline picking up an O'Brien pass, beating two defenders and scoring a fine goal.

He scored another in the second half, as did Reilly and the wonder was that Dunfermline didn't win by a larger margin.

Indeed it was Dundee United's goalkeeper Alec Edmiston who defied the Dunfermline forwards. He even got a sympathetic round of applause from the Pars supporters at the end, who could not understand why this most placid of men was booked by the slightly over zealous referee, Mr R. Yacamini of Perth, after a fairly innocuous clash with a Dunfermline forward.

This may have been Dunfermline's turning point. Last week they lost 1-2 at Forfar, but next week they beat Albion Rovers 7-0!

November 14 2009

Dunfermline Athletic were now on a good run of form.

There had been a shocking run of four defeats in August and September leading to many calls for the head of Manager Jim McIntyre, but the team had steadied and rallied in October.

The rehabilitation was now complete with a 2-1 win over Raith Rovers last week at Stark's Park in which they had come from behind after being 0-1 down at half time.

Now this success was consolidated by a 3-1 win over Partick Thistle at East End Park on a dry and by no means unpleasant day which sent the 3,111 fans home happy.

The crowd showed their respect at the start for Hugh Whyte, former goalkeeper with the club and later the club doctor, who had passed away recently at the tragically young age of 54.

Andy Kirk was away on International duty with Northern Ireland and this gave an opportunity for young Steven McDougall — who had only played twice before for the club — and he took full advantage of the opportunity; he scored his first goal in the 5th minute.

Willie Gibson then scored before half time to make it 2-0 and the Pars looked totally secure until Paul Cairney scored for Thistle early in the second half.

A draw would have been a travesty of a score-line given the run of play, but Pars supporters had to wait until stoppage time before another Willie Gibson goal made the victory secure.

The news of another final score – Morton 5 Raith Rovers 0 - added to the joy of the Dunfermline fans as they left the ground.

November 15 1924

There was a spring in the step of the Dunfermline supporters as they headed to East End Park today.

Yet they were bottom of the League, and had been playing poorly, and today's opponents were Dundee United, until recently known as Dundee Hibs, who were top of the League!

What was the reason for this? It was all about a man called Bobby Skinner who now, after a few legal questions had been settled, was a Dunfermline Athletic player having been signed for £100 (some say £75) from St Mirren.

Skinner had played a few games for Dunfermline at the end of last season when he was "on loan", but now, Athletic having warded off counter bids from Ayr United and Morton, had their man, and the whole town was enthused as a result.

A crowd of 8,000 appeared today, and Skinner was cheered to the echo every time he touched the ball. He did not score – indeed he missed a good chance near the end – but his very presence made a huge difference to the side as he led the line with "a degree of aplomb", as *The Dunfermline Press* put it.

Even the defence tightened up and held back the Dundee United forwards. Dundee United had expected a comfortable win today but were thwarted, and a 0-0 draw was the result.

It would be some time before the Dunfermline fans saw Skinner at his best, but he would be largely responsible for the team winning the Second Division the season after this one.

The significance of this game was that it gave the supporters and the players a much-needed shot in the arm.

November 16 1996

Although Dunfermline's form had been disappointingly poor in the Premier Division this year, today they notched a valuable away win against Raith Rovers.

A derby victory is always satisfactory, but there was an added edge to this one called relegation. The Pars were on the edge of the relegation zone, and Raith Rovers were definitely in it.

Dunfermline had already beaten them at East End Park in late September, and today they made it a double by winning 2-1 at Stark's Park, thanks to a fortuitous own goal and a strike from Hamish French.

It was 2-0 at half time and although Peter Duffield pulled one back in the second half for the Kirkcaldy side, Pars held out and took the three points which temporarily at least moved them up the table.

The crowd was given as 6,762 on what was a typically dull, dreich November afternoon. It was difficult not to feel sorry for Raith Rovers for they were, not for the first or last time in their lives, in total chaos.

Ian Munro, for example, was the fourth Manager in this calendar year of 1996! Jimmy Nicholl had unaccountably left them in February to go to Millwall (yes, Millwall!); they had Jimmy Thomson for a spell. Tommy McLean managed for a week, (yes, a week!) before leaving to join brother Jim at Dundee United.

It was crazy, and in comparison with all this, Dunfermline under Bertie Paton were organised and calm. Not that it was likely to last forever, but at least for the moment the Pars were the better placed club in Fife.

November 17 1962

The conditions were absolutely Arctic as Dunfermline set out for Dumfries today with Jock Stein making several phone calls to make sure the game was on.

However, conditions slowly improved as the team travelled south, and the problem became one of sleet and then rain.

Only one game was off today in Scotland in the First Division and that was at Motherwell where Aberdeen would have been the visitors.

Had it been a home game, Dunfermline's game might not have been played (Cowdenbeath's Second Division fixture with Forfar was off), and it might have been better for the Pars if this one had been off as well.

After a steady start to the season, the Pars had slipped recently, losing at home to St Mirren last week, whereas Queen of the South had, last week, pulled off one of their best ever results by beating Celtic at Parkhead.

Today's game was described in an *Evening Times* headline as "Mudlark of the South", but the pitch was definitely playable, although certainly difficult.

It did not lend itself to any sort of close-passing game, and the one goal that Queen of the South scored was quite certainly "route one" football with a long ball out of defence going over the heads of the Dunfermline defenders to Murray who also lofted the ball over the advancing Herriot.

That was just before half-time and hard though the Pars tried in the second half, no further goals were scored. "Nae day for fitba'" was the excuse, but then again you have to take the rough with the smooth, and Scottish football is no place for softies!

November 18 1905

On a frost bound pitch at East End Park today, Dunfermline had a good 3-1 win over Lochee United of Dundee.

This was in the Northern League, a curious competition which did not always seem to provide regular fixtures for all teams. This, for example, was only Dunfermline's fourth game whereas Montrose had played 12!

Such a gross disparity can partially be explained by Dunfermline's commitments in the Qualifying Cup and various local competitions, but it does seem odd. However Dunfermline had now won three of the four games that they had played.

Today's game was played in front of a sparse attendance and "was by no means characterised by football of a first-class order" as *The Courier* rather brutally puts it.

Dunfermline scored twice in the first ten minutes through Pitblado and Allan, Pitblado's goal coming from a "curious" penalty awarded by Mr McKenzie of Dundee, a man who was clearly no lover of Lochee United.

Dunfermline were giving a trial to two men from the Highland Light Infantry, Lawrie at centre half and Greer at centre forward and it was Greer who scored the third goal.

Both soldiers impressed the Dunfermline supporters but Greer had to be taken off after aggravating a knee injury sustained in a previous game against Dundee Hibs.

The fans were quite happy with this game, but much speculation centred on the future of the Conservative Government and the position of the very unpopular Prime Minister, Arthur Balfour, who seemed incapable of dealing with the problems of unemployment and poverty.

November 19 1966

This was one of the best games of football that one could imagine for breath taking excitement, comebacks and sheer good football.

It was just a pity that Dunfermline Athletic were on the wrong side of the 5-4 score line.

A draw would have been a fairer result, a point conceded by Celtic themselves whose supporters were heard to say that they would like to come back to East End Park every Saturday.

Celtic would of course go on to win a grand slam of all honours that season including the European Cup, but they would never have a more difficult game than this one.

It was a raw, typical November day, but no-one really noticed. Hugh Robertson opened the scoring and then Pat Delaney (whose father Jimmy was of course one of Celtic's all-time greats) put the Pars two ahead.

Bobby Murdoch then pulled one back for Celtic, Bertie Paton then put the Pars 3-1 up before Jimmy Johnstone scored Celtic's second just before half time.

Enough to be going on with, one might have thought, but then Alex Ferguson scored a fourth after he had been mysteriously ignored by the Celtic defence.

4-2 seemed to be it, but Celtic's superior training then told with a goal from Bertie Auld and another from Joe McBride.

4-4 would have been a fair result, one thought, but in the very last minute Celtic were correctly awarded a penalty kick by referee Tom Wharton when Roy Barry handled in the box; McBride scored with it.

The 18,000 fans gave both sides a standing ovation, but while Celtic deserved to win, Dunfermline simply did not deserve to lose.

November 20 1926

This was a terrible day for Dunfermline as they went down 0-6 to Celtic on Celtic's first ever visit to East End Park on Scottish League business.

The Glasgow giants cannot have been in any way impressed by the ground at East End Park, which had already been described as substandard by many clubs.

Today Willie Maley, Manager of Celtic and President of the Scottish League, had an opportunity to see for himself just how poor the facilities were at East End Park.

There had been a great deal of rain the past week (as is often the case in Scotland in November) and one of the corners was under water in spite of the valiant efforts of the Cowdenbeath Fire Brigade to pump it away.

Referee Mr Bilney was reluctant to start the game, but eventually about 20 minutes late, he agreed that the game could go ahead.

Dunfermline must have wished that he hadn't bothered, for their team was never in it and went down 0-6 to a superb Celtic team, for whom Jimmy McGrory scored four goals and Adam McLean two.

At the other end of the park, Dunfermline never got going, with a young man called Peter Wilson — who would one day be a Dunfermline Manager — totally blotting Jimmy Dickson and Bobby Skinner out of the game.

The day was not without its entertainment with Celtic's clown Tommy McInally pretending to swim every time the ball went into the corner where the wet patch was.

The crowd was a disappointing 8,000. On a dry day, it might have been double that.

November 21 2015

It is very easy to scoff at Albion Rovers, a team who have not exactly walked hand in hand with success since their foundation in 1882.

They play in Coatbridge, a town which owes its existence to the Scottish Industrial Revolution of the 19th century and in particular the influx of Irish immigrants after the Potato Famine of 1846, and they have never been a wealthy club.

Nevertheless they reached the final of the Scottish Cup in 1920, and their players have included Jock Stein.

Today the Pars travelled to Cliftonhill (by no means the greatest stadium in the world – "it made Cowdenbeath look like the Nou Camp" was one particularly waspish comment from a Pars supporter!) as second top of Division One and with a niggardly defence that had not conceded a goal since Moffat of Airdrie did the job on September 26.

The trouble was that they were not really scoring all that many goals at the other end with two recent rather drab goalless draws.

Nevertheless the supporters were reasonably pleased with them, and today Dunfermline probably added about 400 or 500 to boost the crowd to over a thousand, when the average home gate was less than 500.

They actually saw a good game with Dunfermline going ahead through an Andy Geggan goal in the 15th minute. Five minutes later however, the proud defensive record was gone when Josh Mullin levelled the score.

From then on, all hammer and tongs football but no further goals, nor indeed any great quality football. But a draw it was and another blip for the Pars. There would not be many more such blips as the Pars now stepped up a gear and won the Division One title with a degree of ease.

November 22 1919

Once again, Andrew Wilson was the talk of Scotland.

Today he scored "six bull's eyes", in the words of the papers, as Dunfermline "whacked" King's Park of Stirling in a Central League match at East End Park.

Today Dunfermline, playing magnificently, delighted their supporters this fairly mild November day with an 8-2 victory.

The other goals were scored by Gow and Kennedy – and these were good ones too! – but the talk of everyone was Andrew Wilson, who scored two goals in the first half.

Of the four in the second, three of them were scored in five minutes — one of them when he picked up the ball immediately after King's Park's kick-off from the centre, beat a couple of men, then charged forward about 30 yards and scored.

This was nothing short of phenomenal, and his feeding of the wings was equally impressive.

Of course, the critics were not slow to say that the opposition was not great in the Central League and certainly King's Park were at the bottom of it, but six goals in a game was good in any language.

He gave the supporters a lot to talk about and to be happy about, and goodness knows, there was little enough to be happy about other than the goal scoring of Andrew Wilson.

The war had been finished over a year ago, but there was still trouble going on in Ireland, Russia and other places, and industry was generally struggling largely due to the collapse of the German and Russian markets.

Jobs were scarce, but at least Dunfermline fans could discuss the prospects of Andy getting a Scotland cap in the New Year!

November 23 1963

Today's home game against Rangers, which normally would have been one of the showpieces of the season, was played in conditions of wind and rain which did not exactly ruin the game but certainly detracted from it.

For Rangers and their fans, there was a huge disappointment in that Jim Baxter (who was, of course, a local boy) was not playing, but the big topic of conversation all day was last night's assassination of President John F Kennedy in Texas.

A minute's silence was held, and although most supporters in the 18,000 crowd stood bareheaded and respectful, even on the uncovered terracing, a section of Rangers supporters (not all of them, it must be stressed) sang and chanted during the silence, for Kennedy, of course, had been a Roman Catholic with undeniable Irish Republican sympathies.

When the game started, Rangers, even without Jim Baxter and Davie Wilson, showed why they were the best team in Scotland this season.

They were 2-0 up at half time, with goals from Bobby Watson and Willie Henderson, Henderson's goal coming when the wet ball squirmed out of Jim Herriot's grasp.

Dunfermline fought well, and scored through George Peebles from a Charlie Dickson cross, but Rangers scored another two from Jim Forrest and a spectacular one from Bobby Watson.

This result put Rangers clear at the top ahead of Dundee while Dunfermline were respectably placed at fourth.

The evening newspapers that night and the television bulletins confirmed the news that an ex US Marine called Lee Harvey Oswald had been arrested in connection with the shooting of the late President.

November 24 1979

Late November at Boghead in Dumbarton doesn't really sound very good at all, does it?

And no, this one wasn't great. In persistent rain bordering on sleet, Harry Melrose's men continued the depressing form which been all too evident this season, their first in Division One (the middle tier) since last year's promotion.

Colin O'Brien scored for the Pars, but Dumbarton had scored first and then scored again.

The game limped to its conclusion at the soulless Boghead before a very small crowd with only a few brave Pars supporters among them.

This defeat left Dunfermline second bottom and looking likely to go straight back down again – but the club had at least been paid one very substantial compliment: a semi-final of the Scottish League Cup was being played in Dunfermline today between Dundee United and Hamilton Academical.

It was the first time that East End Park had hosted a semi-final, and there was little doubt that geographically it was an excellent choice. The crowd was 10,000, an attendance which would have been dreadful in the huge bowl that was Hampden but was well suited to East End Park.

The weather, sadly, was atrocious in the east as well as in the west, but there were plenty of goals with Dundee United winning 6-2.

But the big headlines today were reserved for Love Street, Paisley where Hibs visited with a new player on board, one George Best.

This move was not exactly a long term success, but at least it gave Hibs a brief moment in the limelight. Sadly, there was no limelight for the Pars at the moment.

Dunfermline Athletic 1911. Back Row - TA Robertson (Vice President), A Liddell, W Crichton, R Philp (Secretary); Second Back Row - E Miller (Treasurer), J Philp (Trainer), D Donaldson, D Izatt, J Brown (Captain, holding trophy), A Wilkie, J Thomson, T Ballantyne, J Bewick (Secretary); Second Row - G Anderson (Vice President), J Murray, M Slavin, F Gibson, G Newlands-Robertson, J Farrell (President); Front - J McLaughlan, C Duncan

November 25 1911

This was the greatest day so far in the somewhat impoverished history of Dunfermline Athletic Football Club.

They won the Scottish Qualifying Cup, a competition perhaps comparable to our present Scottish League Challenge Cup in that the top teams do not compete.

A successful run in this competition, as its name suggested, also allowed teams to play in the "real" Scottish Cup, and that was an honour in itself and would allow Dunfermline to play Celtic in the New Year.

Today however, the opponents were Dumbarton, the team who had won the Second Division last year and who had in their ranks the great Finlay Speedie, now nearing the end of a career in which he had played with distinction for Rangers and Newcastle United.

The game was played at the Gymnasium ground in Edinburgh, the home of St Bernard's, before a large crowd of 8,300, many of whom had come from Dunfermline in special trains put on for the occasion.

The game was described as "tight" with Dumbarton getting the better of the early exchanges, but it was that interesting character Fred Gibson, born in South Africa but happy to call himself an Englishman and who flitted between Raith Rovers and Dunfermline at this stage of his career, who scored the only goal of the game.

The Courier is delighted with the success of a local team, and has a long piece written by captain James Brown. Brown just made the game because he had been suffering from influenza in the week before and said that had he been "in tip top condition" he would have been able to put more vigour into his play.

Finlay Speedie seems to have upset him by his over-confidence, being "the life and soul of the forward line" but Brown affirms that he did not do so well once "our halfs tumbled to his game.

"There will be no holding of the Dunfermline enthusiasts now" continues Brown. "It was a popular victory. The crossing of our wing men was great and with Wyllie always up and ready, the Dumbarton defence had a worrying time." "Cooper and Wyllie have perhaps been the most criticised of our players. It was particularly gratifying for me that both came off…Their performance will surely close the mouths of their critics".

At full time Dunfermline fans invaded the pitch. Some of them had climbed to "elevated positions" in the grandstand, so it looked as if some damage might be done to the property of St Bernard's.

The writer in *The Courier* hoped that the SFA would return to their habit of presenting trophies at a social function after the game.

The Scottish Qualifying Cup, a huge and none too beautiful piece of Victorian silverware, was presented by Mr Robertson, President of the Scottish Football Association.

The team then moved back to Dunfermline.

A brake was awaiting the players at the Lower Station; they were feted on a drive through the town as they returned home with President Mr Farrell holding up the huge trophy.

The High Street was "a seething mass of humanity and passage was almost an impossibility".

The "auld grey toon" had never seen anything like this before, and people said that the scenes were reminiscent of Mafeking night and the Coronations of 1902 and 1911, but this was for football!

It was hoped that this might be "lift off" time for the Dunfermline club, but that was a long time in the future.

Nearly 50 years would pass before the team would carry a Cup through the streets of Dunfermline again.

November 26 2005

Dunfermline today delighted their small band of travelling supporters by beating Celtic at Parkhead 1-0.

It was a victory that came totally out of the blue, for Dunfermline were in the middle of an injury crisis and had lost the last seven games in a row.

But 58,203 looked on in amazement as Greg Ross in the 17th minute put the Pars into the lead.

It all came from a free kick from Iain Campbell which found the head of Andy Tod and he headed it down to Ross, who managed to get there before a posse of Celtic defenders and squeeze the ball past Artur Boruc in the Celtic goal.

Celtic themselves were struggling through injury and were missing Shaun Maloney and Shunsuke Nakamura, and the creative skills of the Japanese artist were particularly lacking.

The second half was very much a "backs to the wall" job from the Dunfermline defence but they were helped by so many of the Parkhead men having a bad day, and the attitude of the huge Celtic crowd who turned against their team.

The Pars indeed might have scored again with Noel Hunt and Derek Young coming close, but the bulk of the pressure was Celtic's with Chris Sutton and John Hartson missing chances, and a feeling all round Parkhead that a penalty should have been awarded.

Twice near the end we had the spectacle of Celtic goalkeeper Artur Boruc joining the attack for a corner kick, but the full time whistle brought triumph to the somewhat incredulous Pars supporters.

It showed at least that the Pars were occasionally capable of doing well!

November 27 1994

Oh, what a difficult day this was for Dunfermline supporters!

There had been little to get enthused about in yesterday's performance - a boring goalless draw at Stranraer which seemed to have been a long way to go for some miserable football.

That was bad enough. But today there was a football match on the TV, and it was the Scottish League Cup final between Celtic and Raith Rovers.

It would have been nice to say that all Dunfermline supporters in an impressive show of solidarity with their fellow Fifers got together in their pubs and on their living room sofas to support the men from Kirkcaldy.

After all, so many of the Raith Rovers men had strong Dunfermline connections. Some of them even lived in Dunfermline! But we all know that life doesn't work that way.

For the average football fan, petty mindedness and jealousy rule the roost. You do not really want your local rivals to win, for you would never hear the end of it. "But, but…we beat you about a month ago" would have cut no ice at all with the gloating "neeburs of Geordie Munro" as Raith fans liked to call themselves.

So, there are probably three ways of dealing with this conundrum. Either feign disinterest and watch a film on the other channel, or discover a passion for the green and whites and talk a lot about Jock Stein, or be two-faced and try to cheer as Raith Rovers scored their late equaliser, and as the crucial Celtic penalty was missed.

It would have had to be a very stout-hearted Par, however, who was able to watch them poncing about with the Cup without vomiting!

November 28 1908

Dunfermline sustained their first home League defeat of the season today when they went down to Aberdeen A in the Northern League.

The *Aberdeen Press and Journal* is more concerned with the defeat of their first team to Motherwell at Pittodrie, but is naturally consoled by the triumph of their second XI.

Both the *Courier* and the more neutral *Scottish Referee* are of the persuasion that Dunfermline were very unlucky and that they would have won comfortably if their forwards "had had their shooting boots on".

Hay scored first for Dunfermline but then Aberdeen equalised and then scored what proved to be the winner. Referee Mr McArthur's decision to award the goal was received with "considerable dissatisfaction" by the home supporters; they also had cause to complain when Dunfermline's goalkeeper, Savage, was "savagely attacked" by three Aberdeen forwards when he had the ball in his hands, one of them even being seen to put his arms round Savage's neck!

It is important to remember however that referees in the Edwardian era had no great training in the rules of the game, and certainly for the Northern League, they were usually enthusiastic volunteers from some other club in the League to guarantee neutrality. They were not particularly young or fit necessarily, and often, as here they could be the targets of abuse and even violence.

Today was a bad blow for Dunfermline, who were now third in the Northern League behind Dundee A and Lochgelly United, and did little to help the club achieve what would be its ultimate ambition, namely to gain entrance into the Second Division of the Scottish League.

November 29 2014

Dunfermline to Stranraer in midwinter is a long way, even for a Scottish Cup tie, and, not surprisingly, there were very few Dunfermline fans in the 489 crowd that assembled at Stair Park.

The weather was actually quite decent for the time of year, and the few fans did see quite an entertaining game of football, even though it was ultimately disappointing for Jim Jefferies and the Dunfermline fans.

Dunfermline, wearing red for no obvious reason, scored first; it was a strange goal coming from a free kick inside their own half. It was lofted high into the penalty area. The Stranraer goalkeeper came out and mistimed his jump so that Andy Geggan got up higher and nodded into the net.

It was another header from a free kick that put Dunfermline further ahead and this time it was Gregor Buchanan who did the business.

2-0 up with an hour gone should have made life easy for the Pars, but this was no vintage Dunfermline side with defenders like Norrie McCathie or Roy Barry, and Stranraer were able to pull one back — another strange goal.

Ten minutes of frantic football now remained, with Manager Jim Jefferies being invited to watch the game from the stand after getting rather too "het up" and voluble in his opinions of the refereeing.

Dunfermline seemed to have weathered the storm, until in the 95th minute (an inordinate time having been added).

In a last desperate Stranraer attack, a corner kick was sent over, about half a dozen players went up for the ball and the next thing anyone knew was that the ball was in the back of the net.

Oh dear, Andy Geggan had scored an own goal, and everyone had to reassemble at East End Park a week come Tuesday! And if this one was sore, the replay would be short on joy also...

November 30 1968

St Andrews Day saw a marvellous performance by the Pars as they beat Aberdeen 5-1 at East End Park today, thus consolidating fourth place in the Scottish League.

Aberdeen had been struggling a little of late, but they still had some great players like Tommy Craig, Jimmy Smith, Martin Buchan and Jim Forrest.

Today after a reasonably even first half which saw the Pars go in possibly slightly fortunate to be 2-1 up, Dunfermline turned it on in the second half and a Pat Gardner hat-trick saw then win 5-1, a performance which earned them a standing ovation from their supporters and plaudits in the following day's Sunday newspapers.

The other goals were scored by Alex Edwards and Bertie Paton, and all-in-all it was a grand day for the Pars.

Indeed it was heady days all round at East End Park, for the team were cheered onto the park by their fans for their success in the Cup Winners' Cup where they beat Olympiacos of Greece on the previous Wednesday in a game that sounded like a bit of a rough house.

They had actually been beaten 3-0, but had held out to win 4-3 on aggregate. Thus the prospect of Christmas and the New Year was a pleasant one – comfortably placed in the League, still in Europe, and the defence of the Scottish Cup to look forward to in the New Year.

There were also loads of bullish and optimistic statements from Manager George Farm who even occasionally, supporters were reliably informed, had been seen to smile!

December

December 1 1979

Dunfermline, whose form had varied between the dismal and the dire this season, today showed what they could do as they defeated League leaders Airdrie 1-0 at East End Park.

This was their first season in the First Division (the second tier of Scottish football after the formation of the Premier Division in season 1975/76) after three years in the Second Division.

It was a dull but fairly mild day for December, but by half-time darkness had fallen. The crowd was 3,500, the largest crowd in the First Division today, but still a good deal below what Dunfermline would have expected.

The standard was not great. Only one goal separated the teams and it was scored by the ever popular Jim Bowie; this goal — a real cracker from well outside the penalty area — went down particularly well, for Jim had suffered several serious injury problems of late.

Airdrie were not top of the table for nothing, and fought hard in every sense of the word, but could not breach the Dunfermline defence which had a certain solidity about it today which had been lacking recently.

Referee Douglas Downie's full time whistle was greeted with much relief for it moved the Pars out of the relegation zone as Motherwell and Clyde could only draw.

Today also saw one of the Scottish League Cup semi-finals being played – Aberdeen v Morton before a small crowd in the huge Hampden Stadium.

It was a depressing experience unless you were an Aberdeen supporter for the Dons won 2-1 to set up a final against Dundee United next week.

December 2 1944

Football in war-time was a funny, ad hoc sort of business with teams doing as best as they could with such players as were available.

It would be a mistake to assume however that the game was not taken seriously. Like the cinema, it was vital for the morale of the nation and helped take minds off the real horrors of Europe and the Far East.

Today at Tannadice Park, Dundee, 5,000 were there to see Dunfermline beat Dundee United 7-2 in the North Eastern League.

The main reason for the emphatic victory was the presence on leave from the RAF of "Willie" (sic) Liddell, a Scottish wartime International. Liddell was a Townhill boy, a former pupil of Dunfermline High School and after the war he would become famous as Billy Liddell of Liverpool who sometimes became known as "Liddellpool" as a result.

Today he was home and available to play for Dunfermline, and he simply set Tannadice alight "elusive, confident and clever with great positional sense" in the words of "Ben Bow" of *The Sunday Post*.

He scored once himself and made five goals for Jackie Hunter. It was clear that there was a war on, for "Ben Bow" says that "the Fifers carried heavy artillery and the Tannadice men had only pom poms and the ammunition for these ran short".

The war was indeed continuing. The Normandy landings in June had not yet brought the rapid end to the war that some had expected, but France was now more or less liberated and progress was being made.

It was confidently hoped that 1945 would see an end to it all. For Liddell and a few others however, it was back to their units very soon.

December 3 1966

A great day for Dunfermline as they beat Rangers 3-2 at East End Park.

The weather was cold and frosty with a little fog around, but the pitch was perfectly playable.

The crowd of 18,000 saw a great game in which the Pars emerged victorious, although most Rangers supporters would argue that their side was worth a draw.

It was the first visit of Rangers to East End Park since they had bought Alex Smith in the summer, and hardly surprisingly, he was the target of a great deal of justified and understandable vitriol from the home support for his perceived gold digging in the summer.

Alec was never in any case half as good a player for Rangers as had been for Dunfermline, even though today he managed to score Rangers' second goal.

Dunfermline had unaccountably lost 6-2 to Motherwell last week – something that was totally out of character for this season – and today they lost an early goal to Jim Forrest who was unmarked as a high ball came across the goal.

But the Pars now fought back; by half time they were ahead, first from a bullet header by Alex Ferguson, and then from a penalty kick after Ferguson had been brought down – a decision that did not meet with the approval of some of the less well educated of the blue boys.

Idiots threw bottles and one of them narrowly missed the head of a young fan as Alex Edwards slotted home the spot kick. Alex Smith equalised for Rangers in the second half, but it would be Alex Ferguson who would have the last word.

December 4 1982

It was never what one might have called torrential, and the saving grace was that it did raise the temperature a little, but it was still rain – incessant, miserable and dark.

The floodlights were on well before the 3.00 pm kick-off for the game against Airdrie.

In the circumstances, it was hardly surprising that crowds did not flock to East End Park today; although the club were coy about saying what the exact attendance was, the cynics said that you could count them if the game got boring.

Dunfermline were in one of their many troughs of the 1980s but today's victory (their second of the season) did at least bring them up to third bottom of the First Division.

The team had suffered when Pat Stanton had left his job as Manager to return to his beloved Hibs, and Tom Forsyth had been appointed.

Forsyth, a tough defender who rejoiced in names like "Jaws" and "Iron Man" seemed to lack the temperament to be a Manager at a struggling First Division club, but today at least brought two welcome points.

The only goal of the game came on the half hour mark when Bobby Forrest was on hand to take advantage of a goalkeeping error, and thereafter the Pars did tend to get first to the ball.

It was blood and thunder, typical Scottish stuff, and enjoyed by the Dunfermline support who did at least appreciate the effort put in by the players.

News of the defeats of Queen's Park and Falkirk did not exactly release an orgy of celebration on the streets of Dunfermline tonight, but there was a certain relief that the Pars were no longer bottom.

December 5 1914

The war had been going for four months, and all those who had made absurd statements about it "being over by Christmas" were now looking rather foolish.

Football had survived the attempts to get it stopped, but it was clearly struggling with so many players either abroad or doing their training in England.

Casualties were already high; today it was announced that six Dunfermline Athletic players were among twelve people from the local district who had joined the "Footballers Battalion" of Colonel Sir George McRae of Edinburgh.

Dunfermline were still playing in the Scottish League Second Division. They were sixth in the League, but today they had a bad result as they travelled to Dunterlie Park, Barrhead to play against Arthurlie.

Arthurlie had famously defeated Celtic in the Scottish Cup in 1897, but did not make any long-term impact on the game. Nevertheless a crowd of about 2,000 were there at their ground with the famous slope.

Their own team played well but it was a disjointed performance from Dunfermline, something that was hardly surprising given the amount of youngsters and veterans that they needed to deploy.

Pearson, Crichton, Rae and Cameron are singled out for having played well, but the other seven are ignored in the "eloquent silence" which means that they did not have a good game!

The future was of course very obscure for Dunfermline and for football in general in the circumstances; of course, there was little to cheer anyone up in the town, not so much nowadays "the auld grey toon" as the "auld dark toon" with the blackout in force in fear of shelling from same brave German ship that might have sailed up the Forth!

December 6 1919

Just where would Dunfermline be without Andrew Wilson?

Certainly everyone knew where they were with him and that was at the top of the Central League.

Today, on a dull but mild day, they made the short trip to Brockville in Falkirk to play Falkirk A.

Falkirk's 1st XI was at Aberdeen today playing a 1-1 draw, and the very fact that this was Falkirk's Reserves or their Stiffs — or their Ham and Eggers, so called because they were not paid, but were given their tea, invariably ham and egg, after the game — was a source of hurt to Dunfermline and their supporters.

Dunfermline and Falkirk were towns of similar sizes; Falkirk had already won the Scottish Cup before the war in 1913, and were at the moment in the First Division, whereas Dunfermline were still in the Central League.

The first step forward would have to be winning the Central League, and this now looked like a possibility in 1920.

Today Wilson scored two magnificent goals. The first one was despatched into the net "as if it had been deposited there by the touch of a magician", and the second came after a neat one-two with Meaney which he hammered into the roof of the net.

Falkirk A's goal came from a penalty kick, but it was a good victory for Dunfermline before a crowd of 2,000, some of whose supporters had travelled there by motorised omnibus, a frightening looking contraption but certainly a phenomenon of the new post-war world.

December 7 1985

It was not often in 1985 that a game had to be delayed in order to allow the crowd in.

This was precisely what happened today in the First Round of the Scottish Cup at East End Park. A large arrival of spectators swelled the attendance for the Dunfermline v Raith Rovers tie.

It was sad to see both Dunfermline and Raith Rovers in the Second Division these days — the reason for them having to play in the First Round of the Cup — and the Pars were one of two former Scottish Cup winners (Queen's Park being the other) who found themselves playing in the Scottish Cup today.

The country was on a high, for Scotland had qualified for the Mexico World Cup on Wednesday morning (!) when they beat Australia in a breakfast time kick-off watched avidly on TV.

Dunfermline were currently top of the Second Division, but Raith were struggling, and this was reflected in the play today on this dull, dreich December day when the Christmas lights were beginning to appear in houses (they had been on in shops for weeks).

The Pars scored in the first minute when Ian Heddle drove home a low cross from Bobby Robertson which the sleepy Raith defence failed to clear, and then just on half time John Watson scored a second.

Raith tried hard in the second half, but basically lacked any sort of skill to get through a Dunfermline defence in which Norrie McCathie was outstanding.

Long before full time the Raith supporters were heading homewards.

December 8 1984

To say that Dunfermline were struggling at this time would be an understatement.

Stuck in the bottom tier of the senior game, promotion seemed unlikely at best with the club having picked up only 16 points from 17 league matches .

New manager Jim Leishman found football management to be a tough game.

Hard as it was to see things getting much worse, today, somehow, they did.

In a break from league football, fellow Second Division strugglers East Stirlingshire were the visitors at East End Park for a first-round Scottish cup tie and they won comfortably on a glue-pot surface.

A header from a corner early in the second half by centre half Rennie had 'Shire 1-0 up before a John Watson shot from inside the box gave the Pars an equaliser.

That was as good as it would get; two further goals, another close range Rennie effort and a late Doig lob from distance over goalkeeper Hugh Whyte, put East Stirlingshire through to the second round.

It was only the second time in 25 years that Dunfermline were not in the draw for the 'all-in' round of the cup.

This was, perhaps, the lowest point of the Second Division seasons of the 1980s, though the rest of season 1983/84 would bring equally little joy as the club finished 9th in the second division, 33rd of the 38 league clubs.

With results generally terrible, a ridiculously young manager who seemed as hopeless as those before him and a ginger-haired striker signed from Hong Kong, where did Dunfermline go from here?

Jenkins, McCathie and Watson in 1984

December 9 1978

It was the famous analogy of two old enemies wakening up in hospital after some disaster and seeing each other in adjacent beds.

Here we had East Fife and Dunfermline playing at Bayview in front of a small crowd on a dark depressing December day in Division Two, which of course since 1975 had been the third and bottom tier of Scottish football.

It would be fair to say that Scottish football was generally at a low ebb this season following the cataclysmic events in Argentina in the summer.

There was a particular cause for depression for these two teams in that their supporters had seen a great deal better and, rightly, expected more from their teams.

They had languished in the bottom tier for two years, but East Fife had only joined them this year. Clearly the re-arrangements in the Leagues in 1975 had not worked in the interests of the Fife clubs.

Today Harry Melrose took his men along the coast to Methil, but it was East Fife who went ahead within the first ten minutes.

Dunfermline's equaliser had a touch of the Christmas pantomime about it when an anodyne cross from Bonar Mercer was dropped by East Fife's young goalkeeper and Mike Leonard was there to prod the ball home into an empty net.

The second half was even, tough from time to time with no lack of crunching tackles, but it was East Fife's Methven who got the winner.

The mood of the Dunfermline supporters was not helped by the news that Falkirk, the main rivals, had scraped home against Meadowbank Thistle.

December 10 1921

Today at Station Park, Forfar, Dunfermline Athletic notched their first away win in the reformed Scottish League Second Division.

This was now more or less half way through its first season since it had replaced the Central League in the summer.

Home form had been good, but away form had been far from convincing, and even today, the victory was achieved as much by lackadaisical Forfar defending as by any penetrative play from Dunfermline.

A fairly large contingent from Dunfermline had gone to Forfar to see this game, attracted by Station Park's proximity to the station and the Forfar club's reputation for hospitality.

Soon after half-time with the Forfar club 2-1 up and deservedly so, they must have wondered whether they made the right decision to go to this cold town in the darkness of December for a 2.00 pm kick off.

Even with the early kick off there was a struggle to get the game finished in daylight, with the teams having a cup of tea on the field and a quick turn round.

Shearer and Gray had scored for Dunfermline and Forfar respectively in the first half, then a Scottish Cup winner (with Dundee in 1910) called George Langlands (who rejoiced in the unlikely nickname of "Purkie") put the home team ahead; Forfar remained on top for long spells in the second half.

But then with darkness rapidly descending, Gilmour equalised after some good play from ex-Rangers Jimmy Gordon, then with the Forfar defence beginning to argue among themselves, Cruickshanks nipped in to score what proved to be the winner.

Seconds later, the referee pointed to the pavilion.

December 11 2010

It is of course impossible to say what is the coldest football match that there has ever been, but this one must be in with a shout.

December 2010 was one of the worst winter spells of them all in recent years, but there was another bizarre factor as well this winter – namely a referees' strike in protest about unfair criticism.

The Pars had for one reason or another not played a game for nearly a month, and it was only through almost superhuman efforts by a few volunteers that this game against Queen of the South was played.

But of course when you are doing well in the League, you want your team to play, and the fans (2,062 brave souls which included a few from Dumfries!) were rewarded with a game.

In truth, no-one would have said that this was the best game they had ever seen. Willie Gibson would certainly agree with that statement, for he got a red card.

All those who jump on the bandwagon of "summer football" seemed to be winning their argument against the more traditional "Scottish football is no place for softies" brigade until late in the game when substitute Joe Cardle tapped home a David Graham cross with his first touch to give the Pars a 1-0 victory.

It was so late that some fans had already departed to face the tricky roads or a warm house or pub, and although compassion is a rare emotion among football fans, a thought or two had to be spared for those travelling back home to Dumfries after their late heartbreak.

It was not as if the Pars had never been there themselves!

December 12 2015

The previous season had been a disaster – as one of two full-time clubs in the third tier, Dunfermline had somehow managed to finish 7th, the worst league finish in 30 years.

However, under new manager Allan Johnston, things had improved in 2015/16 and the season started with consecutive 4-1, 5-1, 6-1 and 7-1 wins, but as this December day began, Ayr United were three points clear at the top of the league.

A big game, therefore, as Dunfermline travelled to Somerset Park for the top-of-the-table clash.

The Pars took a first half lead through Michael Moffat's header, but it lasted only a minute as Gerry McLauchlan immediately headed in a corner. Things turned Ayr's way early in the second half when Joe Cardle was harshly sent off – the club later appealed the decision and won.

With the Pars team forced to defend deep, it looked a matter of trying to see the game out and hold on to take a point but then suddenly, from nowhere, David Hopkirk was put through on the keeper, calmly went round him and slotted in.

As the joy of the goal faded, one felt that 20 minutes of torture were about to follow, as indeed they did.

But, in a display of heroic defending, an equaliser was prevented, the final whistle blowing with the team defending in their box.

Every football fan loves good football, but there's nothing quite like a successful backs-to-the-wall defensive effort to stir the emotions and really get into a game.

At the time it felt like a big win, and that feeling too would be proved correct. Although Dunfermline would ultimately win the league by a large margin, this was the game that turned everything.

Moffat scores with a header against Ayr United in 2015

December 13 1947

Dunfermline sadly came off second best to Raith Rovers in today's Fife derby at East End Park.

In spite of the dull and cold weather and the fact that this was a Second Division game, over 8,100 appeared at East End Park, with many trains arriving to disgorge Raith Rovers supporters at Dunfermline Station.

This was said to be "austerity" Britain, but in fact with everyone in full employment as the nation recovered from the war, things were a great deal better than they had been in the 1920s and 1930s, and this was reflected in the tremendous enthusiasm for the game of football, which had never made the mistake of pricing itself out of the market.

Today's game had some interesting visitors. At least eight English clubs were represented in the old "hen house" stand (as it was affectionately named) watching Jackie Stewart of Raith Rovers and Bert Kinnell of Dunfermline. Neither player really shone that day, however.

The Pars were off with a bang and in the first quarter of an hour, the noisy neighbours from Kirkcaldy had been silenced as Dunfermline were 2-0 up with fine goals from Wright and Keith over table-topping Raith Rovers. But then Raith were awarded a penalty by referee Mr Jackson of Glasgow.

It was much disputed, but this was far too early for TV replays or VAR, and Raith duly pulled one back, then crucially equalised through their talented winger Johnny Maule just on the stroke of half-time.

Dunfermline never recovered from this psychological blow, and the challenge subsided pitifully as Raith scored twice in the second half to retain their spot at the top of the Division while the Pars languished in the lower half, well below the other three Fife teams – and that hurt!

December 14 1968

The Pars today recorded a great victory by beating St Mirren, a team who had been having a reasonable season so far, 6-2 at East End Park.

Celtic drew 0-0 at Falkirk. This cheering news meant that Dunfermline had strengthened their title challenge and allowed Pars fans to dream of a Scottish League flag to follow their Scottish Cup of April this year.

The manner of the win was also praiseworthy for St Mirren were actually twice ahead before Dunfermline made it 2-2 at half time, and then in the second half, they simply clicked into gear.

The pitch was hard but definitely playable, and a good crowd of about 9,000 was there. The two St Mirren goals were preventable – one was an interception from a John Lunn throw-in to goalkeeper Bent Martin, and the other was when Blair lofted a ball over Martin's head before tapping the ball in.

However a good goal from Pat Gardner and another from Barrie Mitchell levelled matters and soothed the wrath of Manager George Farm at the half time interval. However Mr Farm's strong words of encouragement at half time meant that Dunfermline came out of the blocks and took command.

Alex Edwards was virtually unstoppable on the wing and he fed Jim Fraser and Ian Lister for another two goals before Gardner scored again and near the end John Lunn added a sixth.

St Mirren had simply no answer to this power play, and the Pars fans, now thoroughly warmed up in spite of it being a very cold day, departed happy, their team second equal in the League and only three points behind leaders Celtic.

December 15 1956

Although defeated in the pouring rain at Celtic Park today, the Pars had reason to be happy with their performance.

The 1-3 defeat (the goal coming from George O'Brien just after the start of the second half) could well have been a real thumping, but sensible play prevented this from happening.

Indeed it was only 1-2 until the last minute when Fifer Willie Fernie scored Celtic's third.

Some of the Pars' play was respectable and considering that they were without the injured Charlie Dickson, it was all in all not a bad result especially as most of the other teams threatened with relegation didn't do all that well either.

Today some Pars supporters decided to be brave and to enter the cowshed shelter at Celtic Park commonly referred to as "the jungle".

Normally only home supporters went there but the crowd was not a huge one today and the Pars supporters enjoyed the Glasgow banter with the Celtic fans.

Today however "the jungle" resembled more the Amazon rain forests, for there were holes in the roof! No-one was ashamed of East End Park any more after they had seen that!

Everyone was aware however that the rest of the season would be a grim relegation struggle. In the meantime, it was now obvious that the days of Anthony Eden as Prime Minister were numbered.

Having led the country into the disastrous Suez adventure a month ago, (which could well have led to World War Three!) he was now ill and seemed to be suffering from a nervous breakdown from which he was trying to recover in the West Indies.

December 16 1961

Dunfermline's remarkable year of 1961 was coming to an end, and today, on a dark and foggy day, the Pars beat Rangers 1-0 in a great game of football, full of some grand moves and a few feisty encounters — one or two players on each side were lucky not to have been sentenced to the long walk for the legendary early bath.

Dunfermline were more or less up to strength, but Rangers were without their two best ball players in Jim Baxter and Ian McMillan.

Both teams had won Cup ties in midweek, and Rangers were due to play in the replay of the Scottish League Cup final against Hearts on Monday night. 18,000 crammed into East End Park today and they were well rewarded.

Referee Mr Cook from Edinburgh was kept very busy as well, not least in the very last minute of the first half when a confrontation between George Peebles and Bobby Shearer might have become a great deal worse than what it was.

Still 0-0 at half time and almost impossible to predict the winner, Rangers' famous left wing of Ralph Brand and Davie Wilson were the ones who were looking most likely.

In fact it was Harry Melrose, a one-time free transfer from Rangers, who broke the deadlock for the Pars, picking up a Peebles pass and lashing home.

Ten minutes remained, but goalkeeper Eddie Connachan was able to repeat his heroics of last year's Scottish Cup final, and the Pars held out for a famous victory, much appreciated by Dundee who also won today, beating Airdrie to remain top of the Scottish League.

December 17 1969

No-one realised it at the time, but this was Dunfermline's last European competition for thirty years. They would duly lose the second leg in a month's time, and would never again qualify for Europe in the Twentieth Century.

There was something rather poignant and appropriate that the glory which started in the early 1960s finished at the end of that tumultuous decade. Those Pars fans who lived through those years remain the envy of those who didn't.

Tonight George Farm's men travelled to Anderlecht in Belgium for the first leg of the Fairs Cities Cup third round tie. They lost 0-1 but that was not necessarily considered a bad result.

The problem was that there was now a rule about "away goals" and it might have been better if the Pars had scored a goal even at the expense of losing two. (As it happened, "away goals" were their downfall at East End Park.)

Anderlecht's goal came, distressingly, at the very bad psychological time of just before half time, and it was scored by Belgian International Johan Devrindt who headed home a cross from Puis.

In the second half, Dunfermline had one or two half chances which the hard working Mitchell might have put away, but most of the traffic was one way towards the goal of Willie Duff.

However full backs Willie Callaghan and John Lunn were both outstanding, and the full time whistle came with the tie still open and Dunfermline still in with a chance. It was not a bad way to spend Christmas!

December 18 1965

A blow to Dunfermline's chances of winning the Scottish League came today with the visit of Celtic to East End Park and two goals from Stevie Chalmers in the middle of the second half.

The weather was cold, as one would expect at this time of year, but a crowd of 15,000 were there neglecting their Christmas shopping duties in favour of a game of football between Scotland's two form teams at the moment.

A couple of weeks ago, Scotland had been eliminated by Italy from the 1966 World Cup due to be held in England, and that was a bad blow, but there was little wrong with the Scottish domestic product at the moment as this game showed.

Dunfermline, playing in an unusual strip of bright red with pin stripes, survived the early Celtic barrage and held their own until half time, while also being able to give veteran goalkeeper Ronnie Simpson a lot of bother.

The game began to look as if it might end up in a goalless draw until a long ball from John Cushley — who would play for Dunfermline in future years — found Chalmers.

A few minutes later the normally very reliable Jim McLean got himself into an awful mess with a pass back and Chalmers once again took advantage.

This was Jock Stein's first full season as Manager of Celtic, and they were looking a great side, but Dunfermline also played well under Willie Cunningham, and would not be far away when the honours were to be handed out at the end of the season.

December 19 1962

This was one of the most remarkable nights in the history of Scottish football when Dunfermline, 4-0 down from the first leg of their Inter Cities Fairs Cup tie against the holders Valencia in a very naïve performance, managed to level the tie on aggregate with a 6-2 win at East End Park.

The late Bob Crampsey recalls coming to Dunfermline that night and enjoying the sight of all the Christmas lights on trees and in houses — a feature of what was then called "the affluent society" — but also wondering whether there really was any point in him being there to commentate on the game for STV, for the Pars surely had no chance against the Spaniards.

But the Spaniards suffered from the intense cold of a Scottish midwinter and a hard (but playable) pitch, and Jock Stein's tactics were to hit them hard from the start.

He had the players to do this job as well, and by half-time, the tie was levelled with the Pars winning 5-1 thanks to two goals from Jackie Sinclair and one each from George Peebles, Jim McLean and Alex Smith.

This was barely believable stuff and the 15,000 crowd (more than one might have expected in the circumstances) were going mad. It couldn't last, it was felt, and when Jim McLean managed to get in the way of a ball to divert it into his own net, it looked as if the dream was about to end, but Alex Smith scored again to make the final score 6-2.

In modern times, the Pars would have been defeated on away goals, but in 1962/63 a deciding game was to be played in Lisbon in February. Christmas in Dunfermline in 1962 became a merry one!

BIENVENIDA al VALENCIA CLUB FUTBOL

Inter Cities Fairs Cup

6 DUNFERMLINE versus VALENCIA 2

EAST END PARK :: DUNFERMLINE

Wednesday, 19th December
1962

KICK-OFF, 7.30 p.m.

Official Souvenir Programme . . 6d.

December 20 1958

"Firhill for thrills" was the slogan for Partick Thistle in the 1950s, for the Jags were so mercurial and unpredictable that anything could happen.

This game certainly lived up to that category with those who had left early to do some Christmas shopping missing something.

The weather was dull and drab but it was also midwinter and there was no problem with either rain or frost so that a full card of football was played.

Glasgow was actually quite a bright place with loads of Christmas lights, and Firhill's floodlights, switched on only quarter of an hour after the 2.00 pm start, were very bright and the game was a good one.

Thistle were neatly placed in the middle of the table but DA were in their far from unaccustomed place of the fringes of the relegation battle.

Both teams served up a great game of football for the 10,000 fans who included a healthy contingent from Fife, the pattern being that fathers and sons went to the football while mothers and daughters went Christmas shopping in the bright lights of Sauchiehall Street.

Those who went to Firhill saw George Peebles put the Pars ahead, but nevertheless the half time score was 2-1 for Thistle with legendary winger Tommy Ewing — "Ewing is the best buy, the best buy in years!" — in dazzling form.

And that was what it looked like ending up until the Pars got a penalty which Harry Melrose put away. Then Ewing scored what looked like the winner for Thistle in the last minute, but Pars were not to be denied when Melrose scored again in injury time. It was better than Christmas shopping!

December 21 1935

Midwinter's day saw a remarkable game of football at East End Park with the score line a very unusual Dunfermline Athletic 5 Albion Rovers 5.

Nothing however was more remarkable than the pitch which was in fact totally covered with sand!

The conditions were hard frost and freezing fog and the only chance that there was of the game being played was to cover the pitch in sand.

The result was, in the opinion of "Lynx-eye" in *The Sunday Post,* a remarkably good game of football.

These two teams, keen rivals, had actually been promoted together in 1934, and were more than holding their own in the First Division with Dunfermline in particular enjoying a good season.

At Celtic Park today, Jimmy McGrory established the world record for goal scoring, which was rather a shame for it rather detracted from Dunfermline's game in the newspapers.

At the 60th minute mark the score was 5-2 for the Coatbridge men after a swift orgy of goal scoring in which Albion Rovers, Dunfermline and Albion Rovers again scored well inside three minutes!

Dunfermline now seemed to have shot their bolt, but Dunfermline kept fighting and by the 70th minute, Morrison and then Bob McGowan had pulled it back to 5-4.

Even at that, Albion Rovers seemed to be edging over the winning line until in the very last minute McGowan tore through the defence and levelled the game to a great shout of approval.

"Lynx-eye" even expressed the hope that the frost would stay, for he hoped for more games on the pitch that resembled a beach!

December 22 1923

It was midwinter and dark as the crowd made their way to East End Park to see Athletic take on the "Red Lichties" of Arbroath.

The crowd was reasonable for the time of year, for it wasn't particularly cold although there had been a great deal of rain, something that made it difficult for players to keep their feet on the wet surface.

Arbroath were having a bad season and were very close to the bottom of the Scottish League Division Two whereas Dunfermline, whose form had been inconsistent this season, were nevertheless in the top half.

Dunfermline won 2-1 but it was a far from convincing victory as Arbroath belied their lowly position in the League. Dunfermline scored first from the penalty spot, although it looked to be a case of "it played him" i.e. the ball actually hit the arm of the defender rather than that the defender deliberately handled.

Nevertheless, Strachan did not argue and scored from the spot. After that an "undesirable element of rough play" made its appearance as Arbroath resented the penalty kick award, but it was Dunfermline who went further ahead when Joe Sutton pounced on a poor clearance.

Arbroath did pull one back, and in the second half had hard luck on several occasions with Dunfermline heavily indebted to goalkeeper Mackie for their victory.

It was a good day for Dunfermline, but there was a distinct uncertainty about where the country was going, for a General Election on December 6 had produced a "hung" Parliament with no party having any kind of majority.

There was the distinct possibility, however, that in the New Year, there might be a Labour Government for the first time, albeit a minority one.

December 23 1971

A great night for Dunfermline as they won the BBC Quiz Ball tournament by beating Leicester City 3-1.

This was a rather popular quiz programme involving invited English and Scottish football teams.

There were four players in the team, and each team was allowed a supporter. Sometimes it is believed that football clubs are not necessarily over-endowed with intelligent people, but at this point the Pars had Manager Alec Wright, Jim Fraser and John Cushley.

Their "supporter" had been Jimmy Logan, the Scottish singer and entertainer, but he was "subbed" in the final by Jon Pertwee, one of the many actors who played Doctor Who.

The rules were complicated with routes to goal, tackles, etc., but the Pars won tonight, thanks mainly to John Cushley, a much underrated player. He was a teacher of French and Spanish, and came to Dunfermline via Celtic and West Ham.

He possibly could have been Celtic's centre half for many years but had the misfortune to be at Parkhead at the same time as Billy McNeill and had to move on.

He was good enough on the field for Dunfermline, but he was certainly the star in the quiz show. He was well supported by the other three as well, and the victory in the quiz broadcast tonight was a great boost to Dunfermline and their supporters.

1971/72 was, of course, Dunfermline's relegation season, the season that brought to a temporary end the good times of Stein, Cunningham and Farm, but at least the Pars supporters could boast of something this Christmas and New Year!

December 24 1921

This was an odd Christmas Eve for Dunfermline Athletic, for although they beat Bo'ness very comfortably 4-1, this game was actually played at Central Park, Cowdenbeath.

This was because Dunfermline were serving a punishment of having their ground closed for a month from early December.

It so happened that on December 10 and 17 they were away from home in any case, but today they had to find another ground, in this case Cowdenbeath – something that would have cost them a fair amount of money.

All this followed some thuggery by their supporters in a game against St Johnstone in mid-November where the referee was jostled and threatened.

Sadly it appeared that rather too many supporters, those from Dunfermline not excepted, had learned rather too well how to be violent in their years in khaki, and football in the early 1920s was full of such behaviour from disturbed and unhappy young men.

Today, however, in weather that was not too bad for Christmas Eve, Dunfermline played very well and won deservedly with Smith scoring two and Gilmour and Strachan the other ones, with the half back line of Mercer, Fyfe and Gordon in total command.

The left half was Jimmy Gordon, a man who had excelled for Rangers before and during the war before he became a Sergeant in the Highland Light Infantry where he served with distinction.

This result maintained Dunfermline's position in the middle of the table, a position which did not please some of the disgruntled support. But it was a satisfactory Christmas, at least.

December 25 1926

Christmas Day was not a public holiday in Scotland until 1958 (such was the grim Presbyterian desire to see everyone unhappy!) and if Christmas Day fell on a Saturday, football was played as per normal.

This was Dunfermline's first Christmas in the First Division, and they celebrated it (if that is an appropriate term for a team at the bottom of the League) with a 1-1 draw when Morton came calling.

The attendance was low; many of Dunfermline's supporters were miners who had just returned to work after a long and painful strike and had little money for Christmas presents, let alone football matches.

The weather was not great but the game was a decent hard fought one against a team who looked to be about much the same standard as Dunfermline.

Bobby Skinner remained the man of the moment for the home side, and it was he who put them ahead after missing an absolute sitter a few minutes earlier.

It was the first goal scored at East End Park since October 16, although the offside laws of the game had recently been modified to make it easier to score goals!

Morton scored after a shocking defensive error, so that it was "peels" i.e. a draw at the interval. The second half, in indifferent light throughout, saw Dunfermline on top but they were profligate with chances.

Skinner in particular had a real shocker of a game, so much so that the question was asked by some fans whether there had been some "nobblings" or "taking bribes"– a feature all too prevalent in football in the 1920s.

Not on this occasion, however. Bobby was simply having a bad day.

December 26 1989

This was a grim Boxing Day battle at East End Park on a cold, frosty but clear day, and Dunfermline emerged 1-0 winners over Dundee.

More or less half way through the season and everyone knew that survival in the Premier Division was what was at stake.

The tackles were grim and uncompromising and we had the sight of a Dundee player, Mark Craib, being shown a yellow card after less than 10 seconds play for clattering Istvan Kozma!

Thereafter referee Michael McGinley of Clydebank was a busy man. In the circumstances he had a good game; he managed to keep the lid on things.

Most Dunfermline supporters tended to agree that Dundee deserved a penalty late on in the game when Tommy Wilson brought down Joe McBride junior.

The only goal of the game came in the last minute and was a funny one when a high ball from Ray Sharp beat everyone and came to Kozma on the edge of the box.

The Hungarian hit the ball hard; the ball eventually went in, having ricocheted off quite a number of legs on the way and eventually almost crawling over the line.

The game was much enjoyed by the 9,282 fans, in spite of the lack of flowing football, and it meant that Jim Leishman and his men could now enjoy some breathing space at the bottom of the Premier Division.

For Dundee, however, this was a hammer blow from which they did not recover.

December 27 1919

The decade of the 1910s (has there ever been a more dramatic or tragic decade in world history?) was coming to an end, and Dunfermline played their last game in this decade today when they entertained Broxburn at East End Park in a Central League game.

The 1-1 draw meant that they maintained their position at the top of the Central League but it was a far from impressive performance.

The Courier stated that "even Wilson was off form", a reference to Andrew Wilson, the man who had lit up East End Park this season with his fine goals and superb play.

The weather had been awful this week with both frost and deluges of rain, but the pitch had stood up to it remarkably well. The cold conditions and intermittent rain and wind meant however that only a very sparse crowd turned up with the papers guessing at something like 2,000.

Man of the match was Dunfermline's right back Jack Baird, who was "wonderfully energetic and accurate with his clearances".

Dunfermline were quite easily the better team but the problem was that they could not convert all their outfield pressure into goals.

Wilson had one or two rocket shots but was nothing like his best and it was Cobben who scored the only goal for Dunfermline.

Broxburn's equaliser came from "an oblique shot" and caught everyone by surprise.

Although today had not been one of the better performances, nevertheless, the future was looking good for Dunfermline.

It was looking less good for the world however. The war had been over for more than a year, but it had not yet gone away. It stayed in everyone's minds and consciousness.

December 28 1968

It was second v third at East End Park today as the Pars took on Dundee United.

The game was in doubt for some time, for the pitch was hard and a fall of snow round about lunch time caused more problems. But if anything, the snow gave the players a grip and in any case the snow also brought a slight rise in the temperature, so that Mr Willie Syme, the referee, was happy to let the game go ahead, especially when the sun came out.

The Dundee United squad were given the false news that the game was off, returned to Tannadice but then heard that the game was on!

So back they came!

However at 3.00 pm everyone was in place, and the Pars were off to a blistering start. Bertie Paton scored with a header but it was chalked off, then Alex Edwards scored direct from a corner kick, a goal which owed something to the hard turf.

Just before half time, Pat Gardner was brought down in the box, and Hugh Robertson made no mistake from the spot. So far, so good and Dunfermline looked to be going well at half time.

However, Dundee United were not second in the League for nothing and fought back well, taking advantage of defensive frailties to score twice through Ian Mitchell.

The game finished with both teams missing chances, and although the Pars were disappointed not to win, the general agreement was that a draw was a fair result in this, the last game of the wonderful year that was 1968.

December 29 2010

The Pars made sure that their fans would have a very Happy New Year with a very comfortable 5-0 West Fife derby over Cowdenbeath.

They ended the year not exactly as the runaway leaders of the First Division (second tier) but going well in the promotion battle with local rivals Raith Rovers and Falkirk.

Derby games between Dunfermline and Cowdenbeath possibly lacked some of the edge that derby games v Raith Rovers, for example, had, but they were still important.

Today 2,942 were there to see Cowdenbeath get the better of the earlier exchanges but it was Andy Kirk who opened the scoring for Dunfermline.

Kirk then picked up a knock and had to be taken off, but it was his replacement, Pat Clarke, who scored twice in the second half, with Nick Phinn scoring as well.

Just at the end, Cowdenbeath conceded an own goal when Scott Linton miskicked into his own net to complete a very sad day for the Blue Brazil.

It was a very odd season, however, although Dunfermline won the Division One title by ten points from Raith Rovers.

The real challengers would have been Dundee – but they were deducted 25 points for going bust and having to enter administration!

For Cowdenbeath, things looked black. Already out of the Scottish Cup before today's game, they found that 2011 brought them very little consolation for they ended up second bottom with only Stirling Albion beneath them and were relegated by means of a play-off.

December 30 1989

Dunfermline Athletic finished the 1980s on a high.

Having defeated Dundee on Boxing Day, they today won unexpectedly at Celtic Park, a place where they seldom did well.

Granted, it was against one of the weakest Celtic teams that one is ever likely to see, a team obeying the apparently unalterable law of Glasgow that if Rangers are going to be good, Celtic have to be bad – and vice versa.

But today before a large holiday crowd of 30,548 Stuart Rafferty scored the first goal in 20 minutes off the post after a run by Ross Jack.

When Celtic were awarded a dubious penalty kick, Andy Walker lofted it over the bar, and that was the score line at half time.

The second half saw some resolute Dunfermline defending with Rougvie and McCathie outstanding against almost constant Celtic pressure, although most of it was desperate and hysterical rather than creative and inspired with the constant high ball down the middle food and drink to the Dunfermline defence.

Yet, one always felt that Celtic would have to score some time, but when the goal came it was at the other end when Ross Jack broke away to score.

This victory, as pleasant as it was unexpected, probably played a big part in saving Dunfermline from relegation at the end of the season, for the rest of the season would not be quite as good as this for Jim Leishman's team.

On January 3 for example, in the first game of the new decade, they would lose to Dundee United.

December 31 1977

There was something appropriate about 1977 finishing with a goalless draw against Berwick Rangers at a desolate East End Park on a dull, mild sort of a day of the kind that one associates with Hogmanay.

In truth the game wasn't all that bad, and the Pars had real hard luck in the shape of narrow misses and a few refereeing decisions towards the end, but the 2,500 crowd were far from impressed.

The 1970s had been cruel to them, and the League restructuring had done them few favours; here we had Dunfermline with undeniably the best stadium in the Second Division but a poor, mediocre team about half way up the bottom tier of Scottish football.

A decade ago, things had been totally different, but today's crowd could be divided into three groups:

(a) the still enthusiastic who believed that 1978 would see the Pars bounce back,

(b) the angry who were now turning on the Directors and Manager Harry Melrose (a man who was more acutely aware of the change of fortunes than most),

and (c) the biggest group which were those who were quietly and philosophically resigned to what was going on, and saying to each other that "You have to take the rough with the smooth!"

No-one was sorry to see the back of 1977 – but there were good things as well, not least the prospect of Scotland playing in the World Cup in Argentina in summer 1978.

Scotland doing well and a resurgence in the fortunes of the Pars were high on the wish lists for 1978 as the bells tolled.

January

January 1 1953

New Year's Day, and possibly for the first time ever, there is a hint that things are getting a little better.

The infant National Health Service is now beginning to kick in, houses are beginning to be built and unemployment is virtually a thing of the past.

In addition, there is the Coronation of the new Queen to be looked forward to with the date set for early June. But for Pars fans, is there any chance that things might begin to improve on the football field?

Certainly today's game against old rivals Cowdenbeath at East End Park was a great cure for hangovers as a crowd of 5,000 watched Dunfermline beat Cowdenbeath 2-1.

Cowdenbeath played well, and certainly at half time they left the field well worth their 1-0 lead, brought about when Jimmy Clarkson conceded an indirect free kick. Paton slipped the ball to Allan who hit the ball into the roof of the net.

A few boos were heard from the Pars fans as their team left the field, but then Dunfermline reshuffled their forward line in the second half, and the effect was more or less instantaneous with wee George O'Brien collecting a ball from Durkin and running on to slip the ball past the Cowdenbeath goalkeeper.

In the 70th minute Muir hit what proved to be the winner when he tried a snap shot from a difficult angle and caught the goalkeeper by surprise.

Cowdenbeath tried hard, but the heavy ground took its toll, and Dunfermline finished the game comfortably on top.

January 2 1954

However Dunfermline Athletic celebrated the New Year, it seems to have worked, even though the supporters were still tearing their hair out at the inconsistency of their team.

Still in 1954 a Second Division team, Dunfermline had started the League season very well after being ousted from the League Cup by those League Cup specialists East Fife.

They had suffered a dip in form in the month of December before a creditable 1-1 draw in the West Fife derby at Central Park against local rivals Cowdenbeath (visits to Cowdenbeath in the recent past hadn't always been so rewarding!) and then today they suddenly went crazy and beat Dumbarton 6-1!

George Henderson scored four goals (one of them from the penalty spot) but the man of the match was Willie McSeveney, who scored one himself at the end and was largely responsible for all the other goals.

This sort of form was very welcome of course to the Dunfermline fans but it made them worry just how long they could hope to hold on to him. They were well aware that Middlesbrough had already made at least one bid for him, and it was no secret that several other teams were also interested.

He would at the end of this season go to the ambitious Motherwell side, but for the moment at least he was still a Dunfermline player, and more pertinently, Dunfermline by this thrashing of lowly Dumbarton, had put themselves back into the promotion race.

That meant a Happy New Year to the Pars supporters.

January 3 1970

Dunfermline had begun the New Year and the decade of the 1970s with a good 3-0 win over Raith Rovers at East End Park.

Today they were brought back down to earth with a dull thud at Tynecastle as they went down 0-2 to Hearts.

The sun was out, but the pitch was hard and the low winter sun was not able to reach some areas of the pitch. The pitch, however, survived an inspection by referee Mr Robert Henderson of Dundee and the game went ahead.

Some other grounds were not quite so lucky, but 11,000 turned up to see this game.

Hearts' New Year's Day game had been a disappointing 0-0 draw with Hibs at Easter Road, but they played a great deal better today and scored twice in the first 25 minutes – a header by Murray and a prod home by Ford after an appalling mix up in the Dunfermline defence.

Roared on by a substantial support, the Pars fought back but simply failed to find the net. Once or twice they were thwarted by offside decisions, but basically Hearts' defence remained on top.

This result more or less killed whatever chance Pars might have had of making an impact on the Scottish League, but of course there was still Europe and the Scottish Cup.

For Hearts on the other hand, it was an indication that they were slowly improving. Yet it was only a temporary and superficial improvement, for the decade of the 1970s was fated to inflict some horrors on the supporters of both these teams.

January 4 1964

Heavy rain which had been falling steadily all morning briefly threatened the visit of table topping Kilmarnock to East End Park.

The pitch survived the inspection, but the attendance was badly affected with the crowd of less than 8,000, including a fair few from Ayrshire with blue scarves, huddled under the shelters.

The floodlights were on at full blast from the very start even though it was still only 3.00 pm! The crowd actually saw a very good game, as often happens in wet conditions in Scotland.

Managers Jock Stein and Willie Waddell had enjoyed a healthy rivalry with each other since the days that they played on either side of the Old Firm.

They had both expressed interest in learning from the methods of Helenio Herrera on Inter Milan, and they had a great respect, if not liking, for each other.

It was Dunfermline who scored first through Jim Kerray and three minutes later Willie Callaghan put the Pars two up after picking up a pass from George Peebles.

But Kilmarnock were not top of the Scottish League for nothing, and before half-time Brian McIlroy had pulled one back.

Half time saw a little potential crowd trouble with policemen taking up position between the two sets of fans, but in the second half, such was the standard of football that everyone was engrossed in what was happening on the pitch.

Any thought of trouble had disappeared, but the second half did not make for happy watching for Dunfermline fans, as McIlroy headed an equaliser early on, and then in the closing stages after close things at both ends, the same man completed his hat-trick with a late, depressing winner.

January 5 1924

Dunfermline had enjoyed a good New Year, a creditable draw with Alloa on New Year's Day and a 6-1 defeat of Lochgelly United on the 2nd, so they embarked on their trip to Volunteer Park, Armadale in good spirits.

The conditions were very good for the time of year, but it was an odd game with two penalties, correctly awarded for handling, one for each side; Dunfermline were distinctly unlucky not to get at least something out of this game.

The first goal came in the first minute with goalkeeper Paterson having no chance because he was unsighted by a combination of the low winter sun and one of his own defenders.

Both teams then got their penalty on either side of half-time, before Armadale scored the best goal of the game with a fine header scored by Ramsay from an inch perfect cross.

This was a disappointment for Dunfermline and their gallant band of supporters who had made the short trip to West Lothian, and a draw would have been a fairer result, it was felt.

If one could have gazed into a crystal ball however, one would have seen less than a decade away the demise of Armadale, a victim of the collapse of local industry and the general inability of West Lothian to sustain its football teams.

The main topic, however, in early 1924 would have been politics. The General Election of December 1923 had produced a hung Parliament.

Everything had then been suspended over Christmas and the New Year, but now the intriguing question was "Could there be the first Labour Government?" Dunfermline and West Fife MPs Willie Watson and John Adamson certainly hoped so.

January 6 1962

The weather was still cold, and it was still touch and go, as far as pitch inspections were concerned. There was certainly a great improvement on the weather which had devastated the New Year programme, and the go ahead was given for the game against Dundee United at East End Park today.

The 10,000 crowd contained a large element from Dundee supporting the Tannadice Terrors who were now in their second year in the First Division and showing clear signs, like the Pars themselves, of being upwardly mobile and ambitious.

The game was a very good 4-1 win for Dunfermline and contained one of the strangest goals that one could ever have imagined.

The Pars were already 1-0 up through a Tommy McDonald header when, early in the second half, they forced a corner on the right. McDonald would have been vexed with his effort.

It was sailing gently into the hands of the goalkeeper, Alec Brown, who rose confidently to collect, but he had come too far out and had to bend back to get the ball. Sadly he stumbled upon landing and rolled into the net with the ball still in his hands!

It was bizarre, but welcomed by the Pars fans. Alex Smith then scored again after a classy move involving Peebles and Melrose.

Although Dundee United pulled one back from Irvine, Alex Smith scored again to give Dunfermline a good start to the New Year and to consolidate their position near the top of the First Division.

January 7 1922

Vale of Leven were visitors to East End Park for this second division match, their first trip to the ground in eight years.

The Athletic took the lead with a goal *The Dunfermline Press* made doubly certain to report as being on the fortunate side, describing it as a 'lucky and at the same time "fluky" goal'. An equaliser before half-time made it 1-1 which is how the game finished.

During the 1920s, Vale were a club on the way down. Based in Alexandria near Dumbarton and one of the early powerhouses of the Scottish game, the club had been the second to win the Scottish Cup, winners in 1877, 1878 and 1879.

Despite being a founder member of the Scottish Football League, their decline in the 1920s was steep, firstly being relegated to the short-lived Third Division before ceasing playing altogether in 1929.

While Vale of Leven were on the way down in 1922, Dunfermline were very much on the up.

Before World War I, promotion and relegation had not been automatic. Dunfermline were among the leading voices arguing against this blatant unfairness that required clubs to apply to move up a division rather than have it decided on results.

When football resumed after the war, Dunfermline resigned from the SFL and played for a season in the rebel Central League, the success of which forced the SFL to reinstate Division Two, but this time with automatic promotion and relegation in place.

A mid-table finish meant that Dunfermline were not the first club to be automatically promoted — Alloa had that honour — but a series of similar league finishes laid the foundations for the second division title win in 1926.

January 8 1996

This Monday night, Norrie McCathie and Mandy Burns were found dead after suffering carbon monoxide poisoning.

McCathie had played in the loss at Love Street two days earlier, his 497th league appearance for the club and 576th in all competitions – easily the most of any Dunfermline player.

His time with the club included successive promotions in 1986 and 1987, as well as famously scoring the winning penalty in the League Cup semi-final shoot-out win over Airdrie in 1991 to take the club to their first final since 1968.

The week after was a time of great sadness, but a decision was taken to play the following Saturday's match with Clydebank at East End Park as scheduled on January 13.

The minute's silence was unbearable and the game had an atmosphere that has never been experienced since.

In normal circumstances the Pars would be strong favourites in this game and, after going 3-0 up in the first half, things were going to plan.

However, maybe as a result of the emotional stress on everyone, things started to go wrong and the Bankies came back, eventually levelling at 3-3 with 5 minutes left.

The emotion in the roar of encouragement that went up as the equaliser went in was astonishing, and it had the wanted effect. Straight from the restart, a shooting chance fell to new captain Craig Robertson 20 yards out and, despite a touch from the keeper, it flew into the top corner for a 4-3 win.

On its own it was a good goal but, given the circumstances, it ranks as one of the greatest in the club's history. A fine tribute to the man he had just replaced as captain.

While McCathie is well-known, it should always be remembered that two young people – Norrie and Mandy – tragically died that January day.

January 9 1926

Dunfermline today registered a good 6-2 away win at Dunterlie Park, Barrhead, home of Arthurlie, thus maintaining their position of 3rd in the Second Division of the Scottish League, tucked in behind Stenhousemuir and Clyde and in a good place for a promotion push.

The weather was not at all bad for the time of the year with a certain amount of sun around, but there was rather too much of a wind.

Arthurlie won the toss and chose to play against the wind, their idea being to hold or restrict Dunfermline until half time. This plan clearly back-fired, for Dunfermline were three goals up at half time, two from Skinner and one from Stein.

"None of them were great goals" according to the curmudgeonly writer of *The Sunday Post* and "goalkeeper Rundell should certainly have saved Stein's", but the virtue of Bobby Skinner was his ability (like all good strikers) to read the game and thus to be in the right place at the right time for a simple tap-in.

He scored again early in the second half, revealing his ability to understand the new offside law which was designed to encourage the scoring of more goals.

Arthurlie fought back to an extent with two headed goals, but their shooting was wild, revealing a clear misunderstanding of the strength of the wind.

Dunfermline scored two late goals through Herd and Stein, and the train journey back home was a pleasant one for the team and the few fans who had travelled with them.

The New Year had been mixed so far – a good 5-0 win on January 1 but a 0-1 reverse the following day – but this was a good result.

It did not take a genius however to work out that in 1926 there was real trouble brewing in the coal mining industry.

January 10 2019

Stevie Crawford was today appointed Manager of Dunfermline Athletic following the departure of Allan Johnston.

Crawford had been with the club since the start of the season as a coach. A local boy who had been a youth player at East End Park, success came at Raith Rovers with whom he won the Scottish League Cup in 1994/95, scoring in the final.

After a spell in England, he came to East End Park as a player, initially on loan from Hibs. 16 goals while on loan helped the club to promotion in 1999/2000.

After signing permanently the following season, perhaps the best spell of his career followed. Forming an impressive partnership with Craig Brewster, his scoring form was such that he regularly played for Scotland and helped take the club to the 2004 Scottish Cup final.

After moving to Plymouth there were spells at Dundee United and Aberdeen, another at Dunfermline, before coaching under Robbie Neilson at Hearts and briefly managing East Fife.

His time as East Fife manager had been largely unsuccessful, so, with no other experience in management, it was something of a gamble that he should be appointed Pars manager.

This appointment came at a difficult time – Allan Johnston was sacked after letting a 2-0 lead slip against Alloa, which was just one disappointment too many in a largely uninspiring season.

In the middle of a tight league, a good run could see a push for promotion play-offs while a bad one meant relegation danger. Of more immediate concern, however, was a big cup tie at Stark's Park.

January 11 1947

The weather was foul, something that reduced the attendance to about 1,500 when on a drier day some 7,000 or 8,000 might have been expected to see the Fife derby.

Ex-servicemen were grateful for the demob hats with the broad brims which had been issued to them when they came back, and they were put to good use today.

Earlier in the season, Raith Rovers had beaten Dunfermline comfortably at Stark's Park, so today's 4-1 reply was sweet revenge, even though most honest Pars supporters would have admitted that the score line should have been a lot narrower than that.

The rain which fell heavily more or less all day rendered the pitch difficult at the best of places and an absolute quagmire at the worst. Credit is due to the players for serving up any kind of football at all in the conditions, even though they clearly tired at the end.

Bert Kinnell scored twice in the first half as the Pars went in at half time 3-0 up, although the best goal of the game was that of Willie Irvine just after half time.

He caught everyone by surprise with a shot from the wing. Davie Kinnear scored the other goal for Dunfermline and half way through the second half Lawson got one back for Raith Rovers.

Both teams were round about the middle of the Division "B" table, currently led by Dundee, but there was still a long way to go.

1947 is famous for being the one of the worst winters of the 20th century and it would play havoc with the fixtures in February – but it hadn't started yet!

January 12 1974

Wind and rain lashed Scotland last night and this morning causing the postponement of several fixtures.

However, by the time that Partick Thistle came to Dunfermline today for their Scottish League game, the worst had passed; although the pitch was far from perfect, it was certainly playable with what was left of the high winds drying it out.

This was of course the winter of 1973/74.

Industrial problems abounded.

Inflation soared to such an extent that it was believed to be getting out of control altogether.

War was threatened in the Middle East again (there had been one a few months ago).

The net kept tightening on US President Nixon for his part in the Watergate burglary.

In the midst of all that relegation from the Scottish First Division remained an ever present possibility for the Pars, and the visit of Partick Thistle, who had a similar problem, became a vital occasion.

A crowd of 3,500 including a fair amount of red-and-yellow bedecked Partick Thistle fans turned up in spite of the conditions which were far from pleasant.

Manager George Miller had signed Willie McCallum from St Mirren in midweek and he was given a game today at centre half.

He was obviously finding the conditions and his new surroundings difficult, and at half-time it was the Glasgow side that was leading 1-0 thanks to a goal scored by Ronnie Glavin, and at the other end some good saves from goalkeeper Alan Rough.

Alex Kinninmonth, however, managed to notch an equaliser for the Pars in the second half, and a draw was possibly a fair result.

January 13 1962

Jock Stein's men came back virtually from the dead to register a good 2-1 win over Falkirk to-day at Brockville in the Scottish League.

These two are near neighbours of course and enjoyed a healthy rivalry, although it would have to be said that in recent years Dunfermline were getting the better of things.

Dunfermline were Scottish Cup holders, competing in Europe and respectably placed near the top of the First Division, whereas the Bairns were engaged in a relegation dog fight.

Brockville is a ground that is sadly no longer with us, having been replaced by the Falkirk Stadium near the Kelpies. In 1962 however it was a good, atmospheric ground and had been the scene of many great matches over the years.

Today's crowd of over 8,000 contained a good few black and white scarves, and they were rewarded with a very good game in the watery winter sunshine. There had been frost overnight, but it had melted and there was no problem with the pitch.

Both goalkeepers Eddie Connachan and Willie Whigham were kept busy but were dealing with it all until, seconds after George Peebles had missed an open goal, Innes of Falkirk picked up a ball in the Dunfermline penalty box, and then dribbled round Connachan.

That seemed to be it, but then within the last five minutes of the game, the Pars got a deserved equaliser when Tommy McDonald scored.

Just as both sets of supporters were reconciling themselves to a draw, George Miller popped up to give Dunfermline both points.

January 14 1928

This was one of Dunfermline Athletic's darkest days as they went down 0-9 to Celtic at Celtic Park in the Scottish League.

It was also a very famous day in Scottish football history for it was the day that Jimmy McGrory scored eight of the nine goals! He also managed to have another two chalked off for offside, and missed a few chances as well.

Celtic's other goal was scored by Alec Thomson, a Fifer from Buckhaven.

For Dunfermline, it was just a case of being outclassed. There were a few first team men out with injuries, but relegation was now clearly beckoning.

A surprise in the reports of the game is that the attendance was little more than 3,000 at Parkhead but then again, the weather was foul and January is not the best time for attendances.

So where did the Pars go from here? Oddly enough, although they did indeed experience relegation, there was a reasonable Cup run before they went down to Hibs in the quarter final.

But at least one of the very few Dunfermline supporters who had gone to Glasgow (it was perhaps a blessing that hardly anyone was there!) came back and showed that he had not lost his sense of humour, for he came in to the pub and said "Well, they couldn't give us ten!"

By Monday, however, a more sober reckoning of the situation was that Jimmy McGrory was simply a brilliant scorer, and that Celtic (who had beaten Rangers 1-0 at the New Year) were a good side.

It was simply a bad day, and that Dunfermline should really be measured against the likes of Bo'ness and Raith Rovers rather than Celtic and Rangers. But in fact, the Athletic really were poor this season and ended up rock bottom.

January 15 1969

It is not often that East End Park is sold out other than for a Celtic or a Rangers game, but that is what happened tonight when Dunfermline took on West Bromwich Albion in the European Cup Winners' Cup before 25,000 fans.

The weather was remarkably clement for the middle of January and huge traffic jams and queues were visible outside the ground. League form had been nothing to write home about recently, but this was a European tie with the added attraction of it being a Scotland v England tussle and everyone remembered the games against Everton.

West Bromwich had a good few fans with them and in those still unsegregated days, mingled, if not happily then certainly peacefully, with the Dunfermline supporters.

West Bromwich were in this tournament because they had defeated Everton in last season's English Cup final, and they were generally regarded as being a good team with Jeff Astle in the forward line as well as a fresh faced young Scotsman called Asa Hartford.

Dunfermline started the stronger and for a moment looked well on top, but then West Brom regained the ascendancy in such a way as to suggest that they were different class from their Scottish opponents.

The crucial thing was that West Brom had not scored, but then again neither had Dunfermline. The second half ebbed and flowed and it is not often than a goalless draw is so exciting, but at the end both teams felt that they had done well enough.

Dunfermline were still in the tie, but the men from the Midlands felt that they now would have the advantage at The Hawthorns.

European Cup-Winners' Cup

3rd ROUND (1st LEG)

Dunfermline Athletic
(SCOTTISH F.A. CUP-HOLDERS)

versus

West Bromwich Albion
(ENGLISH F.A. CUP-HOLDERS)

Wednesday, 15th January 1969

KICK-OFF, 7.30 P.M.

Official Programme - 6d

January 16 1965

Dunfermline had a good 1-0 win over Kilmarnock before a large crowd of 14,000 at East End Park today on the slightly cold and wet but otherwise comparatively pleasant January day.

It was in fact the most exciting League race for years, with Hearts, Kilmarnock, Rangers, Hibs and Dunfermline all in with a chance as no team had emerged as any better than anyone else.

Today on a wet, slightly muddy pitch, the tackles were fierce and injuries were frequent. In the very first few seconds, after a clash with Tommy Callaghan, Ronnie Hamilton of Kilmarnock was carried off with what looked like a broken leg.

It wasn't, as it turned out, for Hamilton was able to resume a quarter of an hour later with his leg heavily bandaged, and he was gradually more and more able to get full function back.

But Kilmarnock trainer Walter McCrae was a frequent visitor to the pitch, treating Sneddon, McGrory, Beattie and Hamilton again. As a result of all this, (no substitutes were allowed until 1966/67) Dunfermline had the bulk of the play but were not able to convert their superiority into goals until the 80th minute when Bertie Paton hit home a drive from about 12 years.

This triggered a tiresome pitch invasion by youngsters and the throwing of toilet rolls in triumph (two of the annoying phenomena of crowds in the 1960s).

When the pitch was cleared of both, the Pars had a good ten minutes of Kilmarnock pressure to sustain until referee Mr Crockett of Dundee blew for full time.

Hearts, having beaten Celtic 2-1 today, were top of the League.

January 17 1959

Only eight games were played in Scotland this Saturday; East End Park — which generally in those days had a good record of getting games played — was one of them.

It was a vital one against neighbours and possible relegations rivals, Falkirk.

As late as 24 hours previously there had looked to be no hope for any game in Scotland, all of which had been covered in hard frost.

A thaw arrived quickly overnight, and a little hard work on the Saturday morning by Dunfermline's dedicated ground staff and a few volunteers ensured that today's game went ahead, in front of a crowd of about 6,000.

Dunfermline were on the fringes of relegation, and although New Year form had been reasonable, last week had seen a bad 1-0 defeat at Kilmarnock. Possibly as a result of this, Manager Andy Dickson today decided to recall his namesake Charlie Dickson for the arrival of the men from Brockville.

The move seemed to have borne fruit when in the first minute Alex Smith put the Pars ahead. Just before half-time Dickson scored twice for Dunfermline. One was a simple tap-in after a goalkeeping error, but the other was a good header from a delicate lob from Harry Melrose.

Thus it was a good 3-0 lead for Dunfermline at half time, and although Falkirk pulled one back through Doug Moran, Pars stayed on top and Charlie Dickson notched his hat-trick just on the full time whistle.

The significance of this game became apparent at the end of the season when Dunfermline finished third bottom and Falkirk finished second bottom and were relegated.

January 18 1964

Remarkably, considering the temperature and the prevalence of freezing fog throughout the country, not a single game was postponed in Scotland today, and Dunfermline Athletic travelled to play Dundee United at Tannadice.

Form had been quite good this season but already in the New Year there had been a couple of defeats to Kilmarnock and Hearts, teams whom Dunfermline felt that they should now be beating.

Dundee United were also considered to be in that category as well, and a crowd of 8,000 appeared at Tannadice to see the game.

The first half was hard but goalless, with Charlie Dickson coming very close in the first minute with a low header, and United having a few chances as well.

It was United who took the lead early in the second half when McManus was on hand to bullet home a rebound from a Rooney shot after the ball had come back from a defender.

Dunfermline fought back and Jim Kerray (a man who tended to divide opinions among the supporters) silenced his doubters by scoring twice, the first being a sweet finish to a cross from Alex Edwards on the right, and the second a mere tap-in.

Roared on by their always fanatical fans, the Tannadice Terrors pressed hard but at full time it was the ever gentlemanly Jerry Kerr who shook hands and congratulated Jock Stein.

The big sporting news of the day however was in rugby where Scotland drew 0-0 with New Zealand. Apart from being a great result for Scotland, a 0-0 draw in rugby was odd enough to be considered a statistical curiosity.

January 19 2019

A truly awful day for Dunfermline as they exited the Scottish Cup, losing 0-3 at the hands of their old rivals Raith Rovers at Stark's Park.

What made matters worse was that this defeat was technically a giant killing as Raith were in Division One and the Pars were in the Championship.

Those who had hoped that a 4-2 win at Falkirk the Saturday before the New Year was a return to winning ways were sadly disillusioned with a miserable draw with Alloa and a defeat by Dundee United, but this was the nadir.

The first half was reasonably even, with the Pars possibly marginally on top, but the turning point seems to have been the sending off of Lee Ashcroft by referee Bobby Madden for bringing down Chris Duggan.

Reduced to ten men, Dunfermline then conceded a penalty which was converted by Lewis Vaughan. A brilliant diving header from the same player made it two, and then he completed his hat-trick with another.

By this time the Pars fans in the 6,000 crowd were on their way home, and new Manager Stevie Crawford, (who had only been in his post a matter of days), trying to make the best of a bad defeat, said that "we have a bit of work to do to get the supporters back onside".

That was stating the obvious, and for many supporters, it was the last game of the season. There was a slight upturn in fortunes in February and March but it was temporary and the club finished a miserable seventh.

And thanks to today, a much-needed run in the Scottish Cup was not forthcoming.

January 20 1906

Dunfermline today beat Lochgelly United 4-0 in the Northern League but not in a way that reflected any credit on them.

The Courier reporter was distressed at the amount of "rough play" and suggested that the referee was not perhaps as on top of things as he should have been.

The writer of *The Scottish Referee* on the other hand is very impressed by Dunfermline and says that they have as much chance of winning the Northern League as do Arbroath and Kirkcaldy United.

Not only that, but he is confident of their chances next week in the Scottish Cup when they travel to Scottish League First Division Aberdeen. (In fact, they lost that game 0-3).

Today's game saw Lochgelly United concede an own goal, then Dunfermline scored "rather cleverly" through Ferguson.

Ferguson then scored again early in the second half, by which time Lochgelly had been reduced to 10 men with Gray having been taken off injured, and then Low completed the scoring in a rather impressive display.

The roughness of the play was put down to the fact that they were both Fife teams and maybe even "knew each other rather too well", but it was a good day for Dunfermline who would end up second top of the Northern League that year.

They then applied for membership to the Scottish League but were not voted in (automatic promotion and relegation did not yet apply) to their intense disappointment.

During this time, the General Election of 1906 was going on. In those days, it took about three weeks with all the constituencies voting at different times, (in the case of West Fife on Tuesday January 23 where the sitting Liberal would win comfortably) and it was already clear that the Liberals were going to have a large majority.

January 21 1989

There was never any great love lost between the supporters of Dunfermline Athletic and Airdrie, and today at Broomfield there was an added ingredient.

Both teams were battling for the First Division Championship and entry to the Premier League which had now streamlined itself down to 10 teams. Therefore there would be only one promotion spot.

The Pars had, of course, had a taste of the Premier League and rather fancied another go, and therefore they took a huge away support with them to Airdrie.

The official crowd was given as 9,100, leading the *Glasgow Evening Times* to say that "it has been a long time since Broomfield witnessed an atmosphere like this", as Airdrie were top and Dunfermline were second.

Rae Farningham, who had recently been bought from Motherwell, was in the team today, as was Norrie McCathie who had been on loan to Ayr United.

The first half was fast and furious with Dunfermline coming close to scoring when John Watson managed to kick an easy chance over the bar to the groans of the Pars supporters.

But in the second half, Jim Leishman's men turned it on and scored twice, once through Ross Jack (his fourth goal this year) and then Norrie McCathie added another, as the Pars ran out clear winners.

This game meant that the two teams effectively changed places with DA now top of the League, a position that they did not relinquish for the rest of the season.

There would be a few stumbles on the way – losing to Falkirk and Raith Rovers, for example, and a run of draws, but this was the game which turned it all.

January 22 1972

It was a result that no-one could have forecast from a scan of the League table before the start of the game.

Dunfermline today beat Aberdeen 1-0 at East End Park.

Dunfermline, clearly now in decline from their great days of three or four years ago, were battling relegation for the second year in a row, while Aberdeen were challenging for the League title.

Aberdeen were well supported as usual in a reasonable crowd of 7,243 on a cold day, and for a while both teams were well balanced, and a stranger would have been hard put to it to say which team was in the higher League position.

It was actually a mistake by Aberdeen goalkeeper Andy Geoghegan, deputising for the injured Bobby Clark, who gave away a bizarre goal late in the first half.

He failed to deal with a pass back from Stevie Murray, which he allowed to slip through his fingers; Jim Gillespie ran round the back of him and prodded the ball into an empty net.

It was not exactly a deserved goal, but was gratefully accepted by Dunfermline's players and fans.

The second half has been described as a "war of attrition" as both teams played it tight, Dunfermline for obvious reasons of "what we have we hold" and Aberdeen for reasons of their strange policy of trying to score on the break when a more directly attacking approach was clearly called for.

Full time came to great scenes of joy among the Dunfermline support, but any hope of a sustained improvement came to nothing.

January 23 1926

An astonishing crowd of 15,000 turned up at Shawfield today to see Clyde beat Dunfermline 3-0 in the Scottish Cup.

The crowd was astonishing because it actually was several thousand more than the crowd which turned up at Ibrox to see Rangers v Lochgelly United!

Clyde and Dunfermline were the two teams who were going head to head for promotion from the Second Division.

Dunfermline had defeated them handsomely at East End Park in December, but today there was little doubt that Clyde, at home and in a competition that they tended to do well in, were the better side.

Clyde had never won the Scottish Cup, but they had reached the final of two occasions to lose to Dundee in 1910 and Celtic in 1912, whereas Dunfermline had no Scottish Cup tradition at all.

The best you could say about the Pars today was that they simply had an off day.

Pearson scored for Clyde early in both halves and then Kennedy finished it off in the latter stages.

Against that, Dunfermline's talisman, Bobby Skinner failed to perform, being well policed by centre half Neil Gibson, son of a famous Rangers player of the same name.

It is often said that an early exit from the Scottish Cup is a blessing in disguise so that the team can then concentrate on the League. Frankly, this is moonshine.

The Scottish Cup is a great money spinner, and Dunfermline players and fans were thoroughly depressed as they headed home tonight. But there was indeed still the Scottish League.

January 24 1970

Dunfermline had real bad luck today; they went down 1-2 to Celtic in the Scottish Cup at Parkhead before a huge crowd of over 50,000, such was the power of these two teams to attract the crowds in those days.

In that context it is perhaps worth noting that Manager George Farm took along to Parkhead some tickets for the projected replay at East End Park on Wednesday night.

This may have been simply George Farm trying to make a propaganda point, but there were those who "wondered" about that!

After all, allegations of Cup games being fixed as a draw for another big gate in a replay are not new! But if this game was "meant" to be a draw, no-one seemed to tell the players who served up a great game of football for the fans on this dull January day.

Celtic were the better team but it was Dunfermline who went ahead on the hour mark when Jim Gillespie took advantage of two separate mistakes by McNeill and Brogan, at a time when the Pars were temporarily down to ten men as Thomson was off receiving attention!

The Parkhead crowd now recalled the game two years ago at a similar stage of the Scottish Cup when the Pars won 2-0, but this was a stronger Celtic team, and in the 80th minute John Hughes equalised.

It now began to look as if Farm's decision to bring the tickets along was justified (and it would have looked bad if the Press got wind of it!) but in the very last minute Harry Hood scored the winner with a glancing header.

January 25 1969

Dunfermline's first game in the defence of the Scottish Cup was, ironically enough at Stark's Park, the home of old rivals Raith Rovers, a club whom Dunfermline had rather overtaken now in the race for the honour of being the best team in Fife.

It was also the former home of men like Manager George Farm and free scoring forward Pat Gardner, both of whom were given a reception from the Rovers fans which was less than welcoming.

The weather was surprisingly good for the time of year, and a crowd of 11,000 turned up to see a game which might have gone either way until half time, but then Dunfermline took command and goals from Pat Gardner and Bertie Paton saw the Pars home in a game which ended up surprisingly one-sided.

There had been the threat of crowd trouble from the less intellectually gifted members of either support. The Pars supporters started to sing a song that seemed to be wishing Raith Rovers as Happy Birthday. If you listened carefully however, it was actually "Relegation to you…" etc.

Nor was it any idle threat, for the fans of the Kirkcaldy side were a little depressed by their exit from the Scottish Cup, and now had what seemed like their annual battle against relegation to contend with.

They had made a splendid effort to save themselves last year, and they were similarly in trouble this year. But it was still a great day for the Pars whose supporters were now fancying another Hampden triumph.

January 26 1927

It was a Wednesday afternoon, and the weather was far from pleasant with frequent rain showers and a strong wind.

Dunfermline Athletic and Bathgate did well to attract a crowd of 3,300 to East End Park. This was to see the replay of the Scottish Cup First Round tie which had been drawn at Bathgate on Saturday.

Dunfermline were struggling in the First Division, but Bathgate were similarly struggling in the Second Division in early 1927, and the 2-2 draw at Bathgate on Saturday had been a disappointment in every respect.

Today, however, Dunfermline were seldom stretched, even though Bathgate shocked them by taking an early lead. By half time however they were 3-1 up with goals from new man Williamson, Bain and Stein.

The second half became a bit of a bore, enlightened only by some of the songs sung by the fans!

There was nothing unpleasant or partisan about them, nothing even to do with football, more to do with the great songs of the War years or songs of Robert Burns whose birthday it had been yesterday!

It was a clear sign that the football was uninteresting but late in the game with Dunfermline well on top, Bobby Skinner nipped in to score a couple as the Bathgate defence tired.

This made it 5-1 for Dunfermline, and most of the crowd were on their way home by the time that Bathgate scored a late irrelevant goal, something which earned them a cheer from a happy and now chivalrous Dunfermline crowd.

January 27 1968

This was a very fine win indeed for Dunfermline at the home of the European Cup winners at Celtic Park.

The Pars beat Celtic 2-0 in the Scottish Cup on a cold, raw but dry January day in front of a crowd of 47,000 fans which included about 5,000 or so from Dunfermline.

Jock Stein was magnanimous in his congratulations to his old team in the wake of this victory in which Dunfermline were simply faster to the ball and seemed to want to win the game more than their illustrious opponents.

Celtic had scored in the first half but the goal was disallowed for offside.

In the second half, it was Dunfermline who took more and more control, scoring first through Hugh Robertson in a goalmouth scramble in the 64th minute.

In the 75th minute Pat Gardner (whom George Farm had brought from Raith Rovers) took full advantage of a mistake by Celtic's David Cattenach.

The silent emptying of the Parkhead terracings after that told its own tale and full tribute was paid to the Pars by the Press.

Tommy Callaghan of Dunfermline (who would one day join Celtic) and Bertie Auld were booked, but it was never really a dirty game.

Indeed it was a welcome piece of revenge for Dunfermline who felt that they were unlucky in their 3-2 defeat at the same venue on the last Saturday in December in the Scottish League.

This was of course the Pars first step in their attempt to win back the Scottish Cup, and it was a mighty one.

Not often that Dunfermline score against Wigtown and Bladnoch, but here is Harry Melrose doing just that in January 1962 as the Pars win 9-0!.

January 28 1961

No-one really realised at the time what was going on or where this particular adventure would eventually lead us, but the Scottish Cup got off to a good start today with a 4-1 win across the border in Berwick.

The weather was cold – it was, after all, January – but a little milder than in parts of England where a few fixtures were affected by the bad weather.

The visit of the rejuvenated Pars was welcomed at Shielfield Park by a crowd of about 4,100 fans including a fair sprinkling of Fifers.

It was generally agreed that this was a team which had improved since Jock Stein had arrived almost a year ago for the purpose of saving them from relegation.

There was now an air of professionalism about the players, and the whole ethos of the club was improving with a lot of talk about a new stand at East End Park - something that was badly needed.

Today it was Berwick who scored first when Kennedy ran about 20 yards with the ball at his feet before lobbing young Herriot in the Dunfermline goal.

Danger signals were up, but the Pars rallied and before half time, they were 2-1 up with Charlie Dickson scoring first and veteran Tommy MacDonald setting up Dan McLindon for the second.

A further two goals were scored in the second half by Alex Smith and Charlie Dickson. It was a happy party that headed home that night, looking forward to the draw in the second round.

Someone even suggested for a laugh that 1961 might be the year that Dunfermline would win their first ever Scottish Cup.

Honestly! Those young people! What nonsense they utter sometimes!

January 29 1977

The time was when a Scottish Cup tie between Dunfermline Athletic and Aberdeen at East End Park would have been the game of the day in Scotland.

Sadly now two divisions separated the two clubs with Dunfermline languishing in Division Two and Aberdeen challenging strongly for the Premier League.

They had recently won the Scottish League Cup and under effervescent Manager Ally MacLeod, who talked a good game, there seemed no limit to their ambitions — particularly in a city which was taking off in the financial sense as well with the recent discovery of North Sea oil.

However it was like old times again when a crowd of only slightly less than 12,000 turned up, causing the game to be delayed by quarter of an hour to let people get in.

The curse of the 1970s was football hooliganism, and we had some pathetic examples of this here, as the police took away some dreadful looking specimens of not very bright young men from both the Dunfermline and the Aberdeen support.

The pitch was hard but playable, and for the first half, the Pars, although in danger of being outplayed held out to keep the game goalless at half time.

Aberdeen upped a gear in the second half, and Joe Harper scored the only goal of the game about half way through the second half, with Ally MacLeod earning himself no affection among the Dunfermline support with his exuberant and provocative celebrations.

Hard as Athletic tried, they could not get back into the game, and thus they found themselves with only the Second Division promotion race to get bothered about.

January 30 1974

An Ian Campbell goal was enough to get the Pars into the next round of the Scottish Cup this Wednesday afternoon at East End Park.

The afternoon kick-off was all to do with the Miners v Conservative Government confrontation which had started in the autumn and would eventually lead to a General Election at the end of February.

The miners were not yet on strike, but their overtime ban and work to rule was enough to put the country on a three day week and to cause severe restrictions on the use of electricity.

The Pars had drawn with Falkirk at Brockville on Sunday in the Scottish Cup in their first ever Sunday fixture, and the replay had to take place without floodlights with an afternoon kick-off.

The rain was incessant and the ground was borderline unplayable, but the experienced Bobby Davidson of Airdrie decided that play was possible.

Not surprisingly, there was not a great turn-out but those who did brave the wrath of wives, bosses and headmasters by coming along saw a good game in wet conditions.

According to *The Glasgow Herald,* Falkirk were actually the better side but could not score against Dunfermline's Norwegian goalkeeper, Geir Karlsen, who was well supported by full backs Leishman and Wallace and helped by the profligate shooting of the Falkirk forwards.

Dunfermline's goal came when McCallum found Mackie who beat a defender and chipped the ball across the penalty area for Campbell to apply the finishing touch.

The full time whistle came to a great cheer from the crowd which had slowly augmented particularly when school finished for the day. Dunfermline now played Queen of the South in the next round.

January 31 1959

The Scottish Cup draw this year threw up a cracker in a West Fife derby at Central Park, Cowdenbeath considered important enough by the SFA to have Jack Mowat, generally agreed to be the best referee at the moment, appointed to take charge of it.

It was a comparatively rare occasion these days for Dunfermline and Cowdenbeath to meet for they were now in different divisions of the League, but 10,206 were attracted to see this game on a cold and still slightly frosty day.

It would be true to say that neither side were exactly setting the heather on fire in their respective League divisions, and indeed Dunfermline would soon be involved in a relegation dogfight, but this was the Scottish Cup with the prospect of big money in the next round, and of course local pride was very much at stake.

It turned out to be a very even game in which Cowdenbeath scored first and were generally given a great deal of credit in the Sunday papers for their part in the game.

Dunfermline were indebted to Harry Melrose for his two goals in the 2-2 draw in which no quarter was sought or given.

It is of course very tempting to be cynical and point out that a replay brings another lucrative gate, but in fact the replay on Monday February 9 (the match was postponed on Wednesday February 4) was a low key affair which the Pars won 4-1 before a low crowd.

The Pars then went to Montrose in the next round, so the Scottish Cup was not yet a pot of gold this year.

February

February 1 1967

The Scottish football world was still reeling from Berwick Rangers defeat of Glasgow Rangers in Saturday's cup shocker.

This Wednesday night, Dunfermline tonight edged into the next round of the Scottish Cup by beating Kilmarnock in the replay at East End Park.

This had followed a 2-2 draw at Rugby Park on Saturday, and although it was generally agreed that the standard of football was not as high as that of the first game, Dunfermline did well enough to deserve to win through.

The only goal of the game came in the 26th minute when a long clearance from Bent Martin deceived Kilmarnock centre half Frank Beattie (who may have lost the ball in the glare of the floodlights) and came to Alex Edwards who pushed it on to Alex Ferguson to score.

After that it was grim defending from the Pars, but they always looked a better team than Kilmarnock, and the full time whistle was greeted with great joy from the 19,000 crowd.

Both Dunfermline fans and Kilmarnock fans had often been vilified in the past for not supporting their teams in big enough numbers, but that could not be said tonight, for the atmosphere was first class throughout.

The game was well controlled by the huge referee Tom "Tiny" Wharton. It might have become silly, because both teams had men who "took no prisoners", but Mr Wharton was always in charge, never being afraid to give the odd controversial decision now and again.

Dunfermline now go to Partick Thistle at Firhill in the next round.

February 2 1918

The problems of war time football were highlighted to-day at Tannadice Park.

Dunfermline's train to Perth was late, and therefore they missed their connection to Dundee, all of which meant that the game could not start at its appointed time of 2.30 pm.

The team did eventually arrive, the crowd in the meantime having amused themselves by impromptu community singing of "It's A Long Way To Tipperary", and a couple of young men in military uniform, clearly home on leave, having a race up the touchline – activities quietly tolerated by the local Constabulary.

However, the game did start, about 45 minutes late, and this Eastern League game between Dundee Hibs and Dunfermline Athletic ended in a 1-1 draw.

It was obvious that both teams were scratching around to find eleven men, for some players were merely schoolboys and others, by their girth, indicated that perhaps their best days were behind them and they might not have been chosen in other times.

Dunfermline's goal was not over the line, *The Courier* says, but the goal was given even though Willie Fisher miskicked because the huge figure of Balfour, the Hibs goalkeeper, obscured the view of Mr Martin the referee.

Hibs did equalise near the end, and a draw was a fair result.

A "draw" was looking a fair description of affairs in Europe as well, with no resolution looking likely, although the British were now doing well in the Eastern theatre with huge gains in Palestine.

The Russians had now lost and were out of the war, and the Western Allies were now looking for the Americans to make a difference in Europe. They had money and equipment, but were taking their time about arriving.

Scott Wilson scores against Hearts in 2007

February 3 2007

Dunfermline, whose Premier League form had been dreadful and who looked as if they were heading inexorably towards relegation, once again proved that they kept something special for the Scottish Cup.

In the last round, they had astonished the world by removing Rangers and now it was last year's Scottish Cup winners Hearts.

In both cases of Rangers and Hearts, it would have to be admitted that their opponents were suffering from crazy management decisions in team selection, but full marks to Stephen Kenny and his men for beating them.

The first half was candidly described by the BBC website as "woeful", and if anything, in the second half it was Hearts who looked the more likely team to score in the opinion of the 9,597 East End Park crowd.

A reasonable penalty claim for Hearts was turned down by controversial referee Mike McCurry and goalkeeper Dorus De Vries made an outstanding save from a Pospisil downward header so as full time approached, a replay at Tynecastle looked the most likely scenario.

Yet Dunfermline picked up their game; very few of the crowd were showing signs of going home, for there was always the feeling that something was likely to happen.

And indeed it did. Adam Hammill sent over a cross. It found the head of Scott Wilson who directed the ball past goalkeeper Steve Banks, who had been preferred to Craig Gordon and who had earlier shown a few signs of nervousness.

The goal was greeted with joy by the Pars fans, but for the men from Edinburgh "we wuz robbed" simply did not cover it.

It was a rare night of celebration in Dunfermline in 2007!

February 4 1928

Dunfermline played new opposition today when a team called Leith Amateurs came to town to play in the Scottish Cup.

Dunfermline duly won 3-1, but it was not an easy game and Dunfermline were accused in the Press of taking them too easily, particularly in their constant desire to shoot from far out.

Williamson scored first for the Pars with both Dicksons, J Dickson and TW Dickson scoring as well.

This game was almost a source of relief for Dunfermline who had won only one single point in the whole of January — this had included the 9-0 hammering by Celtic at Parkhead — in the First Division of the Scottish League, where they had now been for two years after their winning of the Second Division in 1926.

In addition to the poor run of form, there was the other problem of simply not having the money.

The chill winds of austerity had compelled them to sell to Airdrie their best player, Bobby Skinner, something that had the effect of further depressing their attendances with not very helpful rumours being spread around about bankruptcy etc.

Ironically in these dire circumstances, the team used this win against Leith Amateurs as a springboard for a decent Scottish Cup run.

They beat Dundee in the next round, 2-1 at Dens Park, contrary to all expectations, before reality came with a 4-0 beating by Hibs in early March.

The sad fact was that the Pars were out of their depth this season. Today however was a welcome exception.

February 5 1966

The Dunfermline ground staff had this morning worked miracles to get the pitch playable for the Scottish Cup game against Partick Thistle. The problem was surface water.

Other grounds in the east of Scotland – Cowdenbeath, Hearts and both Dundee teams - had been less fortunate (or had employed less diligent ground staff) but today on the soft pitch, the two teams served up a really good game for the 7,000 crowd.

Heavy conditions do not necessarily prevent good football – indeed they are almost a Scottish stereotype in November and February!

Today the Pars won 3-1 thanks to two first half goals from Alex Smith and Bertie Paton, and a second half goal from George Fleming.

Partick Thistle and their brightly clad, cheerful fans — who denounced Celtic and Rangers in equal measure — contributed hugely to the occasion.

It was generally agreed that the best man on the pitch was the man who scored Thistle's goal and who would one day become the Manager of Scotland, Andy Roxburgh.

The opinion of the Press was that Partick had as much of the pressure as the Pars, but that Dunfermline were more "scientific" (whatever that meant!) in their approach and were good enough to win through to the next round.

Some of the Thistle supporters at the end were heard to express their opinion that they wanted Dunfermline to win the Scottish Cup this year on the grounds that they were neither Celtic nor Rangers!

In fact, the Pars were enjoying a good season, still handily placed in the Scottish League, and still very much involved in Europe.

February 6 1965

Today Dunfermline travelled to Palmerston Park to play Queen of the South in the Scottish Cup.

Since winning the Scottish Cup in 1961, the furthest that Dunfermline had got was the semi-final last year when they had lost to Rangers.

Now under new Manager Willie Cunningham, they were having a good season both in Scotland and in Europe and today gave them a chance to meet up with ex-Par Charlie Dickson who had been transferred to Queen of the South earlier this season.

Queen of the South were third in the Scottish League Second Division and they put up a good fight against First Division opposition before one of their better crowds of 6,700.

The weather was good, a little chilly and the pitch was rather heavy but the teams put up a good show.

Dickson almost scored for the home side in the very first minute but his effort was well saved by Jim Herriot.

Before half time, however, the Pars had gone ahead when Bertie Paton from the edge of the box shot through a forest of legs to beat goalkeeper Ball who had hitherto been outstanding for the home side.

Then early in the second half Dunfermline were awarded a penalty by referee Mr Paterson when Sinclair was brought down in the box.

John McLaughlin took it, the ball was parried and McLaughlin netted the rebound which effectively put the Pars into the next round, the last 16 of the Scottish Cup.

Their reward was a trip to Third Lanark at Cathkin Park.

Noel Hunt about to score against Dundee United in 2004

February 7 2004

There was some excitement about this fourth round Scottish Cup tie, with Dunfermline meeting Clyde for the first time in a decade.

Jimmy Calderwood's side were involved in a 3rd/4th place battle with Hearts in the SPL, while Clyde were flying at the top of the first division.

Both clubs had overspent to reach their respective levels and would suffer for it in years to come.

On this winter day Noel Hunt put the Pars ahead before Barry Nicholson made it 2-0 as light snow began to fall.

When Clyde pulled a goal back after half an hour the snow was gradually getting heavier, but with the pitch still green there wasn't too much concern.

Come the second half, things were considerably different with heavy snow falling, a yellow ball brought out; referee Charlie Richmond (with snow covering his head and shoulders) eventually had enough.

Although the chances of the game finishing seemed slim, a tannoy announcement of a delay for the lines to be swept gave some hope of a result on the day.

Perhaps the most memorable moment of the day was an enthusiastic ball boy taking a brush to shouts of 'sweep, sweep, sweep!' from the away fans.

It was not to be, as abandonment was confirmed with slightly less than an hour played.

The Broadwood announcer must have enjoyed his music choice, with the fans carefully leaving the snowbound ground to U2's 'Beautiful Day'.

The rearranged game 17 days later was a more straightforward affair, with Dunfermline leading 3-0 against 10 men at half-time. This win would be another step along the road to the May final at Hampden.

Clearing the snow at Broadwood

February 8 1913

Today saw Dunfermline's first ever visit to Tynecastle for a competitive fixture.

They had done well in the Scottish Qualifying Cup and were thus awarded a place in the Scottish Cup proper.

In this competition, they were drawn to play at Tynecastle against the mighty Hearts, a club who had won the Scottish Cup as recently as 1906, and who had the advantage of a huge support.

It was possibly as good a draw as Dunfermline would have wanted, for it wasn't too far for their supporters to travel.

In addition there would be a big cheque at the end, something which would be very welcome as East End Park was in urgent need of ground improvements.

Today, a crowd of 25,000 appeared at Tynecastle, including a fair smattering from Dunfermline; they saw a result that was perhaps inevitable, but of which Dunfermline did not have any reason to feel ashamed.

Indeed several of them said that it was a privilege to play on such a huge ground and against men like the great Bobby Walker, commonly referred to as Houdini for his mesmeric twists and turns and his ability to escape the clutches of the opposition defence.

For Hearts, however, it was a question of whether they could beat Maurice Slavin, Dunfermline's personality goalkeeper, who defied them until well into the second half, before Ernest Bannister scored once and Englishman Percy Dawson twice.

Although Alex Hall pulled one back for Dunfermline, the Second Division team were well beaten by a team that would reach the semi-final of the Scottish Cup that year.

February 9 1929

There were goals galore for Dunfermline Athletic today as poor Bathgate were hammered 8-0 at East End Park.

The game described as "too one-sided to be interesting" was significant, however in Bathgate's history.

Indeed it was somewhat of a hollow victory for Dunfermline, for it was no secret in Scottish football that Bathgate, given the decline of local industry and the general economic depression, were struggling.

They had managed to get a draw last week in the Scottish Cup against Raith Rovers, but the Kirkcaldy side had overpowered them in the replay on Wednesday afternoon and this had deprived them of a much needed financial boost.

In fact, they would play only another two games before they found the financial burdens too much and had to withdraw from the League at the end of February.

Today at East End Park, the writing was on the wall.

No supporters with them, and two men called "Newman" in their side – in both cases a young man from a local junior team called up for a trial as an amateur because they could not afford wages for a professional.

Their goalkeeper, a man called Dempster, was singled out as being one of their better players, and as he had lost 8 goals, that does not say very much for the rest!

For the record, middle of the table Dunfermline's goal scorers were Syme (4) Miller (2), Dand and Hamilton but the game itself did not really tell us much.

It was a day of high scoring all over town, for Dunfermline's rugby team at McKane Park beat St Andrews University 45- 0.

February 10 1934

The world-wide economic depression was supposed to be on the mend, but unemployment was still high in the Dunfermline area, something that perhaps explained the low attendance to-day on a reasonably pleasant day to see the visit of Dumbarton.

Those who did attend saw Dunfermline consolidate their position at the top of the Second Division with an easy 3-0 win over the struggling Dumbarton side whose financial problems were well documented.

It was of course not unknown for clubs to go out of business in the 1930s, and many were really in a bad way, Dumbarton being one of them and suffering from their close proximity to so many other clubs in the West of Scotland.

Yet they had a great tradition, having won the Scottish Cup in 1883 and the Scottish League in 1891 and 1892.

The Pars on the other hand, while not without their economic problems, were doing better than some and of course a winning team does cheer everyone up.

Although missing some chances today, the Pars took three great goals. The first one was Watson heading home a great cross from Garland, the second one was from Garland himself with a fine solo run and a thunderous shot.

The third goal was a carbon copy of the second, but this time it was the slight, diminutive figure of Dobson who scored the goal.

Dunfermline's two challengers, Albion Rovers and Arbroath, were both in action today, Albion Rovers drawing 2-2 with Raith Rovers and Arbroath beat Stenhousemuir 3-0.

Willie Knight's side would eventually win promotion but would not win the Second Division Championship which went to the excellent Albion Rovers side of that year.

February 11 1961

Having won at Berwick in the last round of the Scottish Cup, the Pars went even further away, this time to the south-west to beat Stranraer.

The 3-1 victory was possibly better than it seemed, for Stranraer were doing well in the Second Division, and Dunfermline, although playing a little better than they were last year at this time, were still not entirely free from worries about relegation.

Harry Melrose, Andy Dickson and Tommy McDonald scored the goals that saw the Pars into the last sixteen.

The very few Dunfermline supporters who made the trip thought that it was worthwhile, but this was a day of very high scoring.

Celtic beat Montrose 6-0, Rangers (more surprisingly) beat Dundee 5-1, Motherwell beat Cowdenbeath 4-1, and Brechin City beat Duns 5-3.

The biggest score of them all was Hibs 15 Peebles Rovers 1, with Joe Baker scoring nine, a record for modern times. At one point he looked like challenging Jocky Petrie of Arbroath who apparently scored more than 20 in their 36-0 defeat of Aberdeen Bon Accord in 1885.

Such results led to some people challenging the wisdom of allowing teams like Peebles Rovers to play in the Scottish Cup but the Hibs fans weren't complaining.

Across the city at the Rugby International at Murrayfield, Scotland beat Wales 3-0, and that was tame in comparison!

Not that this was of much relevance to the Pars fans, who now awaited the draw for the next round.

It was not very often that the Pars got this length, and there was no doubt that Jock Stein had made a difference.

February 12 1955

In the Second Division game of the day, Dunfermline and Airdrie, both serious promotion contenders, drew 2-2, Airdrie thus preserving their unbeaten record.

Snow was falling heavily at the start of the game, but fortunately the referee, Mr Fitzpatrick from Edinburgh, decided that the game should go ahead.

The pitch was indeed tricky but not unplayable, and although snow fell intermittently throughout the game, there were dry and even sunny spells as well.

After an hour's play the Dunfermline fans in the 8,000 crowd must have wished that the game had been postponed for their team was 0-2 down to a slick Airdrie team in which Ian McMillan was the star.

The goals had been scored by Welsh and Reid, but now the Pars had the advantage as they were playing towards the Halbeath end goal with the sun behind them and the wind blowing the snow into the Airdrie players' faces.

Airdrie conceded a penalty when O'Brien was brought down, and Duthie converted. 1-2, but it was what happened next which impressed Colin Glen of *The Courier*.

Straight from the kick-off, the snow covered ball came to dark haired left half Jim Chalmers, a student at Aberdeen University.

He simply ran for goal, rounding a few men and hammered home an unsaveable shot — "a screamer" — from the edge of the box. There was a split second's pause before East End Park erupted in applause for such brilliance.

Naturally they wanted a repeat but it was not forthcoming, and the game finished in a 2-2 draw, enough to keep the Pars in second place.

February 13 1962

In the quarter final of the European Cup Winners Cup, Dunfermline lost 3-4 in Hungary to Ujpest Dozsa — whose very name caused a little ridicule in Scotland — but were generally agreed to have upheld the prestige of Scotland.

Not very many people from Scotland in 1962 had ever been to Hungary, and it was very much a trip into the unknown, with undertones of a James Bond film or novel.

From the mid 1950s onwards however it had been obvious that the Hungarians were good at football.

The game was played in sleet and very cold conditions at the Nep Stadium which could hold 100,000 but tonight there was little more than 20,000.

Jock Stein's men scored twice in the early stages of the game through Tommy McDonald and Alex Smith, clearly adapting better to the conditions which of course were by no means unfamiliar to those who played in Scotland!

But the Hungarians gradually got back into the game and by half time had equalised.

The second half was very even, but Ujpest Dozsa got a penalty (which they might not have been given in Scotland), scored from that and then as the Pars were still reeling from that blow, the Hungarians scored another.

4-2 was a poor reward for what Dunfermline had put into the game, but Tommy McDonald put a better gloss on the score with a late goal.

The small Scottish party with Dunfermline (mainly Press but with a few wealthy supporters as well) agreed that Dunfermline were very capable of overturning that result at East End Park in a week's time.

In the meantime it was back to a slightly more mundane task – that of facing Stenhousemuir in the Scottish Cup at East End Park on Saturday.

February 14 1948

Events off the park were almost as interesting as the game itself to-day at East End Park.

Kilmarnock were the visitors and neither they nor Dunfermline were having a good season in the middle of Division "B".

They were both also already out of the Scottish Cup, and today on a reasonable (for mid-February) day, only 3,000 turned up – a poor crowd for the boom years after the Second World War.

This may have been St Valentine's Day but little love was shown to Dunfermline's Chairman Mr Tom Gibson who was booed before and after the game by a crowd of Dunfermline supporters who were unhappy about the resignation of Manager Bobby Calder a couple of days ago.

In an attempt to appease the crowd, Mr Gibson had read out Mr Calder's resignation letter which said that he has resigned because of his wife's ill health.

This explanation did not however please the mob who suspected that there was more to it, and calls were heard for a boycott.

The game itself had been watched by loads of scouts and managers of other teams, notably David Meiklejohn, the Manager of Partick Thistle, and Stan Cullis the Manager of Wolverhampton Wanderers.

The game was a 3-1 win for the Pars but neither team had been impressive and two men, one from each side, had asked for a transfer after the game.

The Dunfermline one was captain Pat MacDonald and the Kilmarnock one was centre half Bob Thyne.

Clearly not everything was rosy behind the scenes at either club.

February 15 1958

Football in general was still trying to come to terms with the Manchester United air crash at Munich of nine days ago.

Matt Busby was slowly recovering, although the news of Duncan Edwards was not so good.

But life went on, and today on Scottish Cup Saturday, Dunfermline produced a piece of technical giant killing by beating St Mirren at Love Street.

St Mirren had been struggling of late in the First Division, having made the crass error of transferring their star centre half Willie Telfer to Rangers and alienating their fans in so doing.

Dunfermline on the other hand were beginning to flourish in the Second Division and a major promotion push was underway.

The Dunfermline supporters seemed to make up about half of the 13,000 crowd that day, and they had a great deal to cheer about in their 4-1 win with Charlie Dickson scoring a hat-trick.

The score was 1-1 at half time and the game was evenly fought, but then St Mirren gave away an own goal when defender Wilson miskicked a clearance of a drive from George Peebles.

Once on top, the Pars were able to stay there and near the end, Charlie Dickson made his namesake Manager Andy Dickson proud of him by scoring another two goals.

The 4-1 score line possibly flattered the Pars – 2-1 might have been fairer – but there was no doubt that they deserved their big reward when the draw for the next round was made on Monday, and they were invited to entertain Rangers!

February 16 1980

Today any hopes that the Pars might have had of a Scottish Cup run evaporated with a severe 0-5 whipping at the hands of Morton at Cappielow.

And yet it was not as bad as it seemed.

Often considered to be a team of the same status as Dunfermline, Morton — in season 1979/80 a more than respectable Premier League team — were currently holding their own against teams with a budget about ten times bigger than what was available at Cappielow.

Dunfermline on the other hand were in the First Division, and rather too close to the relegation zone for their own liking.

They were no strangers to the Second Division, never having really recovered from their disastrous years of the early 1970s.

Today, on this heavy pitch, a watery sun was trying to brighten things up.

The key difference was that Morton had a player of real class on their side by the name of Andy Ritchie, whereas Dunfermline's side was made up of honest journeymen – and some of them not even that, according to a few disgruntled fans.

The Pars did well to hold them until half time – indeed they were not without their own moments, but then Andy Ritchie, who had suffered a lean time recently in the Premier League, took over.

Brown scored for Morton, and then Ritchie scored a goal which Dunfermline fans in the 6,000 crowd simply had to admire when he picked up a pass, beat three defenders on his own and then sent Whyte in the Dunfermline goal the wrong way.

He then had a hand in the next three goals, leaving Dunfermline with nothing left to do this season other than avoid relegation.

February 17 1962

Loud boos were heard all round East End Park today, as Dunfermline Athletic failed to beat Stenhousemuir in the last 16 round of the Scottish Cup.

Stenhousemuir were often looked upon as some sort of joke team in Scottish football, so it was an indication of how far the Pars had progressed that this 0-0 draw was looked upon as a disaster.

After all, it wasn't all that long ago that a 0-0 draw with Stenny would not have been considered a bad result!

The boos reflected the frustration of the fans but they were a bit unfair.

The Pars had just come back from an exhausting trip to Hungary in midweek where, although defeated, they had impressed the Hungarians of Ujpest Dozsa.

Today lowly Stenhousemuir played out of their skins and their goalkeeper Ross in particular had one of these days in which he simply saved everything.

It was a performance which may well have struck a chord with Eddie Connachan at the other end for he had had a similar game in last year's Scottish Cup final!

George Peebles, Harry Melrose and Tommy McDonald all came close, but the Stenhousemuir goal remained intact.

In addition, referee Willie Brittle might have awarded a penalty kick on at least two occasions in the second half, but his full time whistle meant that the Pars would have to face an angry Jock Stein, and would also have a replay at Ochilview the week after next.

It was not what was required, but in general terms, Dunfermline were doing well – still in Europe and third place in the Scottish League, and this was just one of "those" days!

February 18 1976

It may have been too little too late, one fears, but the Pars' comfortable 5-1 win over Clyde did at least give the fans something to be happy about, and also gave them some hope of avoiding the drop into Division Two.

It was a strange and confusing season, being the first of the Premier League, and Dunfermline were playing in the First Division (the second tier!) and trying to avoid playing in next season's Second Division (the third tier).

Confusing, wasn't it? And all the games were to be finished by the end of February as there were only 26 League games.

After that there was to be a competition called the Spring Cup for everyone except the Premier League teams. The Spring Cup was a horrendous idea, and mercifully was relegated to its deserved obscurity after one year, but anyhow Dunfermline now had a chance of staying in Division One.

Ken Mackie opened the scoring early with a great shot from 30 yards, and scored again later with a penalty while the other goals were scored by Hamilton, Hunter and an own goal.

Dunfermline supporters were now talking animatedly of the possibility of winning their two remaining games to save themselves, and they were both at home against Partick Thistle and Dumbarton!

Sadly however, this was 1976 and Dunfermline had to obey the immutable law of their own self-destruction. They lost the pair of them 3-0 and the third tier was awaiting for them next season.

1976 was an awful year for football generally in Scotland and for the Pars in particular, yet it was only eight years since they had won the Scottish Cup!

Roy Barry

February 19 1969

This was one of the best nights in Dunfermline Athletic's history.

They beat West Bromwich Albion 1-0 in the second leg of their European Cup Winners' Cup tie at the Hawthorns, having drawn the first leg at East End Park a month ago.

The weather was foul with wind and snow all over Great Britain and indeed Europe (Celtic played AC Milan that night in the San Siro in a snowstorm!).

The Pars scored early on through Pat Gardner with a goal which owed a little to the wind before West Bromwich could settle.

From then on the defence, well marshalled by Roy Barry and with normally attacking footballers like Alex Edwards and Bertie Paton defending heroically, held out in a tremendous rear guard action in which they had to contend with West Bromwich and the snow!

32,000 were there including about 2,000 from West Fife, but it was also possible to watch the game on closed circuit TV at East End Park.

Sadly the wind destroyed one of the screens but the other one functioned and about 10,000 fans huddled inside the enclosure to see what they could of the game.

The excitement as the minutes ticked away was no less intense at East End Park then it was in Birmingham, but the final whistle was greeted with a huge cheer at both grounds.

The players returned the following day by train arriving at Waverley Station to a heroes' reception and the whole country sent their congratulations to the victorious Fifers.

A win for a Scottish team over an English team is by no means a common occurrence.

February 20 1988

19,360 were at East End Park to see one of the greatest performances of Jim Leishman's managership of the club.

Dunfermline beat Rangers 2-0 in the Scottish Cup, and this was a result that made the rest of the world sit up and talk notice of the Pars.

This was the era of the successful but unpopular Rangers team with their English mercenaries on deals that have since been proved to be decidedly dodgy.

There was an unpleasant, aggressive side of both their players and their supporters with their perceived ability to intimidate referees and their ability to paralyse opponents (including Celtic on occasion) into inaction.

Not today however, for Mark Smith put Dunfermline ahead with a cross-cum-shot from the right wing in the early part of the game, and then towards the end of the first half John Brown was rightly red-carded for a blatant body check.

The referee, Alan Ferguson of Giffnock, widely suspected of being a Rangers sympathiser, was clearly not on this occasion, and after consulting with his linesman, "Bomber" Brown was invited to depart.

He didn't go quietly either!

Then early in the second half, a corner from Stuart Beedie was nodded on by Norrie McCathie to find the head of John Watson, and Dunfermline were 2-0 up.

A great deal of pressure was then put on the Dunfermline defence, but they held out, with their star man being Norwegian Veltle Andersen with the unlikely nickname of "Hakka".

Ross Jack however claimed that the good result was entirely due to the inspired poetry reading of Jim Leishman!

February 21 1914

Dunfermline lost what little chance they had of winning the Scottish League Division Two Championship today when they lost to Dundee Hibs at Tannadice Park.

Dundee Hibs are now, of course, better known as Dundee United. Formed in 1909 specifically to represent Dundee's large Irish population, they never achieved the same success as their Edinburgh or Glasgow equivalents, and their ground at Tannadice was a distinctly primitive one with a pronounced slope towards what is now the Arklay Street end.

Dunfermline started off playing towards that end but although they were on top as a result of pressure they showed a "surprising ineptitude" in front of goal and just before half-time, Hibs ran up to the top end and scored.

Hibs then scored with the "brae" in their favour soon after half-time.

Dunfermline were really struggling until they managed to pull one back through Cole, but were unable to force another goal on this pitch which was still wet and heavy after overnight rain.

All this meant that Dunfermline had now played 21 of their scheduled 22 games and were on 26 points, three points behind Cowdenbeath whom they could not now catch.

This did not in 1914 necessarily mean automatic promotion to the First Division – in any case, it was clear that Dunfermline Athletic were nothing like the standard required – but it was still hurtful to lose the Second Division to the "Miners" of Cowdenbeath, their local rivals.

The Hibs were a mid-table Second Division team, still light years behind their rivals and neighbours Dundee, who had won the Scottish Cup four years ago.

February 22 1967

16,500 were at East End Park tonight to see Dunfermline win their Second Round replay of the Scottish Cup against Partick Thistle.

They had been held to a 1-1 draw at Firhill on Saturday and quite a few of the newspapers had said that the Pars were lucky to get a draw and a replay.

But tonight, a fine dry night which was not too cold for the time of year, the Pars, after an uncertain first half hour, took a grip of the tie and ran out worthy winners over the Glasgow side who, to their credit, never gave up, but were overrun by the end.

It was one of the better games played this season by the team.

The Glasgow Herald is full of admiration.

"Dunfermline's victory was essentially one of team work. There was wonderful pace on and off the ball, an apt incisiveness in much of their running and passing and austereness in defence".

Pat Delaney scored a hat-trick tonight and Hugh Robertson and Alex Ferguson scored one each.

Robertson opened the scoring, but Thistle soon equalised.

By half-time however the game was as good as won with goals from Delaney and Ferguson to make it 3-1 and Delaney completed his hat-trick by scoring twice in the second half.

Dunfermline had not had as good a League season as they sometimes did, and Europe had been somewhat of a disappointment this season, but hopes were high of another Scottish Cup run where Dundee United now awaited them in the next round.

February 23 1927

Rangers' first ever visit to East End Park on League business was an anti-climax in that it was played on a wet Wednesday afternoon when the attendance was not as high as it might have been on a Saturday, but credit must be given to Dunfermline for putting up a great fight before they went down 3-1.

Dunfermline, following their surprise exit from the Scottish Cup at Methil on Saturday, were handicapped by the absence of Stein and Strachan through influenza, and then in the second half goalkeeper Stevenson suffered a knee injury and had to retire, to be replaced by Herd.

In spite of all this, Dunfermline put up a good performance and did a lot to win back the respect of their supporters after their poor showing on Saturday.

For Rangers, Jimmy Fleming got a hat-trick, but their star man was undeniably Fifer Sandy Archibald, with their much vaunted left wing of Tommy Cairns and Alan Morton not performing as well as was expected of them.

Dunfermline were well served by Tom Callaghan (no relation of the 1960s Tommy Callaghan!) and it was he who scored the goal when set up by Bobby Skinner.

Willie Williamson was also singled out as having a good game, and it was generally agreed, even in the Glasgow newspapers that Dunfermline were worth more than a 1-3 defeat.

What shone out was the sheer professionalism of Struth's Rangers and their ability to grind out a victory even on days when their flair players were having an off day. For Dunfermline, a grim battle to avoid relegation now awaited.

February 24 1934

Dunfermline, going for promotion, won 4-0 at Glebe Park, Brechin but were more than a little flattered by the extent of their victory.

Brechin's cricket team was always better known than its football team at this time, but the Angus side, founded in 1906, had been in the Scottish League for a good few seasons now, and although survival was always a struggle particularly in the 1930s when the depression hit hard, they usually put up a good show.

This was a steady, if not brilliant Dunfermline team and manager Willie Knight, a crusty and determined character, had brought together a decent team.

Today Brechin were the brighter team for the first period but it was Paterson who put the Pars ahead after a goalmouth scramble.

Then Dunfermline got a real break when the Brechin goalkeeper McCallum fisted the ball out but it struck the back of his defender and cannoned into the net.

The second half saw little in the way of good football, but Dunfermline scored again through Laidlaw and Watson and remained on top of the hard working but talentless Brechin City.

As rivals Albion Rovers weren't playing today, this result put Dunfermline in a fine position for promotion, and possibly even gave them a chance of winning the Second Division (the two of them were due to meet in March 17).

It raised yet again the inevitable question of whether Dunfermline really wanted promotion? Was it not better to stay where they were among teams of their own standard, rather than go up among the big boys where hammerings were inevitable?

But Dunfermline were ambitious.

February 25 1961

Jock Stein's men recorded a remarkable 6-3 victory over Aberdeen at Pittodrie in the Scottish Cup last 16 tie.

It must be stressed that this was by no means a vintage Aberdeen side (they had flirted with relegation once or twice in recent years) but even so, for Dunfermline to travel to Pittodrie and win in such style was something that made the rest of the Scottish footballing world sit up and take notice.

The weather was not great with a biting east wind coming from the beach end of the ground, and the pitch still sodden from the rain and sleet of the day before.

The defending on either side was not great, but full marks to the forwards who produced nine goals.

The crowd at about 10,000 might have been bigger, and at full time it was noticeable how the Aberdeen support turned on their own team, a recurring phenomenon at Pittodrie in those days.

Yet it was Aberdeen who scored first through Brownlie after a mistake by Jim Heriot.

But the Pars came back and by half time, goals by Alex Smith and Charlie Dickson had put them in front.

Tommy McDonald then made it 3-1 and when Aberdeen pulled one back to give some temporary hope to their fans, George Peebles and Harry Melrose made it 5-2.

That seemed to be it, but in the final minute with the crowd streaming out of the ground, Coutts scored for Aberdeen, only for George Miller to score with a header.

Jock Stein may well have been angry with his defence, but it was great entertainment for the fans, and well worth the long trip in their buses and trains.

February 26 1920

Andrew Wilson today became the first ever Dunfermline Athletic player to play for Scotland.

It was the first full International match since the Great War.

Played eccentrically on a Thursday afternoon in front of a 16,000 crowd at Ninian Park, Cardiff, this game was one of the better International games with Scotland fighting back to gain a draw and Andy Wilson not looking in any way out of place in a Scotland jersey.

He was also of course the first player from a Central League team to be chosen for Scotland, and all Dunfermline awaited eagerly any news from Cardiff, queuing up at newsagents to listen to rumours before the evening paper arrived.

The Courier, as one might have expected from a Dundee newspaper sang the praises of Dundee's Napper Thomson but also praises Wilson.

It also tells a story about how a group of "perfervid" Scottish supporters in the stand, started singing "Annie Laurie" to cheer up their players when they were 0-1 down at half-time, but were drowned out by the Welshmen singing "Land of My Fathers".

Wales had scored first through John Evans of Cardiff City in the first five minutes, and no matter how hard Scotland tried, they couldn't get an equaliser.

Alan Morton of Queen's Park was superb, as indeed were Jimmy Gordon of Rangers, Alec McNair of Celtic and Andy Wilson of Dunfermline, but it was late in the game before the equaliser came, a header from Tommy Cairns of Rangers.

Wilson was described as "splendid" throughout with his ability to lead the line and distribute to both wings.

He would have been disappointed not to get the winner, but his time would come.

As it was, a 1-1 draw was a fair result for Scotland, and Wilson was retained for the next game against Ireland.

February 27 1965

The Scottish League Championship race this year was quite incredible, the most exciting one there had been in years.

Celtic and Rangers were both out of it, and it boiled down to the two Edinburgh teams, Kilmarnock and Dunfermline.

Today Dunfermline were the only one of the four of them not to lose, and indeed they would have won had it not been for an injury time strike by Aberdeen's Danish star Leif Mortensen in a tight 2-2 draw at Pittodrie.

Aberdeen were a poor side in 1965, currently without a manager following the resignation a fortnight ago of Tommy Pearson.

John Kilgannon had opened the scoring for the Pars in front of a 10,000 crowd, but then Joergen Ravn had equalised for Aberdeen.

When Jim Fleming put the Pars ahead in the 60th minute, things looked good for Dunfermline with their famous strong defence, for whom Willie Callaghan was outstanding, looking quite capable of holding out.

Indeed Pittodrie was visibly emptying with disgruntled Aberdonians going home, when Mortensen struck. It was a body blow (and an undeserved one) for Willie Cunningham's men, but when they came off the field, they discovered that Kilmarnock, Hearts and Hibs had all lost, Hearts by the barely believable score line of 1-7 to Dundee at Tynecastle!

All this meant that the Pars were second equal but actually in the best position if they won all their games in hand.

The snag was that the "games in hand" were not easy.

Dunfermline were also still involved this year in the Scottish Cup and still had their Inter Cities Fairs Cup tie against Athletic Bilbao to come.

A pleasant problem, however, for Manager Willie Cunningham as he was about to sign a new contract.

February 28 1996

In a 5-way first division title race, fixture rearrangements meant Dunfermline had the other four to play, all at home, in a 12-day period.

Dundee United had visited the previous Saturday and left with a point, while Morton were due the following Saturday and Dundee the midweek after.

On this Wednesday night, St Johnstone were visitors in what would turn out to be a tremendous game.

There were plenty of scoring chances before Andy Smith slid in to put the Pars ahead but, soon after, the ever-popular George O'Boyle, now playing for St Johnstone, tapped into an empty net for the equaliser as the ball rebounded from the post.

O'Boyle's strike partner had also been a Pars player in the past and while Roddy Grant had rarely impressed in black and white, in Perth he was on the way to becoming a cult figure.

So it was then that he too would score, tapping in at the back post right on the half-time whistle.

The moment for which the game is famous came early in the second half; ambling forward from centre half, John Clark took a pass in the middle of the park but there looked no real danger.

Bang! To say Clark hammered it in doesn't do it justice – hit with almost indescribable power from 35 yards, it flew past an astonished Alan Main in the Saints goal.

Now level at 2-2, Bert Paton's side went for the winner, and it came in the middle of the second half. Derek Fleming got up from full-back to cross from the left and Andy Tod won it with a typical crashing header.

A nervy, thrilling night at East End Park and the latest drama in this incredible 1995/96 season.

February 29 1964

It was a trip to Muirton Park, Perth this Leap Year Day for Dunfermline.

Muirton Park, the home of the prosperous but perpetually underperforming Perth Saints, is now a supermarket.

In 1964 it had the reputation of being the best playing surface in Scotland, and it was also the broadest. Surrounded by a whisky factory and an ice rink, it was the home of St Johnstone until 1989.

Today the Saints and the Pars, both respectably placed in the First Division but hardly title challengers, put on a good game of football for the 7,000 fans but it was St Johnstone who edged it 3-2.

Dunfermline were leading at half-time thanks to goals from Jackie Sinclair and George Peebles as distinct from one from Perth's personality Bill "Buck" McCarry.

The second half however saw the game swing in the direction of St Johnstone with goals from Hawkshaw and Kemp sentencing Dunfermline to a defeat in a game from which they expected and deserved at least a draw.

As it happened, Jim Kerray "scored", but the referee chalked it off for a very debatable offside.

The real significance of this game however was that it was the first game that Dunfermline played after the announcement in midweek that Jock Stein would be leaving the club at the end of the season.

This was a blow to the club, but there was no bitterness about it and it was clear that he simply felt that he had done as much as he was likely to do with a provincial club.

He was clearly angling for a move to the chronically struggling Celtic – but they did not take the hint - at least not yet!

March

March 1 1958

Dunfermline had very few big days at East End Park in the 1950s but this was one of them, when they drew Rangers in the last sixteen of the Scottish Cup.

Tickets were printed for this game, people queued for them and the ground record of 24,377 turned up to see the game.

Rangers had not had the best of seasons – they had lost horrendously 1-7 to Celtic in the Scottish League Cup final in October, and were away behind a very good Hearts side in the Scottish League – but they were still Rangers.

Dunfermline on the other hand, unluckily relegated from the First Division last season had now regrouped and were looking to bounce back.

A good win over St Mirren in the last round had made everyone sit up and take notice of Andy Dickson's side, and here they were off to a very good start.

Gerry McWilliams drove a hard ball into the penalty box and it seemed to be handled by Willie Telfer, but referee Hugh Phillips said no to the ardent screams of the Dunfermline fans.

McWilliams did score with a fierce drive just on the quarter hour mark, and for a while a real Scottish Cup upset looked on the cards.

But Maxie Murray silenced his doubters among the Ibrox diehards by equalising, and then young Ralph Brand put Rangers ahead.

They held on to their narrow lead until half-time and then gradually in the second half Dunfermline tired, and Rangers were able to see the game out without much trouble.

March 2 1988

Dunfermline had defeated Celtic when the Celts first came calling at the start of the season, and high hopes were entertained that the result could be replicated this Wednesday night.

The weather was cold but dry, and a large crowd of 17,446 turned up.

The Celtic fans were already buoyed up with the news that Rangers had gone down 0-2 (and it should have been more!) to Steaua Bucharest in a lunch-time kick-off game that had been beamed live to Scotland.

Celtic were now a different team from August, having ironed out a few problems and bought players like Frank McAvennie.

The Pars had generally regressed, give or take the odd good result like putting Rangers out of the Scottish Cup a fortnight ago.

They were now in a spot of relegation trouble, and really could have done with a point or two here, but Celtic, now scenting the Scottish League Championship, put on a master class of football.

Andy Walker scored in the first minute, then McAvennie with a header before scoring a third with a swivel and shot that was as good as anyone would have wished to see.

Billy Stark headed a fourth in the second half, but by then the game was all over as the streams of departing Pars fans would tend to indicate.

Pars fans consoled themselves with the thought that they still had a considerable amount of games to play, and that they did not have to play Celtic every week, but there was little in this performance to bring very much cheer.

March 3 1928

It was Scottish Cup quarter final day, and for once Dunfermline were in among the action.

Their League form had been little short of deplorable, and they were now well adrift at the bottom of the League, but they had enjoyed a reasonable Cup run, beating Clydebank, Leith and then in an excellent performance Dundee at Dens Park, to reach the last eight where today Hibs were the visitors.

Hibs, even as far back as the 1920s had a reputation of flattering to deceive their supporters.

They had for example been in the Scottish Cup finals of 1914, 1923 and 1924 but had lost them all. Yet they remained a well-supported club and today it looked as if virtually all of Leith had come to support them, singing their unashamedly Irish songs – some of them lovely like those of John McCormack, other less so with comments about partition and the Black and Tans of recent years.

It appeared too that an awful lot of them had come in motor cars, either crossing the River Forth on a ferry or taking the very long way round.

Dunfermline's supporters had rallied today as well and it looked as if there would have been about 16,000 in the rather primitive East End Park.

Hibs' star man was the red headed Jimmy Dunn, nicknamed "Ginger" for obvious reasons.

At the end of the month he would star in the 5-1 demolition of England by Scotland in what became known as the "Wembley Wizards" team, and today he starred for Hibs as well.

Dunfermline showed some early drive and might even have scored in the first minute through Stein, but Dunn scored twice for Hibs and Halligan and Bradley scored the other two as Hibs ran out 4-0 winners, to join Rangers, Celtic and Queen's Park in the Scottish Cup semi-finals.

March 4 1950

Dunfermline had a good run in the Scottish Cup this year, but it had now come to an end.

Today saw a tight 2-1 win over Hamilton Academical in the Scottish League Division "B".

Dunfermline were well behind in the promotion race, but in view of their games in hand (caused by their Cup runs in both the Scottish Cup and the Scottish League Cup and a few postponements) they still had a chance, and their win today did the cause no harm.

A crowd of 4,000 were here to see Jim Cannon score in the first minute, and then Jackie Gallacher score a second before half time.

Jackie Gallacher was, of course, the son of the great Hughie Gallacher, still idolised for his part in the "Wembley Wizards" game of 1928, but it was generally agreed that Jackie was not as good as his father.

Hamilton fought hard today, and were given a real break when right back Kerr conceded an own goal but Dunfermline were good enough to hold out for a narrow 2-1 victory.

A glance at tonight's evening paper confirmed that Dunfermline were seventh in the League, some 16 points behind clear leaders Morton, and it was unlikely that they would catch them.

As the Pars had eight games left to play — as distinct from most of the others who had four — it was not impossible that they might yet reach second spot, and thus gain promotion to Division "A" and big derby gates with Raith Rovers and East Fife.

March 5 1955

Close rivals Airdrie and Hamilton were involved in the Scottish Cup quarter finals today, so Dunfermline were able to consolidate their position at the top of the Scottish League Second Division.

They did this by means of a rather easy 4-1 defeat of Dundee United at Tannadice Park.

Dundee United were having a bad season at the bottom of the Second Division, and their ground was still a poor one.

Dunfermline fans were able to comfort themselves with the thought that the Tannadice Park stand was possibly even worse than the East End Park equivalent.

Dundee United, still called "the Hibs" by their older followers, were looked upon as the poor man's team of the city and still drew their support from the Irish population of Dundee.

Today in front of a very poor crowd, Dundee United were no match for Dunfermline who scored first through Charlie Dickson then after United equalised before half time, the Pars simply took a grip of the game and scored through Dickson (again), Reilly and Anderson.

The train home was full of optimistic talk from the Pars fans about promotion. They were second in the League with some eight games to play, but the encouraging thing about this result was that it did not involve any luck.

Dunfermline Athletic had not been in the First Division since before the Second World War, but Bobby Ancell's men looked likely to do it this year.

It was always a source of distress to realise that both Raith Rovers and East Fife looked like permanent residents of Division One, but Dunfermline seemed anchored in Division Two. This had to change!

March 6 1965

It was Scottish Cup quarter final day.

Although a heavy fall of midweek snow had put the games in some doubt, a thaw on Friday night and early Saturday morning allowed play to proceed in all four games.

The Pars had played Athletic Bilbao in midweek and tied the game on aggregate and there would now be a third and decisive game the week after next.

It was Stirling Albion who were the opponents today at East End Park, and the game was delayed by Archie Webster of Falkirk for a strange reason.

Having seen both teams, he thought that their colours were too similar. Stirling wore white shorts with thin red hoops and this strip was deemed too close to Dunfermline's black and white.

Dunfermline, the home team, had to change into red jerseys with white pants. But changed strip or not, the Pars won today 2-0.

John Kilgannon scored in the first half after a fine move involving Alex Edwards and Alex Ferguson, and then Edwards himself scored in the second half.

Stirling Albion fought well and even scored what looked like a perfectly valid equaliser in the second half before it was chalked off for offside, but the Pars held out to win the game and to enter the semi-final draw for the second year in a row and the third time overall.

Today there were also wins for Motherwell, Celtic and in a thrilling finish at Easter Road, Hibs beat Rangers with virtually the last kick of the ball. Dunfermline were now going strong in three competitions.

Heady days!

March 7 1981

These were dire days at East End Park.

Their position in the First Division (the second tier of three) was once again "on a shoogly peg". Pat Stanton, a maestro of a player with Hibs in particular, had been appointed Manager a few months ago, but his presence was proving less than inspirational. He was by no means the first great player to prove himself an ordinary Manager.

As always happens when you are down, luck went against them once again today at Ayr United. Crowds had dwindled to less than 2,000 for home games, and today saw a mere token support going to Somerset Park. Indeed the whole crowd in unpleasant, damp conditions looked to be a lot less than 1,500.

Dunfermline had the better of the first half with Colin O'Brien crossing for Sandy McNaughton to score a good goal, and at half time things were looking good. However, defensive errors, a recurring theme of this year, appeared in the second half and Ayr United scored twice, so Dunfermline returned empty-handed.

The position did not look good with only Stirling Albion and Berwick Rangers below the Pars as we entered the last phase of the season. The mood of Dunfermline supporters was not helped by the obvious success of Raith Rovers. Rovers won 2-0 at Hamilton today and it looked very much as if promotion to the Premier Division for the first time was a possibility.

But for Dunfermline it now looked as if a major effort would be required if another season or two in Division Two was to be avoided.

March 8 1913

Dunfermline today registered an impressive 5-1 victory, admittedly against Arthurlie, not the strongest of opposition.

This was in the 14 team Scottish League Second Division to which Dunfermline had been elected (automatic promotion and relegation were still some distance away) last summer.

They were about half way up the League, but their last three games had been unsatisfactory — a defeat to St Bernard's and two dull 1-1 draws.

Today, however, in the opinion of *The Courier,* the key thing was that they now knew how to shoot.

They had signed a man called Cooper from Central League side Kirkcaldy United, and he made a huge difference to the forward line. He scored one of the goals, Hall scored a hat-trick "although he did not take all the opportunities he got", and Hemphill got the other.

Hardie is described as a hard worker "although he should use his brains as well as his feet", but the best player of them all was Jimmy Brown. He was "ubiquitous" and his "feeding was much improved" — a reference, one hopes, to his ability to pass a ball rather than a recovery from an eating disorder!

Arthurlie from Barrhead were a pretty poor side. Dunfermline still had seven games to play — most other teams just had two — could still win the Second Division.

They would need to win all their games and hope that the teams above them might drop a few. Certainly, they were making a bit of an impression in their first season in the national League.

March 9 2013

These were dark days.

Serious doubt existed about making it to the end of the season – wages were not being paid on time, a large amount of outstanding tax was due, fan fundraising was ongoing and a series of public meetings had been held.

Before today's game at Airdrie, Jim Leishman spoke very gloomily on Radio Scotland; he had been unable to progress in his temporary role trying to find a way forward and had handed back control to Gavin Masterton.

Against this background, the outcome of the game seemed almost incidental, but there was to be an exciting finish all the same.

It looked all over when the home side went 3-1 up with five minutes left, but a long-range Ryan Wallace strike straight from the restart then an Andy Kirk goal in injury time meant an unlikely point.

The following Thursday saw another open meeting at the Vine Church, many leaving it with the feeling that the club didn't have long to go.

Two days after this, the game at Stark's Park ranks as one of the worst experiences in football: going along to watch your team play and thinking it's the last time you'll see them, made for a horrible, confused set of emotions.

The first time I saw Dunfermline play was at Stark's Park in 1989, so it seemed hideous but somehow appropriate that it was all about to end at the same ground.

Although much of the game was a celebration of the club and its history, the final whistle was unbearable.

'Dunfermline til I die' was the song, but it all became too much as realisation dawned that the club was about to die before me.

A horrible day, but I've never been so glad to have made it to a game.

March 10 2020

This game would turn out to be DA's last game for some considerable time, as football would soon be suspended because of the Coronavirus pandemic which was about to hit Great Britain.

It was against Partick Thistle at Firhill, and Dunfermline looked set to win all three points until Thistle scored in the fourth minute of added-on time.

This sounded like hard luck on the Fifers but in fact, lowly placed Thistle had been the better side, particularly in the first half.

Dunfermline came a little more into the game in the second half, but even so, it was quite a surprise when they went ahead in the 72nd minute as Euan Murray hammered home a low corner kick taken by Dom Thomas.

Thistle then redoubled their efforts, but hard thought they tried, it looked as if Dunfermline's 370 travelling fans were going to depart homewards with all three points.

Brian Graham's late equaliser was objected to on two accounts by Williams and the Dunfermline defence.

Some thought that Graham was offside, and Williams claimed that he had been impeded, but referee Steven Kirkland saw no problem, and in truth, a 1-1 draw was a fair result.

The Pars still had a chance of making the play-offs, they felt, but the crowd departed Firhill that night desperately worried about what the future was going to bring.

All Scottish football was suspended on the Friday, and thus the Pars would not be going to Dens Park on the Saturday.

March 11 1967

Most independent or neutral observers agreed that Dunfermline were unlucky not to get at least a draw today at Tannadice Park in the Scottish Cup Quarter Final.

Both teams were going well, having a good season and over 20,000 were at this game with both teams well supported.

Dundee United and Dunfermline had a lot in common for they were both children of the swinging sixties.

The 1950s had been spent in mediocrity in both cases with poor crowds, indifferent football and each team having a grandstand which earned unflattering nicknames like "the henhouse" and "the cowshed".

Both of them creaked alarmingly on windy days and it was frighteningly easy to get a skelf in one's bottom. Stories however of anti-tetanus injections being offered at half time were possibly not exactly true, however.

The 1960s however had changed all that. Today at a bright and breezy Tannadice Park, although Dunfermline dominated the first half with the benefit of the wind, they could not score against a Dundee United defence which was always, under Manager Jerry Kerr, well drilled.

In the second half, the Pars tired ever so slightly but even so, it looked as if the game was to be heading for a replay at East End Park until Finn Dossing, Dundee United's centre forward from Denmark, popped up to score the winner with just four minutes to go and not enough time to equalise.

At least it quashed all the nonsense about "a fix for another big gate" which even reached the newspapers and may even have had some foundation in other games involving other clubs, but not here.

It was a severe blow to Dunfermline's supporters who had been to the Scottish Cup semi-final every year since 1964.

A disputed equaliser against Partick Thistle in the last game before the 2020 lockdown

March 12 1960

It would have been a very brave man indeed who would have forecast that this game was being contested between next season's Scottish Cup winners and the Scottish League winners of two seasons hence.

Dunfermline were currently manager-less and facing relegation (Again! They were in danger of joining Stirling Albion in being called the "yoyo" team of Scottish football as they flitted between both Divisions).

Dundee had a side which had smartened up of late but who were still failing to satisfy the demands of their large support and the local Press who adored them, although they were not afraid to deliver the odd barbed remark if things were not going well.

The weather was reasonable and the crowd was about 8,000, all of whom were surprised to see the Pars go 2-0 ahead with a header from Harry Melrose and then a fierce drive from George Peebles.

This was the sort of stuff that would have impressed any potential new Manager, but sadly it did not last and before half-time, Dundee had equalised with a header from Alan Cousin and a well-developed goal finished off by Bobby Waddell.

Half time reflections were that this was a great game of football, but this was not really needed at this time of the year – it was a victory and two points that Dunfermline needed.

They certainly had the better of the second half and Dickson, Melrose and Smith all came close, but the man of the match was Dundee goalkeeper Pat Liney who defied the Pars time and time again.

It was an encouraging performance by Dunfermline... but they now needed more than "encouraging performances". There were rumours, however, that the appointment of a new Manager was imminent.

March 13 1920

Andrew Wilson, now known universally as "Andy" was absolutely outstanding today as Scotland beat Ireland 3-0 at Celtic Park before a crowd of 39,757.

It was Scotland's first home International since the war and the victory was greeted with great enthusiasm. The 3-0 score line was no fair reflection on the run of play.

Ireland, hamstrung by the struggle for Independence going on in their country at the moment, were poor.

They were no match for a Scottish side that teemed with talent like Alec McNair, Jimmy McMenemy, Alan Morton and of course Andy Wilson.

It was Wilson who scored first. He scored it with a meandering run past two defenders before picking his spot and placing the ball behind Elisha Scott in the Ireland goal.

Wilson excelled throughout and it now looked as if he would be a cert to start in the England game in a month's time at Hillsborough, even though he played in an "unofficial" League.

The other two goals were scored by Alan Morton of Queen's Park and Andy Cunningham of Rangers.

Meanwhile back home, just how much Dunfermline missed him was highlighted when they were held at home 1-1 by Armadale, a result that imperilled Dunfermline's chances of winning the Central League.

All this did nothing to lessen the speculation about Dunfermline Athletic's alleged "illegal holding" of Andy Wilson, with more legal injunctions threatened from Middlesbrough, and quite a few Chairmen of English clubs telling everyone how much they would be prepared to spend to buy him.

March 14 1960

With the club virtually on its knees, second bottom of the League and facing relegation, Dunfermline Athletic today welcomed as their new Manager 37 year old Jock Stein, Reserve Team Coach at Celtic Park.

Jock had started at Albion Rovers in 1942, had been a tolerable but not outstanding defender, had played for a time in Wales and then had surprisingly returned to Scotland as a stop-gap centre half at Celtic.

He showed leadership qualities, became captain and led the club to the Coronation Cup in 1953 and then a Scottish League and Cup double in 1954.

An ankle injury had curtailed his playing career, and he turned to coaching, where he was doing a good job bringing on players like Billy McNeill and Pat Crerand.

There were those who felt that he might have become Manager of Celtic, but what may have been an obstacle was that Stein was a non-Catholic.

In any case when offered the Dunfermline job, he accepted immediately, admitting that he did not know very much about the club, although as a miner himself, he could identify with many of Dunfermline's supporters.

On his first day in the job, he was heard saying that all the players were on trial, but that he did not have a magic wand and his first job was to save the club from relegation.

In point of fact, subsequent events would tend to prove that he did have a magic wand! Certainly, things were never quite the same again at East End Park!

Andy Wilson

March 15 1958

Rarely have Pars fans left East End Park with such a spring in their step as they did today.

Their team delivered an almighty 8-1 thrashing to an admittedly very poor Albion Rovers team.

The weather was still a bit cold with even the odd flurry of snow around — promotion rivals Dumbarton's game at Forfar had been postponed because of snow — but once the sun got going, it was clear that spring was in the air.

Albion Rovers, a team now beginning to struggle after a few good years in the First Division not all that long ago, had no answer to a powerful Dunfermline side who started well and maintained their good play throughout the game.

Both Jimmy Watson and Gerry McWilliam scored hat-tricks and Charlie Dickson scored two to the delight of his Manager and namesake Andy Dickson, and this result kept DA well in contention for promotion and an early return to the First Division.

The goals were all well taken ones and each player who scored had a header among his tally. Pars simply clicked today.

Unfortunately, promotion rivals Stirling Albion and Arbroath both won as well, but this result did a great deal for Pars goal average.

Dunfermline still had two games in hand over Arbroath and a total of eight games left.

Football was in a funny place in early 1958, still coming to terms with the Manchester United air disaster of February 6, but today it was reported that Manager Matt Busby was now slowly recovering, having been out of bed for a short time today.

March 16 1965

Luck was not with Dunfermline Athletic tonight as they exited from the Inter Cities Fairs Cup to the Basque side Athletic Bilbao, often erroneously called Atletico Bilbao.

The programme for the home game calls them Athletico Bilbao, a name they were forced to use in the dictatorship of General Franco.

They wanted to call themselves Athletic because they had been founded by Englishmen, and the Basques were far more sympathetic to Great Britain than they were to the Spain of General Franco.

Their team was rigidly sectarian in 1965 with only Basques, or men of Basque descent, however tenuous, allowed to play for them. This situation was by no means unique in world football, for Rangers operated a similar policy in Scotland at this time.

This game was a play-off, for both teams had already won 1-0 with home advantage in both cases, but Dunfermline had lost the toss for the play-off venue.

The Basques were awarded a fairly soft penalty kick in the first half; Dunfermline then equalised through Alex Smith early in the second half.

Soon after that the Pars hit the post and claimed that the ball had crossed the line but the Swiss referee Mr Buceli said "no".

Then Uriarte ran through a somewhat static Pars defence to score for Athletic Bilbao with five minutes to go, to put the Pars out.

It was an honourable defeat.

Apart from anything else it put an end to all the silly jokes about how several Bilbao players had injured themselves in the revolving door of the City Hotel (where they stayed when they came to Dunfermline) because they "had put all their Basques in one exit"!

March 17 2007

At last Dunfermline recorded a good Scottish Premier League win.

They travelled to Inverness and beat Inverness Caledonian Thistle 3-1, thus reviving hopes that they might, after all, escape the relegation.

It had been overshadowing them so much all winter that the word "doomed" seemed to be attached to Dunfermline Athletic like glue.

There were clear signs that the winter was over; it was a sunny, albeit blustery day. Dunfermline's "bad spell" (as the optimists put it) was still going strong however, in spite of a much-changed line-up, for they were one down at half time.

But then, things changed just as suddenly as the weather did this March day. Stephen Glass scored, then Jim McIntyre put the Pars ahead; the lead was extended later when the referee, Mr Boyle, awarded a slightly dubious penalty and Glass put Pars 3-1 up.

That was how it finished, but the win was slightly soured by Tam McManus foolishly getting himself red carded.

The long journey home thus passed happily (a snow flurry or two round about Drumochter Pass – but what is unusual about that?) with the small band of fans talking happily about an upsurge in form and even a good chance of reaching the Scottish Cup final if they could beat Hibs in the semi-final.

Ah yes, Hibs. They were in the League Cup final tomorrow against Kilmarnock. That would be a good game to watch on TV.

But in the meantime, what about the Pars? We always did say that Stephen Kenny was the man for the job, didn't we? Even though it was only his second League victory since November!

March 18 1961

What a difference a year makes!

Last year at this time, Dunfermline had just appointed Jock Stein as their Manager in a desperate effort to stave off relegation.

He had beaten his old team Celtic in his first game and had achieved his aim of keeping the Pars in the top flight.

Now mid-table respectability was the order of the day, the players all wore blazers and nice trousers, enjoyed privileges at local golf clubs and restaurants, and everyone was looking forward to a Scottish Cup semi-final date against St Mirren at Tynecastle in two weeks' time.

There was even now talk of replacing the old stand which enjoyed a certain amount of local ridicule as the "hen house" and from where it was remarkably easy to get a stick or a splinter in one's bottom!

Today, St Johnstone, traditionally a rival with Dunfermline in their chronic inability to produce a team to enthuse their sizeable but dormant support came to town.

Normally one would imagine this to be a relegation battle but only the men from Perth had that problem today as the Pars swept them aside 5-1.

9,000 were there to see George Peebles score two goals from a distance, then Harry Melrose score two headers.

The Saints eventually pulled one back, only for Charlie Dickson to make it five.

The DA fans headed home talking animatedly among themselves, about where and when Stand Tickets would be on sale for the semi-final, how many extra Football Specials would be going that day and how it was only a very short walk from Haymarket Station to Tynecastle Park.

March 19 2006

Celtic had put eight goals past Dunfermline in a League game at East End Park exactly a month ago, so not many people fancied the Pars in today's Scottish League Cup final at Hampden Park.

The run to the final had been a difficult one, starting with a tricky away game against Gretna that was won mainly due to a superb goalkeeping performance from Bryn Halliwell.

Next up was Kilmarnock away, with the 4-3 win being the first win on that ground since 1992, a surprising 3-0 home win over Hibs then a semi-final against Livingston at Easter Road won by a Darren Young penalty.

The great Jimmy Johnstone had died of Motor Neurone Disease earlier in the week, and he was given a great round of applause by all players and spectators. All the Celtic players wore no 7 on their pants in honour of the man who is quite rightly regarded as one of the best players of all time.

The Pars did well enough to hold Celtic until nearly half time until an error by goalkeeper Allan McGregor allowed Zurawski to put Celtic ahead.

The second half saw Celtic very much on top but no further scoring until late in the game when Shaun Maloney scored with a free kick and Dion Dublin added a third.

Dunfermline don't get to many cup finals, so it was a real disappointment to go down so meekly without laying a finger on Celtic – there was a real feeling that the team just hadn't turned up.

However, the reluctance to attack when only a goal down was perhaps influenced by that hammering a month before.

March 20 1926

The best crowd seen at East End Park this season (about 10,000 and including Provost Fraser and his wife) saw Dunfermline take a very large step towards promotion to the First Division.

They beat close challengers Ayr United in a very close and hard-fought game.

Ayr United, who had a fairly large and vocal support with them, scored first with a lovely long range shot from Paton and for the rest of the first half, the visitors retained control.

Gradually, however, Dunfermline fought their way back into the game and a Ritchie cross was deflected into his own goal by defender Woodburn.

Dunfermline now pressed but their talismanic goal scorer Bobby Skinner was well policed, and it was eventually a penalty kick, awarded for handball, which separated the sides and was well taken by Wilson.

2-1 it was, but then tempers began to fray. First Herd and Fleming squared up to each other; fortunately they were separated by the referee Mr Martin before things got too far out of hand.

A far more serious flare-up occurred a little later between two other players and this time a spectator jumped the fence to join in, but was fortunately pushed away just as several other spectators looked set to enter the fray.

The police kept the crowd quiet and the referee did likewise with the players and the game finished 2-1 for Dunfermline which suited them down to the ground. There were now only five games to go and another five points were needed to win promotion.

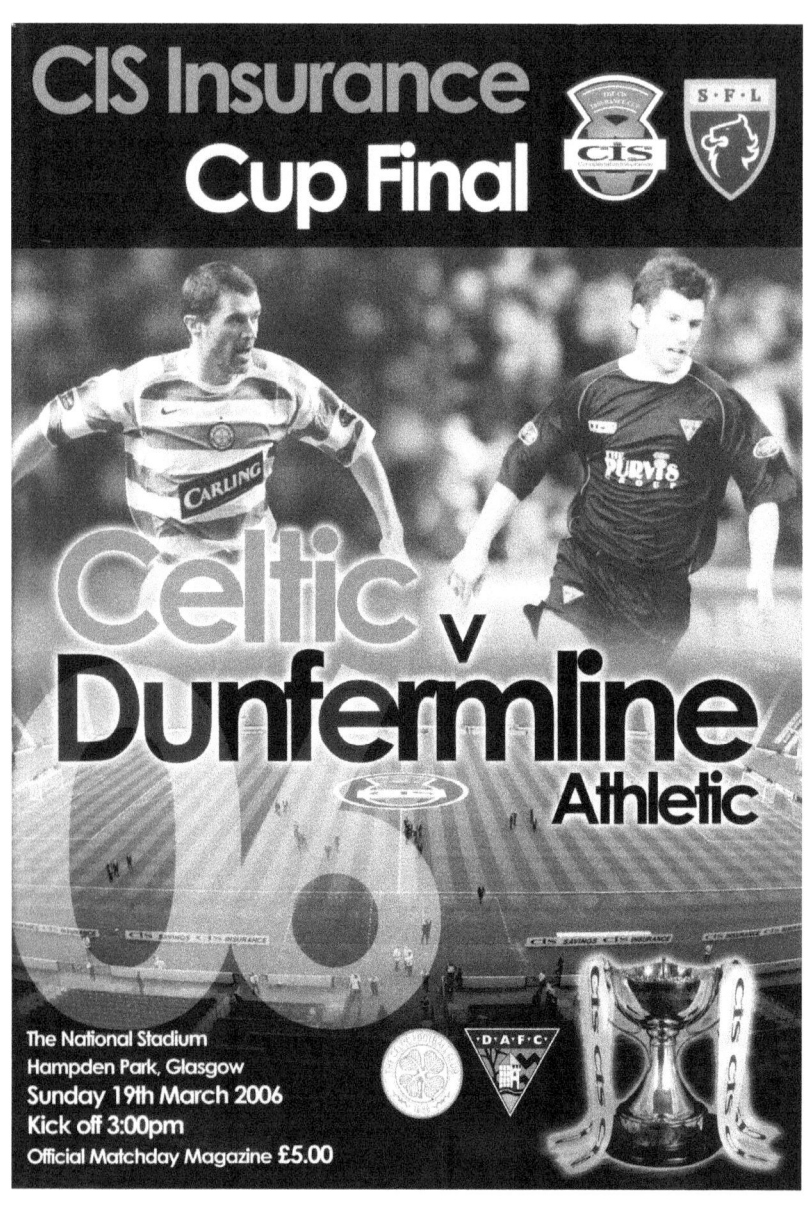

Programme cover, CIS Insurance Cup Final, 2006

March 21 1914

Dunfermline had enjoyed a fairly successful season, finishing third in the Scottish League Second Division, although the fact that Cowdenbeath had been the winners must have been a sore blow.

Today they advanced in the first round of the Fife Cup to meet their rivals Cowdenbeath. They did this by a win at Scott's Park, Pathhead, Kirkcaldy — the ground of their old rivals Kirkcaldy United.

Kirkcaldy United had never achieved Scottish League status, largely because of the presence of Raith Rovers and the belief that Kirkcaldy could never sustain two Scottish League teams – as indeed was proved when the United folded in 1916 and never resumed after the war.

Today was a fine spring day, although with rather too much of a cross-wind. In addition, Scott's Park was built on an incline, so good football was difficult.

The famous Jimmy Gourlay, one time of Raith Rovers, scored for the home side in the first half when they had the benefit of the conditions, but in the second half Dunfermline took over although both their goals "had a flavour of luck about them".

In fact, they were both deflections. Then well within the last five minutes, Kirkcaldy were awarded a penalty kick, but Gourlay's attempt was "rather too elevated".

Dunfermline advanced to the next round, a turn of events not 100% to the liking of some Kirkcaldy youths who saw fit to throw a few stones at their Dunfermline counterparts before a local constable "gave them a lecture on the error of their ways".

March 22 1965

Dunfermline kept themselves in the race for the League Championship with an 8-0 win over Third Lanark at East End Park this somewhat chilly Monday evening.

No-one realised it at the time, but this would be the last time that this famous old Glasgow team would ever visit East End Park.

Third Lanark, traditionally a team with great players – Jimmy Carabine, Jimmy Mason, Ally McLeod, Matt Gray for example – but constant under-achievers had been struggling for some time.

They were suffering from being the sixth team in Glasgow, a city which was itself struggling as its "overspill" population was moving to the new towns of Cumbernauld, East Kilbride and Glenrothes, but there was also rumoured to be a considerable amount of embezzlement and corruption in the Boardroom.

They would be relegated this year and would only survive another couple of years in the Second Division before going out of business altogether.

They had recently been involved in a Scottish Cup saga against Dunfermline which had gone to three games before being settled in favour of the Pars.

Tonight however in a game that should have been played before Christmas, Thirds were simply swept aside by a rampant Dunfermline team.

Harry Melrose scored four goals, Jackie Sinclair had two and George Peebles and Alex Smith one each.

The last ever game between the two of them would be at Cathkin on April 10. Dunfermline would win that one as well but by a considerably smaller margin.

Tonight however the Pars were simply superb and looked well on course for a League and Cup Double, if they could only beat Hibs in the Scottish Cup semi-final on Saturday.

March 23 1991

The Pars had not won a game since February 23 (exactly a month ago) so it was a welcome change to watch a 3-2 win over St Johnstone at East End Park in the Scottish Premier League today.

As with most of the home games this season, there was sadly not a large crowd at East End Park to see what turned out to be a good game.

A main reason for the poor crowd was that the supporters had still not forgiven the Board for their high-handed decision to sack Manager Jim Leishman at the start of the season.

There was a lack of competitive edge this season as there was no relegation; the Premier League was to be expanded to 12 teams – a questionable decision, perhaps, but it had its advantages for Dunfermline!

Yugoslav Milos Drizic was given his debut today in a three-man central defence alongside Norrie McCathie and Davie Moyes, while Ross Jack was the only forward.

It did not seem to be a formula for attacking football, but it worked – eventually. Ian McCall who had a good game sent over a corner to be headed home by Moyes.

This made the score 1-1, then McCall was instrumental in the second goal soon after half time. A cross to Istvan Kozma was well dummied and the ball came to Paul Smith who scored, before McCall rounded a defender to score a third.

He then "scored" again, but it was mysteriously disallowed for reasons that had the Press scratching their heads, apparently for offside.

St Johnstone did pull one back near the end but it was a good victory in an otherwise dull season.

Dunfermline Athletic at the end of the Great War. The trainer, back, far right, was Eddie Dowie.

March 24 1962

Dunfermline had a good victory over Kilmarnock today at East End Park.

This maintained their position as third in the Scottish League and still even with an outside (although fast diminishing) chance of winning the League.

It was annoying to see Dundee (a team whom the Pars had defeated not all that long ago) still in the dogfight with Rangers at the top of the Scottish League, a place where the Pars could have been if it hadn't been for earlier lapses.

Even more frustrating had been the inexplicable loss to St Mirren in the Scottish Cup two weeks ago and this perhaps explained why today's attendance on a reasonable spring day was only 7,000.

Kilmarnock, managed by Willie Waddell, were also having a good season but were, like Dunfermline, likely to finish trophy-less.

Nevertheless there were still places in the Inter Cities Fairs' Cup at stake for both teams today, and Dunfermline opened the scoring through George Peebles in the very first minute following a through pass from Bertie Paton.

Harry Melrose went for the ball, then dummied it and Peebles was on the spot to put the Pars 1-0 up with a great deal of the crowd still queuing at the turnstiles.

There was then a dreadful mix up and comedy of errors when Dunfermline really should have gone 2-0 up.

It was not until the second half that Harry Melrose scored for Dunfermline with a header from a very difficult angle which took everyone (including perhaps Melrose himself) by surprise.

It was a good day for the Pars and with the prospect of the old stand about to be demolished pretty soon, things were looking up.

March 25 1972

A bright but slightly cold spring day, and a performance from the Pars that might indicate that all was not necessarily lost for them this year.

Alec Wright's team of gnarled veterans and raw youngsters were still bottom of the table and facing relegation.

However, having beaten Hibs two weeks ago 2-1, today they beat middle of the table St Johnstone by the same score.

It was a hard-fought but hardly classic encounter, a strange game on a hard, bumpy pitch at East End Park; the start was delayed because of the non-appearance of a linesman and an appeal had to be made to the crowd for a volunteer!

16-year-old Ken Mackie was the star of the match, heading home the first goal from a Gillespie corner, and being perpetually involved in the action.

Dunfermline went further ahead before half-time from a penalty kick when Benny Rooney of St Johnstone brought down Barrie Mitchell in the box, and Mitchell himself scored with the spot kick.

The 2-0 score line at half-time was unbelievable riches for the Dunfermline supporters, a mere 6,000 of them, who had previously all been reconciled to relegation and even saying that it would be a good thing in the long run.

There was now a chance, albeit a slim one, if they could hold out today.

They did not make the mistake of sitting back to defend, and although did concede one goal to Pearson, the Pars defence with John Cushley outstanding, held out for a victory that was much celebrated, and deservedly so!

March 26 2016

With 11 wins from 14 league games since the huge win at Somerset Park in December, coupled with Ayr's loss of form over December, tickets were being sold for next week's game at Cliftonhill, when it was considered most likely that the league title would be sealed.

It could happen today, though that would need Peterhead (19 league games unbeaten) to lose at home to Cowdenbeath, which was long odds against.

Today's visitors to East End Park were Brechin City, a side who had looked certain to be relegated until a recent run of four consecutive wins.

There looked little danger after an early goal from top scorer Faissal El-Bakhtaoui, and the Athletic were in complete control.

When the same player made it 2-0, it looked like being a routine win, but nobody accounted for the superb turnaround from Brechin.

Former Pars player Robert Thomson quickly pulled a goal back and suddenly a game that had looked one-sided became exciting and competitive with both sides playing well.

Brechin looked to have equalised late in the game but it was harshly disallowed for a push.

Meanwhile, the news from elsewhere was good – Cowdenbeath were a goal up at Peterhead so a win would guarantee the title today.

It seems ludicrous when the league was about to be won in March, but the tension around the ground was incredible until a last-minute breakaway saw El-Bakhtaoui score again for his hat-trick.

It was a great way to win a league – a genuinely good game with an exciting ending, against a good opponent who were a little unlucky not to get a point from the game.

With the league title and a return to the second tier confirmed, it somehow felt as if the recent financial collapse, that had brought about relegation, had now been dealt with.

March 27 1965

A great win for the Pars today in the Scottish Cup semi-final against Hibs at Tynecastle to see them into their second Scottish Cup final in five years.

The weather was distinctly unpleasant with wind and rain and there were wet patches in each goalmouth.

There was still a crowd of over 30,000 at Tynecastle, the size of the crowd causing the game to be delayed by a few minutes.

Pars supporters were outnumbered but only slightly, but it was the Hibs supporters who had the most to cheer about in the early stages.

Willie Cunningham's men were pinned back by a Hibs team who were full of confidence after their win over Celtic in a League match in midweek.

It was against the run of play that Dunfermline took the lead when Harry Melrose headed home a John Lunn cross, but from then on Dunfermline never looked back.

They remained on top for the remainder of the first half and then early in the second half they scored again. Once again John Lunn was involved, crossing to Alex Ferguson who nodded on to Alex Smith to finish the job.

From then on Dunfermline were professional enough to hold on, and long before the end Hibs were a beaten team, their supporters streaming out of the ground once again wondering how it was that Hibs could never do well in the Scottish Cup.

Dunfermline, on the other hand, were jubilant, although at this time they did not know who their opponents would be in the Scottish Cup final, for Celtic and Motherwell had drawn 2-2 today.

March 28 1964

68,000 were at Hampden Park today to see Dunfermline exit the Scottish Cup at the semi-final stage to Rangers.

It would have been their second Scottish Cup final in four years, but they were playing under a psychological handicap of knowing that manager Jock Stein was leaving at the end of the season.

Jock would have loved to have finished his time at East End Park with another Scottish Cup, but it was not to be.

Dunfermline started off without centre half Jim McLean but Rangers also had a couple of players injured in Jim Forrest and Willie Henderson. The weather was dull with rain always threatening.

It was possibly true that Rangers were just the better side, but Pars fans would argue that referee Tom Wharton might well have taken stronger action against both Jim Baxter and Bobby Shearer for bad fouls on George Peebles and Jackie Sinclair respectively.

Both in the event were booked but Pars fans and indeed a large section of the neutral Press felt that the long walk to the pavilion would not have been out of place in either case.

This did little to counteract the general feeling in Scotland in 1964 that the real reason for Rangers success was the lack of action taken against some of their players, Jim Baxter in particular.

The only goal of the game came just before half-time when a lob from Baxter found Davie Wilson who scored after he controlled the ball in the capricious breeze.

It was just the wrong time for Dunfermline to lose a goal. They tried hard in the second half, and once or twice came close, but it was Rangers who qualified for the Scottish Cup final. Their opponents were to be Dundee who today beat Kilmarnock 4-0 in the other semi-final at Ibrox.

March 29 2011

It was tight at the top of the first division as Dunfermline travelled to Victoria Park, Dingwall this Tuesday evening.

The season-long battle of the Fifers, where the Pars and Raith Rovers had generally been within a couple of points of each other at the top all season, was now getting especially tense.

This game was brought forward 11 days because of Ross County's involvement in the Challenge Cup final, and approaching the game Raith were a point ahead.

A point would be enough to go top on goal difference (with a game more played), but a win would be a huge result.

County had struggled in the league but had improved after the recent appointment of former Pars manager Jimmy Calderwood, and had taken a point at East End Park three weeks ago.

There isn't much to be said about the first 90 minutes of this game – nervy, edgy stuff where little of note happened, and frankly a dire football match that looked like finishing 0-0 all the way.

Second half injury time was just a bit more interesting, however. With time pretty much up, much-criticised left-back Austin McCann went on a mazy dribble up the wing and was taken down just outside the box.

Martin Hardie went over to take the free kick but eventually took up a position in the middle of the box. Joe Cardle's cross was met by Hardie himself, the header flying past County goalkeeper Michael McGovern.

The restart was delayed by some handbags in the goal net, but when the ball was finally centred, there was all of two seconds' play before the final whistle. A great night in the end, and from here on Dunfermline would never lose top spot, this being the start of a run of six wins in a row.

Harry Melrose has just scored in the Scottish Cup semi-final of 1965 against Hibernian

March 30 1966

In heart breaking circumstances, Dunfermline went down late in extra time to Real Zaragoza in the Romareda Stadium, Saragossa.

They had been 1-0 up from the first leg at East End Park, but tonight went down 4-2, the late winning goal coming only two minutes from the end of the extra time period.

This was in the Inter Cities Fairs Cup (now the Europa League) quarter final, and the Pars would have had a plum draw against Leeds United in the semi-final.

Had the "away goals" rule been in force, Dunfermline would have won, for the score at 90 minutes was 2-1 for Zaragoza.

In retrospect, Dunfermline blamed themselves for not scoring more goals at East End Park and for not adopting a more positive approach in Spain. Isasi and Marcelino had scored for Zaragoza in 90 minutes, beating the outstanding Bent Martin in the Dunfermline goal, but then Alex Ferguson had levelled the tie to take it to extra time.

Villa scored for Zaragoza, compelling the tiring Scotsmen to go for an equaliser, and then in the 101st minute, John Lunn did just that, only for Villa to score again just at the end.

It was a tragedy for Willie Cunningham's men, who had now gone out of two competitions in four days, having lost the Scottish Cup semi-final on the Saturday.

Tomorrow, once the players and fans had returned home, they would have had a chance to vote in the 1966 General Election. Adam Hunter would duly win the Dunfermline seat for Labour with a comfortable majority.

March 31 1928

It was a very bittersweet day for Dunfermline Athletic today.

Funnily enough attention would have been divided between events at the world's two largest football stadia, namely Hampden Park and Wembley Stadium.

One wouldn't have imagined that too many Dunfermline supporters would have gone to Hampden today to see their bottom of the table and already relegated side go down to another heavy defeat.

This time it was 0-4 to Queen's Park, with the newspapers searching for nice things to say about them, coming up with phrases like "hard working" and "one or two good moves, but not enough of them" for the DA side who were already planning for Division Two.

But this was not the only football match that was of interest today.

It was the day of England v Scotland playing at the new fabulous stadium called Wembley. Scotland had already played there in 1924, in 1926 the fixture had gone to Manchester instead, but today it was back at the Empire Stadium.

And there was something else, very indicative of the new age – namely something called a "wireless" or a "radio", and (incredibly) if you were rich enough, or eccentric enough to own one of those machines, you could hear a man called George Allison who was at the game talking about it!

Unbelievable but true, and some Dunfermline cafés in the High Street bought a wireless for the occasion and allowed their customers to listen to it!

So, the price of a cup of tea and a currant bun would allow you to hear this marvel. It was a marvel in more senses than one, for this was the day of the "Wembley Wizards" when Scotland won 5-1! This took the edge off some of the pain involved in Dunfermline's heavy loss.

SCOTTISH CUP — SEMI-FINAL
Dunfermline Athletic 1

v. St. Johnstone 1

Replay = 2-1

TYNECASTLE PARK

SATURDAY, MARCH 30th, 1968   Kick-off 3 p.m.

Official Programme   Price 1/-

April

April 1 1967

Spring wasn't quite here yet this dull and drizzly Glasgow day, but Dunfermline achieved the rare feat of doing a double over Rangers.

Having defeated them at East End Park in December, they now beat them 1-0 at Ibrox, a place where they don't win very often.

The only goal of the game came from Hugh Robertson about halfway through the second half after good work by Alex Edwards.

The game was a poor one with the Rangers fans not slow to voice their disapproval of what they considered to be a sub-standard performance by their favourites.

The Pars fans on the other hand left the ground full of cheer tinged with just a little regret that their team was not involved more intimately in the distribution of the honours.

This in fact was a game that neither side wanted to be involved in, for today was Scottish Cup semi-final day, but Dunfermline had gone out in the previous round to Dundee United and Rangers had infamously exited at Berwick at the end of January.

As it was, the semi-finals saw Dundee United lose to Aberdeen through an own goal at Dens Park, and Celtic draw 0-0 with Clyde at Hampden.

Celtic fans recovered from their depression at a poor show by their own team when they saw some Pars supporters at Queen Street Station and greeted them like long lost brothers, offering them drink and some of their fish supper – and all because of Hugh Robertson!

A statistical peculiarity of this game at Ibrox was that both goalkeepers were called Martin – Norrie of Rangers and Bent of Dunfermline!

April 2 1904

Dunfermline may well have wondered why they bothered travelling to Stark's Park, Kirkcaldy to play Raith Rovers today in this Fife League game.

In the first place the Fife League was by no means the most prestigious of competitions, usually played for at the end of the season when most interest in the season had gone.

Today's weather was also very poor with wind and rain, and as a result the attendance was little more than 1,500, which was considered disappointing for a Fife derby.

For some unspecified reason, presumably the weather, the kick-off was delayed for half an hour, a decision that did not go down any too well with the supporters.

It was the first time these teams had met this season, for Raith Rovers were now in the Scottish League Division Two whereas Dunfermline had spent past the past two seasons in the Northern League, albeit with only mediocre success.

They did have aspirations to reach the Scottish League someday, however, and realised the value of impressing their Kirkcaldy rivals.

Raith Rovers had the better of the conditions in the first half and were 2-0 up at half time. When the teams turned round at half-time, Raith had learned to deal with the conditions which had, if anything, deteriorated.

The game finished 2-0 to the distress and disappointment of the small crowd of Dunfermline supporters who trudged sadly back to Kirkcaldy Station with no real answer to the question of why, whatever Kirkcaldy had in the way of membership of the Scottish League, Dunfermline couldn't also have.

April 3 1968

After some Herculean efforts by the Tynecastle ground staff to get the game on, tonight's Scottish Cup semi-final replay between Dunfermline and St Johnstone proved a disappointment – but not to Pars fans!

Ian Lister's late winner at the end of extra-time was enough to put the Pars into the Scottish Cup final for the third time in the decade of the 1960s. Oddly enough, in almost parallel circumstances, Hearts did likewise against Morton at Hampden.

In a severe and unseasonal spell of weather, four inches of snow covered Tynecastle in the morning; the pitch was cleared as the snow was in any case beginning to melt.

The attendance was a miserable and frozen 9,845 fans, some of whom must have wondered at half time why they bothered, for the standard of football was far from the best.

However, things did perk up a little after Alec McDonald scored for St Johnstone midway through the second half.

Then Bertie Paton levelled things after Pat Gardner had cut a ball back to him, and then the Pars were awarded a penalty, after Lister was brought down in the box.

Poor Hugh Robertson shot too close to the goalkeeper and the same man also saved the rebound.

Robertson's misery continued when he missed a sitter in extra time, but at long last when everyone was thinking of yet another replay (no penalty shoot outs in 1968), Lister fired home a cross from Willie Callaghan.

It was a somewhat lucky victory, for St Johnstone played very well, but in a Cup tie, a win is all that really matters.

April 4 1931

The Dundee Courier on Monday would call it "promotionitis", a situation whereby a team seems set for promotion but nevertheless suddenly blows up and fails to achieve its aim.

Today at East End Park, Dunfermline once again delivered another self-inflicted blow to their promotion chances by going down 0-2 to the Stirling team King's Park.

Supporters, of course, were not slow to see something sinister in all that, arguing that the club were very happy to stay in the Second Division on the grounds that their last spell in the First Division had lasted only two years and had cost the club a lot of money.

Added to that – this was 1931, the very depth of the economic depression – there was no money in the town.

Against this, of course, was the argument that the First Division would guarantee several large "gates" and that this was the way to generate money.

In truth, today's performance against the mediocre opposition from Stirling was lacklustre and, most of the time, fitful.

"The attacks lacked smoothness, passing was often ill judged and the shooting was poor" is the rather damning verdict of *The Courier*.

In the second half with the benefit of the wind and the sun, King's Park took command and scored through right winger Duffy.

Then with time running out, Craigie, from a suspiciously offside-looking position, scored a second to send Dunfermline fans home very unhappy.

The muttering and the gnashing of teeth were fairly obvious to all concerned, but there were still another four games left to catch Dundee United for second place. Third Lanark were unlikely to be caught at the top.

April 5 1961

Dunfermline made history this Wednesday night at Tynecastle before a crowd of about 15,000 when they beat St Mirren 1-0 to reach the final of the Scottish Cup for the first time ever.

It was generally agreed that the first game last Saturday at Tynecastle had been a poor game, and this one was not a great deal better until the 67th minute when the Pars got a slightly fortuitous own goal.

It came about from an Alec Smith free kick when the ball struck Stewart on the foot but then spun upwards, hit the bar and came down clearly over the line.

The game then got a lot better with St Mirren striving to equalise and Dunfermline not making the mistake of sitting back, but instead going forward trying to add another and put the issue beyond any doubt.

There was no further scoring; the full-time whistle came to great cheers from the Dunfermline supporters whose team was now heading for Hampden and a possible 100,000 gate.

Historically, the Kingdom of Fife had generally not done well in the Scottish Cup – East Fife had been to three Scottish Cup finals and Raith Rovers only one – and the triumph of the Pars was all the more significant because St Mirren had been favourites.

The Paisley side had won the Scottish Cup twice, the last time only two years ago when they had beaten Aberdeen in the 1959 final.

Dunfermline's opponents in the final were to be Celtic, the greatest Cup fighters of them all, but the optimistic and perceptive supporters observed that Manager Stein knew the set-up at Celtic, having recently come from there, and could pinpoint their weaknesses.

April 6 1966

Dunfermline strengthened their chances of a place in next season's Fairs Cities' Cup with a 3-2 win over rivals Hibs at East End Park.

It was a fine night, and a good crowd of only a little short of 10,000 were present.

They saw a strange game in which Bertie Paton scored for the Pars in the very first minute and then the Pars retained that advantage throughout, for although Hibs equalised twice, both times the Pars almost immediately went ahead again.

Hibs' first equaliser was with a penalty kick scored by Joe Davis, a decision not 100% agreed with by the crowd, but the anger was forgotten when Paton notched his second.

Later in the game Eric Stevenson scored for Hibs, but this time it was Alex Ferguson who scored what turned out to be the winner. Tommy Callaghan of Dunfermline was lucky not to be booked for holding on to Jim Scott's jersey, and it was Scott who was unlucky enough to be booked for his perceived retaliation.

The full-time whistle came to a great roar of appreciation from both sets of fans for what had been a good game of football.

Some Dunfermline fans would always look upon 1965/66 as some sort of failure, particularly after their defeat in the Scottish Cup semi-final some 10 days ago, but in comparison to where the club had been a decade earlier, these were untold riches!

It was all a question of what people expected. European football, for example, had now become the expected norm for East End Park.

April 7 1962

Dunfermline today played in front of their biggest crowd of the season when they travelled to Ibrox to play Rangers before a crowd of 35,000 spectators.

In fine spring weather, Rangers kicked off and immediately came very close to taking the lead, but Dunfermline fought back well.

Dunfermline were currently fourth in the League and this would be their best ever finish, but Rangers were locked in a thrilling battle with Dundee for the Championship, and were currently one point ahead.

This game was therefore very important. Rangers took the lead towards the end of the first half when Davie Wilson dashed down the left wing and crossed for Maxie Murray, Rangers' sometimes despised and under-estimated centre forward, to sweep home.

In the second half, Dunfermline tried very hard, but Rangers just had the edge and if anything, came closer to adding a second than to losing an equaliser.

However the full time whistle brought a great cheer of relief from the Ibrox supporters, although the wind was somewhat taken from their sails with the news that Dundee had also won, beating Airdrie 2-1 at Broomfield.

Dunfermline had now only two games left against Third Lanark and St Mirren, but Rangers and Dundee had three each beginning with derby fixtures on the Holiday Monday – Dundee at Tannadice and Rangers at Celtic Park.

Then next Saturday was Scotland v England at Hampden. Dunfermline had reason to be happy with their season, and work was soon to begin on their new stand.

April 8 1950

How Dunfermline and their supporters must have rued their loss of form in the early part of the season!

Losing 10 games out of 30 was really an insuperable blow to any hopes for promotion, even if Dunfermline did finish strongly in the Second Division.

Promotion had gone to Morton and Airdrie even before today's very encouraging 4-2 away win over Dumbarton.

Boghead was called "fatal Boghead" because of the traditional ability of the Sons of the Rock to beat Celtic and Rangers there.

Not this season, however, which had been a poor one as Dumbarton finished second bottom.

Dunfermline however, who finished third, were looking good for next season.

McCall gave the Pars a cracking start by scoring twice in the first ten minutes, once with a header and the other with a full-blooded drive from 30 yards.

After the Sons had drawn level just after half time, Dunfermline went up a gear and scored through Mayes and then Clark to finish the game worthy 4-2 winners.

This being 1950, the crowds were huge, interest was high and there was more than a little "hype" already for next week's Scotland v England International.

Billy Liddell, Townhill born and bred, would play for Scotland in a forward line of Waddell, Moir, Bauld, Steel and Liddell.

And what was remarkable about these five? They were all called William (or Willie or Billy)!

If Scotland beat England, they would take part in the World Cup to be held in the exotic land called Brazil this summer; sadly, it finished 0-0.

The SFA decided that they would refuse the invitation and not send a team! What was the point of being Champions of the World, if you couldn't be Champions of Great Britain? Such was the tortuous, bizarre and self-defeating thinking of the SFA in 1950!

April 9 1921

This was a real red letter day for Dunfermline's Andy Wilson as he scored first in Scotland's decisive 3-0 win over England at Hampden.

This meant that Scotland had now beaten all three of the Home Countries this season, and Wilson had scored against them all!

The crowd was a little short of the six-figure mark, something that can possibly be explained by the uncertainty caused by the labour problems of the day, not least in the railway industry.

Dunfermline did not have a game that day, so quite a few Dunfermline supporters travelled to Glasgow to see their hero. His goal, when it came after about 20 minutes, was simple enough.

A hanging ball from Alan Morton drooped over the heads of all the defenders and came to the unmarked Wilson who did the needful into the top corner of the net.

It was a simple enough goal, and England had their goalkeeper, Harold Gough, to thank for several other saves from Andy.

Scotland's other two goals were scored early in the second half by the Rangers pair of Alan Morton and Andy Cunningham, and after that there was no coming back for England.

Peter McWilliam, now the Manager of Tottenham Hotspur but before the Great War, the famous "Peter The Great" of Newcastle United and Scotland, writing in *The Sunday Post,* however damns Wilson with faint praise.

He goes on to say "He's a grafter. He shoots well and he passes well". This opinion was not necessarily shared by all concerned, for certainly all of Dunfermline treated him like a hero, as indeed he was.

April 10 1926

Dunfermline today beat Bathgate 4-2 to clinch the Scottish League Division Two flag.

Quite a few Dunfermline supporters had made their way to Mill Park, Bathgate to see them do so.

The four goals that they scored brought their total for the season to 106, something that beat the previous Scottish League record set by Falkirk.

This season's success owed a great deal to the goalscoring prowess of Bobby Skinner, and indeed he scored one of the goals today.

In total Skinner, who had joined the club from Ayr United about 18 months ago, scored an astonishing 53 goals in 38 games that season, but he was not the only star as the team included men like Jimmy Stein and Joe Sutton.

The Pars were without any sort of doubt the best team in the Second Division, but some of their supporters expressed concern that promotion to the First Division might not be a good idea, given the limited resources of the club.

On the other hand, Raith Rovers (who admittedly were on the point of relegation this year) had shown that it was possible for a Fife club to do well in the First Division, and their budget and support was just about the same as that of the Pars.

No-one worried about that this particular night as the team and their supporters returned from Bathgate, as Second Division champions.

For a few years now their supporters had wondered if they really were interested in promotion, but today had settled the argument.

April 9 1969

Roy Barry exchanges pennants with the captain of Slovan Bratislava in 1969

April 11 1925

Dunfermline supporters leaving East End Park this afternoon were in two minds.

In the first place they were delighted with the performance of their team who had just defeated Stenhousemuir 3-1, but they also regretted that they had not played like this earlier in the season, otherwise they would have been challenging strongly for promotion.

Today's game was played on a bright sunny day and Dunfermline took the lead early through Skinner, then Dickson scored, then Skinner again before Stenhousemuir scored at the end.

Had it not been for Shortt in the Stenhousemuir goal, the score would have been a great deal more; clearly the emergence of a great goal scorer in Bobby Skinner was making a huge difference.

Dunfermline would finish in a reasonable position in the League this year, and the feeling was growing that a team was developing that might just be good enough to take them to the First Division next year.

There were always the two examples on either side of them, Raith Rovers and Falkirk, who had enjoyed moments in the First Division.

Of course Raith Rovers were currently over the moon about Dave Morris, their centre half and captain who had just last week led Scotland to a domestic treble of defeats of Ireland, Wales and England – a triumph in which Dunfermline, like the rest of Scotland, had shared.

Football was in a good place at the moment as the Great War now began to recede into the distance, and Dunfermline supporters were keen to grab a share of the good life.

Dunfermline Athletic Second Division Champions 1925-26. Back Row - T Burns, R Wyllie, E Miller, G Turner; Middle Row - E Douie (Trainer), Bain, Mitchell, Herd, Gibb, Wilson, Clark, Masterton, J Farrell (Linesman); Front Row - S Paterson (Manager), Ritchie, Sutton, Skinner, Dickson, Stein,

April 12 1947

The first official post-war season had been mediocre for Dunfermline, to put it mildly, and today the team travelled to Muirton Park, Perth to play St Johnstone.

They did not play badly but St Johnstone just edged home 2-1. Kinnell scored Dunfermline's goal, but Ferguson suffered the misfortune of missing a penalty kick, which would have earned Dunfermline a not undeserved draw.

It had been a strange season for the club.

Very few games had been played in February in view of the awful weather which had blocked roads and caused snow to be piled up at the side of roads and railway lines.

The club had appointed a new Manager in Willie McAndrew.

There had been some awful beatings from Airdrie (twice), Albion Rovers, Alloa and worst of all a 10-0 hammering at the hands of Dundee at Dens Park. (To be fair, Dundee were a good side and won the Scottish League Second Division very comfortably).

To-day, still visible from the railway line were piles of snow which had not yet melted, although the temperature had now risen considerably.

Scotland were playing at Wembley today in the first official post-war International, and the game ended in a 1-1 draw.

According to the Scottish Press, Scotland were "all over them", but there were other perceptions of the game as well. Prime Minister Clement Attlee, an Englishman from London but anxious not to upset the majority of Scotland who were Labour voters, said laconically "Both sides played well".

Ever the diplomat, the quiet and apparently insignificant little man Attlee is now looked upon by many people as Britain's best ever Prime Minister.

April 13 2013

This was the saddest day in the history of Dunfermline Athletic Football Club when it was announced that the club would go into full administration.

Interim administration had been in place for a number of weeks, and this was a mere confirmation of what everyone had known for some time, namely that the Pars were bust.

It was a time when the word "administration" was on the lips of almost everyone in Scottish football, the most spectacular case being that of Rangers about a year previously in 2012.

As to how it had happened with Dunfermline, it was clear that there had been a degree of maladministration, that they had over-reached themselves, that players earning large salaries were not really paying back enough in terms of achievement and that so many supporters had been alienated.

All this raised the question of the long-term prospects of full time football in Dunfermline, and even whether there would be a football team in the "auld grey toon" ever again.

Yet there was so much goodwill to the club as well, even from some supporters of other clubs at a similar level, who had been rivals on the field but who had no desire to see them go out of business.

There would be a revival – indeed the Pars would be out of administration by the end of the calendar year, but it was also clear that any rebuilding would take a long time.

And yet it was as recently as 2011 that the Pars had earned promotion to the Premier League. That now seemed to be a long time ago.

April 14 1937

This Wednesday afternoon in Motherwell saw Dunfermline Athletic relegated from the First Division after having been there for three seasons.

A draw would have kept the race open, but Dunfermline seemed to have decided to get relegated in style.

They were duly lashed 0-6 by a very strong Motherwell team who, under the leadership of John "Sailor" Hunter, were one of the crack Scottish outfits of the 1930s.

It was a normal working day; the steel factories were now back in full production making things for the war that everyone suspected was coming.

There was a very small crowd here — hardly a Dunfermline supporter there at all, for relegation had been staring the Pars in the face for some time.

The veteran left wing stars George Stevenson and Bobby Ferrier were on song today, especially in the second half after Dunfermline had done well to restrict them to one at half-time.

It was a sad day for Dunfermline, but they had never really looked like making any impact all season.

It was no disgrace to lose to Motherwell, who in little more than two weeks would dish out an 8-0 thumping to Scottish Cup winners Celtic!

Dunfermline, it was felt, would probably now revert to part-time football (they had employed a few full-timers this season) and would listen to offers for their talented right half Bob Bolt (he eventually went to Falkirk).

It was a sad day for Dunfermline supporters, but an inevitable one, and most eyes now turned to the immediate prospect of the Scotland v England International at Hampden on Saturday.

April 15 2007

Scottish Cup semi-final day was a bright and really quite warm Sunday.

Hibs and Dunfermline battled for the right to play in the final against Celtic, who had unconvincingly beaten St Johnstone the day before.

Dunfermline's League form had been shocking, but the Scottish Cup had seen a great run with surprising home wins over Rangers and Hearts, and another against Partick Thistle.

As Hibs had been inconsistent at best, Pars fans certainly felt their side had a genuine chance of making it to another final.

Stephen Kenny, appointed manager earlier in the season after Jim Leishman's resignation in the wake of an appalling home loss to Hibs, was reasonably confident.

25,336 turned up at Hampden for this one and although Hibs had more supporters, Dunfermline were far from being outshouted.

The game finished 0-0 but it was far from the worst game seen at the famous ground as both sides had their moments.

Jamie McCunnie was unlucky in the early stages of the game when he hit a post but Hibs, the Scottish League Cup holders, probably had slightly the better of it overall, with Steven Fletcher missing a golden chance early in the second half.

Right at the end of the game, Dunfermline's Souleymane Bamba made a superb clearance off his own line to force a replay.

Hibs were more disappointed than the Pars to hear the final whistle, but a draw it was, and the replay would be Tuesday April 24, again at Hampden Park, although there were those who felt that changing the venue to Tynecastle might not have been the worst idea in the world.

April 16 1958

A solitary Charlie Dickson goal at Station Park, Forfar this Wednesday night was enough to more or less guarantee promotion back to Scottish League Division One for next season.

They had been playing yo-yo between the two Divisions for a few years now, but the hope was now expressed that this time, they would go to Division One and stay there.

Tonight's game was reasonably well attended by Dunfermline supporters who went there in a fleet of buses and cars — a sign of the times — as well as the more conventional train.

Dunfermline were now six points ahead of Dumbarton.

Although they could theoretically be caught and beaten on goal average, the current goal average situation saw the Pars way ahead.

By the same token, it was unlikely that the Pars could catch Stirling Albion for top position.

It was noted that some of the Dunfermline Directors spent a long time looking at Forfar's new stand, which was being built just behind the somewhat ramshackle main stand. It was felt that East End Park could similarly do with a major face-lift, especially as the big boys were now coming to town.

But that was of little concern to the triumphant Pars supporters as they made their way home tonight.

Promotion would indeed be confirmed on Friday night (just 48 hours away) when Dunfermline beat Berwick in a game brought forward to avoid a clash with the Scotland v England International on the Saturday.

Both these games incidentally ended in a 4-0 score line.

Everyone was delighted at the 4-0 victory for the Pars, but the game on the Saturday at Hampden was one of the more depressing experiences of Scotland's sometimes lamentable footballing history.

April 17 1965

Today the Pars' League challenge (the closest they have ever been to becoming Champions of Scotland either before or since) finally came to an end.

It had been a very close race, but Dunfermline had been faltering for some time. To have any chance, they really had to win today, but they could only draw tamely with St Johnstone, while Hearts and Kilmarnock both won 3-0.

This meant that the League would be won next Saturday when Hearts and Kilmarnock faced each other at Tynecastle with Hearts the clear favourites.

Dunfermline, of course, would have the consolation of playing in the Scottish Cup final next week instead!

But today was really a rather disappointing performance from a tired looking team against St Johnstone for whom there was not little at stake.

The weather was sunny but windy, the pitch a little hard and bumpy as often happens at the end of the season.

It was St Johnstone who scored first when the Dunfermline defence made the fatal mistake of waiting for a linesman's flag as Hawkshaw slid the ball past Jim Herriot.

A few minutes after that, Alex Ferguson revived flagging hopes with a lovely chest-down swivel and shot.

The second half saw Dunfermline with the wind behind them redoubling their efforts but a goal did not come, and in any case the 9,000 crowd knew the progress of the other two games involving Hearts and Kilmarnock.

Perhaps it was a case of too many games finally catching up with the team, after 10 games in March due to involvement in Europe and a long Scottish Cup run.

Speaking of the Cup, how would today's disappointment affect them next week in the final?

April 16 1988

Gary Riddell in action in a game v St Mirren on April 16 1988. The other two Dunfermline players are Craig Robertson and Stevie Morrison

April 18 1959

This was one of the more remarkable days in Scottish football history. It was the last day of the League season, and the title and relegation were still to be decided.

Queen of the South were already relegated but the other spot seemed to lie between Falkirk and Dunfermline Athletic. At the start of the day, the two clubs were level on 26 points with the Brockville side having the better goal average.

This meant Dunfermline needed to score loads of goals against Partick Thistle and hope that Falkirk did not outscore them against Raith Rovers.

Although Dunfermline and Falkirk were in greatest danger, several other clubs were also involved.

Raith Rovers themselves were not safe, and in certain circumstances, Stirling Albion, Clyde and even Aberdeen might have gone down.

Aberdeen were in the remarkable position of needing to beat Rangers (who needed to win to lift the League title) at Ibrox to guarantee safety – and then next week they were in the Scottish Cup final against St Mirren!

Basically, all that Dunfermline could do was look after themselves, but they knew that their safety was not 100% in their own hands.

The trouble was that Dunfermline had conceded 86 goals (nearly three per game on average) throughout the season and it was generally agreed that the defence was not of the best.

In 1959, teams tied on points were separated by goal *average* not goal *difference* — "goals for" were divided by "goals against" so, under this somewhat illogical method, "goals against" were more important.

Conditions were excellent for the visit of Thistle, who did not have much to play for, and it was simply one of these days.

Everything went right for the Pars who won 10-1, Harry Melrose scoring 6 of them! Harry was playing on the wing and six goals was a Scottish record for someone playing in that position.

This would have seemed to make Dunfermline's position in the First Division secure, although there was always the possibility that it might not be enough.

In 1959 there was no instant communication as there is now, and the best hope lay in asking the newspaper reporters who could always phone their office for news of other scores.

The half-time score board told everyone that at Brockville it was Falkirk 0 Raith Rovers 1, so there were certain grounds for optimism.

One could only guess at the reaction at Brockville when they saw Dunfermline Athletic 7 Partick Thistle 0!

Back at East End Park, although double figures were reached in the second half, they still had to wait for the full-time score from Brockville for confirmation that Falkirk had not managed an unlikely second-half turnaround.

That game actually finished 2-2, and the Pars had retained their First Division status. Falkirk had a chance to win from 2-0 down, but missed a late penalty.

The excitement did not finish there however, for at the top of the League we had the bizarre situation of a Celtic win handing the League title to Rangers!

Aberdeen have never been relegated but they came very close this season – had they lost at Ibrox on the last day (as would be expected) and Falkirk's late penalty been converted, down they would have gone.

As it was, they won at Ibrox to stay up while Celtic beat Hearts, for whom a win would have given them the title. Neither Celtic nor Rangers supporters knew whether to laugh or to cry, but Pars supporters celebrated endlessly.

The irony was not lost either that it was, in fact, Raith Rovers who helped save the Pars just as much as the Pars themselves by their high scoring win.

It was therefore a day for the connoisseurs and makes a great quiz question along the lines of "When did Raith Rovers save Dunfermline and Celtic save Rangers on the same day?"

Escape from relegation could be described as an empty victory, and it was clear that long term problems still remained at East End Park, but they were for another day.

April 19 1986

Dunfermline returned to Division One (the second tier of Scottish football) after a 4-0 defeat of a wretched East Stirlingshire team at East End Park.

Ironically, they needed some help from old local rivals Cowdenbeath, who beat Queen's Park 1-0 at Hampden to guarantee promotion for both Dunfermline and Queen of the South.

The Dumfries side beat Arbroath at Gayfield.

East End Park saw a crowd of 3,298; this was huge for the Second Division against East Stirlingshire.

About half seemed to invade the park at the full-time whistle to express their happiness and gratitude to the players and to Jim Leishman for taking them from the Second Division; words like "salvation" and "deliverance" were freely heard and read about in the Sunday newspapers.

The goals were scored, not by John Watson today (although he was still at the top of the Second Division scorers), but by Rowan Hamilton, Gary Thompson, Ian Campbell and Grant Jenkins.

This result guaranteed promotion but there was still the possibility that the title could be won.

Because of the hard winter which had postponed many games, there were still four games to be played, and Queen of the South were only one point ahead.

It was a good day for Pars fans, and the weekend still had more in store because history was to be made tomorrow with the first ever live televising of a Scottish League match.

This was Hearts v Aberdeen at Tynecastle, and was part of a new TV deal agreed recently after a long running dispute.

April 20 2004

A great night for Dunfermline.

They reached their fourth final of the Scottish Cup by beating First Division Inverness Caledonian Thistle in the semi-final replay at Pittodrie.

Although semi-finals had been played on neutral grounds from 1912 onwards, this was Pittodrie's first, and it was controversial.

Everyone agreed that they did not want to go back to Hampden, but both clubs would have preferred McDiarmid Park, Perth, which was smaller but would have attracted a larger crowd, certainly from Dunfermline.

The SFA were obstinate, though, and insisted on Pittodrie.

This behaviour got what it deserved in the shape of a minuscule crowd of 5,728, the lowest ever for a semi-final, with the whole south side of the ground bereft of supporters and the rest of the ground nothing like full.

The sparse crowd did not prevent this from being a good game, enjoyed particularly by the Dunfermline supporters who left the Granite City on a high, having seen the 37 year-old Craig Brewster mastermind a 3-2 win for the Pars.

Inverness had scored early, but an equaliser came from a Brewster pass to Bullen out on the left, and a simple cross in for Darren Young to score. Then, just after goalkeeper Derek Stillie made a superb save from a close-range header, Brewster himself scored the second from a tight angle.

A solo Barry Nicholson effort, that would later draw comparisons with the famous Archie Gemmill goal in 1978, made it 3-1.

Had Inverness's late consolation goal (from the penalty spot) come a little earlier, it might have caused Jimmy Calderwood's men a few palpitations, but as it was, Dunfermline were safely through to the final to meet Celtic.

Nobody would say that this was an easy task, but there was always a chance.

Harry Melrose in 1961

Barry Nicholson scores against Inverness in 2004

April 21 2007

Scottish Cup finalists Dunfermline looked dead and buried in the relegation battle.

Now they are looking as if they might yet pull off a "great escape". 5,131 were at East End Park today to see the Pars beat Dundee United 1-0.

They generally tended to do well against Dundee United, particularly at home; today, although no-one could really get enthused about the quality of the play, the team nevertheless showed enough effort to cheer up the supporters.

It was a great feeling to be in a Scottish Cup final, but most supporters felt that survival in the Premier League was in the long term the more important goal for the club.

The only goal of the game came on the 30 minute mark, and it was scored by Tam McManus who described it thus

> Greg Shields made a run down the wing…I just peeled off the centre half to the far post, and it was a perfect cross for me. I just connected with it really well to get in a header which bulged the net.

From then on, (as relegation battles demand sometimes), it was a question of grim defending.

The Dunfermline defence who had done so well in the semi-final, held out against a Dundee United side who were no great shakes either and were themselves on the fringes of the relegation battle.

Dunfermline were still at the bottom of the league after this game, but now at least almost within touching distance of St Mirren, whom they had to meet a week come Monday.

April 22 1961

113,618 watched the Scottish Cup final today at Hampden Park.

This was the biggest crowd that the Pars had ever played in front of — by some considerable distance, at least ten times more than their average.

It was an odd sort of a day for Hampden with no sign of any wind and the atmosphere, if anything, rather sultry and thunderous.

Scotland was still living in the shadow of their notorious 3-9 defeat at Wembley the week before, but that was of little concern to the thousands of Dunfermline supporters who boarded buses and trains to take them to the ground.

This now being the affluent society, an increasing number of supporters went by car.

The rest of the town, including many people who had never been to a football match in their lives, were listening to the game on the radio, while most shops were decked out in the black and while colours of the club.

The Pars had suffered a bad blow in the week running up to the final when Tommy McDonald took ill with appendicitis; he was apparently listening to the game from his hospital bed.

Manager Jock Stein played Dan McLindon in his place. It was generally agreed that the 0-0 draw was fair in a largely undistinguished Cup final.

Celtic had the best player in Pat Crerand and more chances on goal, but on the other hand Dunfermline had two good chances in the second half.

One was when Kennedy cleared off the goal line, and the other was more or less at the end when Haffey had a good save from Peebles.

Centre half Jackie Williamson was carried off injured, and although he was able to resume, he was ruled out of the replay on Wednesday night.

April 23 2011

Three games to go.

Dunfermline – 61 points, Raith Rovers – 60 points.

Today, the two would meet at East End Park in the biggest Fife derby since 1995, when they had met in similar circumstances late in the season at Stark's Park.

On that spring day of 1995, it had been the Rovers who went into the penultimate game with a lead, but today, with the Athletic holding a single-point advantage, there was real hope that the title could just about be sealed with a win.

The excitement and anticipation during the week had been immense, and on the morning of the game came the news that the ground was a complete sell-out.

It's rare in the modern era for many fans to be in the ground early, but even by 2pm there was plenty noise coming from both ends. Mascot routines before kick-off are usually forgettable, but not so Sammy the Tammy's effort today – with "Two Tribes" playing over the PA system, Sammy wandered onto the park with a cardboard tank, and motioned to shell the away end.

Amusing to most in the ground because of the sheer absurdity of it all, including many Rovers fans who applauded it, local MP Thomas Docherty nonetheless saw fit to criticise it.

With 11,052 in the ground, it was the Pars who got the lift from the crowd and dominated the first half.

Raith Rovers were never really in it, and with their goalkeeper Andy McNeil looking extremely unconvincing, it was surely just a matter of time until Dunfermline scored.

The goal almost came in the middle of the half when a beautiful move saw Andy Kirk's volley hit the bar, but disaster struck shortly before half time.

A weak header from a free kick wasn't held by Chris Smith in goal and the ever-irritating John Baird poked the loose ball in. To be a goal down at half-time, given the way the game had gone, was incredible and an absolute sickener – but 'that's fitba', as many of us will have said with a shrug over the years.

The worry was that Jim McIntyre's Pars side might not recover from this, and indeed the record against the Rovers had not been great this season.

Both games at Stark's Park had been home wins, and at East End Park in November Raith had taken a late point after being 2-0 down. However, the January signings of Martin Hardie and Kevin Rutkiewicz had added a harder edge to the team for the second half of the season.

Although Rutkiewicz wasn't playing today after being sent off in last week's 6-1 win over Queen of the South, the team as a whole had a toughness that had sometimes been lacking when things had gone against them earlier in the season.

This was the day when it really mattered, and the second half started with a similar pattern to the first with McIntyre's Pars side committed to attack. After all the good play that went before it, the equaliser was a very basic goal, Martin Hardie heading in a corner early in the second half.

Now back level at 1-1, still Raith Rovers rarely threatened as McIntyre's team went all out for a winner. In any big game when the scores are close, it inevitably gets tense going into the last 20 minutes. We all want to be there to see our team play in these games, but does anyone with a close attachment to either side actually enjoy this period?

The one moment that was certainly enjoyable to those with black and white sympathies came with little more than 10 minutes to go. Free kick, 25 yards out, Martin Hardie – bang!

What an eruption around the ground, as the Pars finally had the lead they deserved. Further chances came to kill the game, but in the end there was the inevitable need to suffer for a few minutes with Gregory Tade, always a difficult opponent while at Raith and later at Inverness, coming close to getting on the end of crosses a couple of times in the last few minutes.

It was the ultimate 2-1 hammering and could well have been more comfortable, but that feeling when the final whistle is blown, when your team has been defending a one-goal lead in a big game, is surely the most glorious feeling in the world.

April 24 1965

A historic occasion but a major disappointment for Dunfermline today as they went down 2-3 to Celtic in the Scottish Cup final.

The day was sunny with a touch of wind about. The Pars were well represented in the 108,800 crowd.

It was one of those days when there seemed to be no-one left in the town; everyone was in Glasgow cheering on Willie Cunningham's men against those led by Dunfermline's former Manager Jock Stein.

The Pars were twice in the lead through Harry Melrose and John McLaughlin, but it was to be Celtic's day with two goals from Bertie Auld and a famous header from Billy McNeill to win Celtic's 18th Scottish Cup and their first since 1954.

And yet it was a game that might have gone the other way, particularly when goalkeeper John Fallon of Celtic saved a shot from Alex Edwards when the score was still 2-2.

Even after Celtic scored their late winner, a bit of luck might have earned the Pars a replay. But it was not to be, and Dunfermline had nothing to reproach themselves for.

The first goal came early when Dunfermline took advantage of some poor Celtic defensive work, and the second came just on the stroke of half-time when a free kick was passed from Melrose to John McLaughlin to score from well outside the penalty box.

It was generally regarded as one of the better Scottish Cup finals and Dunfermline were well praised for their part in this game but, having seen a real chance of the league title slip away last week, this was a sore defeat.

A league and cup double was genuinely on just a few weeks ago, but the best-ever season in the club's history would now end with neither.

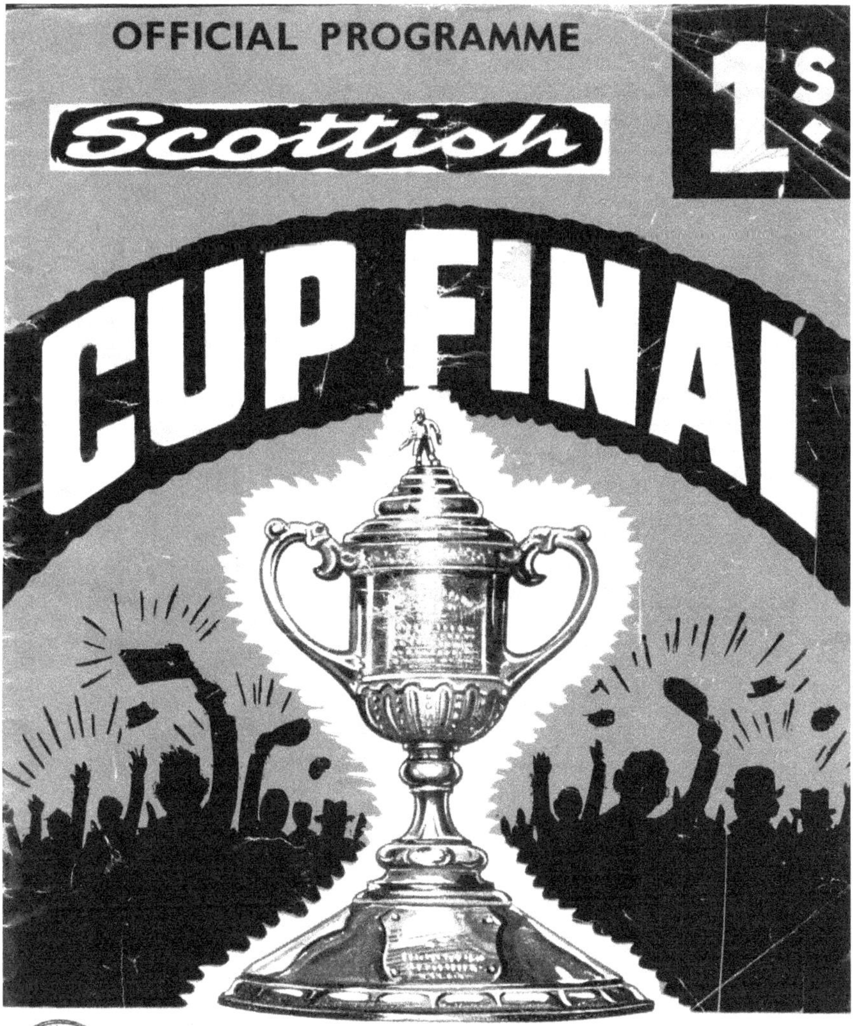
OFFICIAL PROGRAMME
1s.
Scottish
CUP FINAL
THE SCOTTISH FOOTBALL ASSOCIATION LIMITED
CELTIC v. DUNFERMLINE ATHLETIC
KICK-OFF 3 P.M.
HAMPDEN PARK. APRIL 24. 1965

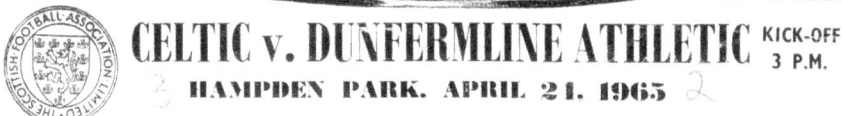

Hardie celebrates in 2011 after scoring against Raith Rovers

April 25 1936

East End Park today was in the odd position of seeing the home supporters outnumbered by the away ones.

It was the last Saturday of the season, and Dunfermline, without having distinguished themselves during the season, had nevertheless guaranteed themselves First Division football next year.

There was not, therefore, a huge turnout of home supporters but the same could not be said about Hibs and their fans.

They really needed to win today at East End Park to guarantee safety and so about 4,000 of the 6,000 fans today had come from Edinburgh, all coming off the trains with that hunted, anxious look that proximity to relegation brings.

Of course, the Hibees knew all about that, for they had recently spent a couple of seasons in the Second Division, a particular humiliation for men from the Capital!

Today on a dry, bumpy pitch (a criticism that was seldom made of East End Park) the standard of football was poor from both sides, the only player of real quality being Peter Wilson of Hibs who would, in a few years' time, become Manager of Dunfermline.

The half time scoreboard confirmed what Hibs already knew – that they really needed to win, but no goal came for either team until late in the game.

The goal when it came was an odd one – an aimless punt up the field was well ahead of the Hibs forward line, but Black chased it and when the ball bounced, he dived forward and headed the ball, catching the Dunfermline defence by surprise.

This goal released hysteria among the supporters from Edinburgh who invaded the field and needed a detachment of the Dunfermline Constabulary to chase them off.

A similar thing happened a few minutes later when, after Dunfermline had claimed half-heartedly that a ball of theirs had crossed the Hibs line, the referee blew for full time.

Dunfermline were not necessarily broken hearted at Hibs' escape, for they were near neighbours and tended to bring a large crowd.

April 26 1961

This was undeniably the greatest night in the history of Dunfermline Athletic Football Club. The Pars won the Scottish Cup for the first time.

It was generally felt that although Dunfermline had done themselves proud on the Saturday at Hampden in the 0-0 draw in their first ever Scottish Cup final, Celtic would assert themselves in the replay.

By a curious coincidence, in the same way that Dunfermline had lost Tommy McDonald to appendicitis, Celtic too lost Jim Kennedy to the same medical problem between the first game and the replay.

This meant that the Parkhead side were compelled to give a debut to Willie O'Neill at left back. They might have recalled Bertie Peacock, the aged Irishman, to bolster the defence but he was allowed to go to Italy to play a friendly for Northern Ireland.

Jock Stein, an old colleague of Peacock, and a man with a great respect for the Irishman was glad that they did!

The game was played a week after a certain drama on the world stage. The USA had seen fit to try to invade Cuba in what became known as the Bay of Pigs incident. It was a total failure and the USA were the subject of a certain amount of ridicule in the world Press, but all of this was of little consequence to the Pars supporters as they headed to Hampden that night.

Dunfermline had made two changes from Saturday. John Sweeney and Dave Thomson replaced Jackie Williamson and Dan McLindon.

87,866 were at Hampden that dull and misty night to see Jock Stein's team win 2-0 over a spirited Celtic side whose finishing let them down badly.

The first half was goalless, but after Dave Thomson stooped to score with a header midway through the second half, Celtic threw everything at Eddie Connachan.

An equaliser was surely inevitable, but no, Connachan could not be beaten; instead it was Charlie Dickson who scored at the death to clinch the biggest of all victories for the Pars.

The Celtic players accepted their defeat gracefully, but not so their fans, some of whom threw bottles and coins in an unacceptable display of hooliganism, as the white coat of Jock Stein "glowed like a

Dunfermline score first goal in 1961 Scottish Cup Final replay

beacon" at the end of the game as he watched his men, some of them with glazed eyes and clearly overcome by the moment, go up to lift the Scottish Cup, presented by of all people, Mrs Kelly, wife of Celtic Chairman Bob Kelly who was also President of the SFA.

Although there was a glow of unreality over many Pars supporters that night who simply did not believe that it had all happened, nothing could detract from the victory of the Pars.

In these pre-floodlight days, the game had kicked off at 6.15 pm, and the 8.00 pm finish allowed the team to get home before it was too late, and the rejoicings in the town were a sight to behold.

The *Courier*'s headline the following morning was the simple, prosaic one that "Dunfermline Have Won The Scottish Cup".

It was generally agreed that although Celtic had the more territorial pressure, Dunfermline were the crisper side and definitely had the better goalkeeper in Eddie Connachan, who defied the Celtic forwards time and time again.

Cyril Horne, the respected journalist of *The Glasgow Herald* sums things up well when he states that "But for all this glorious goalkeeping and for all [that] the reconstructed Dunfermline defence played with tremendous zeal and no little skill, Celtic lost the final through their forward deficiencies."

It was only the second time that a team from Fife had won the Scottish Cup – East Fife had done so in 1938 – and it was now "lift off" time for the great Dunfermline team of the 1960s.

The plans for the building of a new stand were also a sign that the club meant business and they would even be in Europe next season!

The team was Connachan; Fraser and Cunningham; Mailer, Sweeney and Miller; Peebles, Smith, Dickson, Thomson and Melrose.

Dave Thomson stooped to score with a header.

Jock Stein congratulates his players after winning the Scottish Cup in 1961

With the Scottish Cup in 1961

That year they also won the Fife Cup and the Penman Cup. Back: Fraser, Mailer, Connachan, Herriot,

April 27 1968

A disappointing crowd of only 56,366 saw Dunfermline Athletic lift the Scottish Cup for only the second time in their existence.

Today they beat Hearts 3-1 with two goals from Pat Gardner and a penalty kick from Ian Lister, as distinct from a John Lunn own goal for Hearts.

By a long way, Dunfermline were the better side and their victory was a great triumph for Manager George Farm and his team, as the Scottish Cup, once again draped in black and white ribbons, made its way back to Dunfermline for the second time this decade.

The weather was dull, but that didn't entirely explain the low attendance at the start of the game.

It did swell as the first half proceeded, but it seemed that quite a few of the fans from the east of Scotland had left it a little late.

There were a few neutral fans, but not as many as one would have liked, the situation not helped by Rangers' arrogant refusal to postpone their game against Aberdeen and allow the Scottish Cup final to have Glasgow to itself.

Youngster John McGarty was given his third game for the club, and acquitted himself admirably.

The game was goalless at half-time with *The Evening Times* summing it all up quite correctly but unkindly saying that the most polished performance on the field had been referee Willie Anderson of East Kilbride, who had kept a tight rein on things and was controlling everyone's Cup Final nerves. It was not a great first half.

But then Pat Gardner scored for the Pars, after a goalkeeping error from Jim Cruickshank. This was followed by a penalty awarded when Bertie Paton was brought down, and Ian Lister sunk the kick with no fuss. An hour had passed and Dunfermline seemed to be on easy street.

But then ten minutes later Hearts pulled one back with a deflection off John Lunn.

It was desperately bad luck for the hard working Lunn; the Hearts fans began to hope that they might yet save the day, but three minutes later Gardner settled the issue for Dunfermline with a fine shot.

The game finished with the Pars well in control with the half-back line of John McGarty, Roy Barry and Tommy Callaghan outstanding.

383

A major disappointment came in the stubborn refusal of the police to allow a lap of honour. This was in accordance with the policy at Hampden following previous rioting at a League Cup final in 1965 involving Rangers supporters, but it was hardly necessary here, and it caused a great deal of annoyance to Dunfermline players and fans as the players appeared at the tunnel to show off the Scottish Cup but were pushed back by conscientious but overzealous policemen.

The Pars had beaten Celtic, Aberdeen, Partick Thistle and St Johnstone to reach the final.

An interested spectator that day was Jock Stein, the previous Scottish Cup-winning Manager. His team, Celtic, were due to play the Pars today in the League, but the game was obviously off and Jock took his Celtic squad to watch the Cup final.

They had their own reward when they heard that Rangers had lost to Aberdeen that day and therefore Celtic had won the League.

This however was of little concern to the Pars fans on the buses and trains home that night as they lauded the praises of Martin, W Callaghan and Lunn; McGarty, Barry and T Callaghan; Lister, Paton, Gardner, Robertson and Edwards.

Sadly no player won two Cup medals in both 1961 and 1968. The town was in celebratory mode for days afterwards with Cliff Richard's "Congratulations" being sung quite a lot!

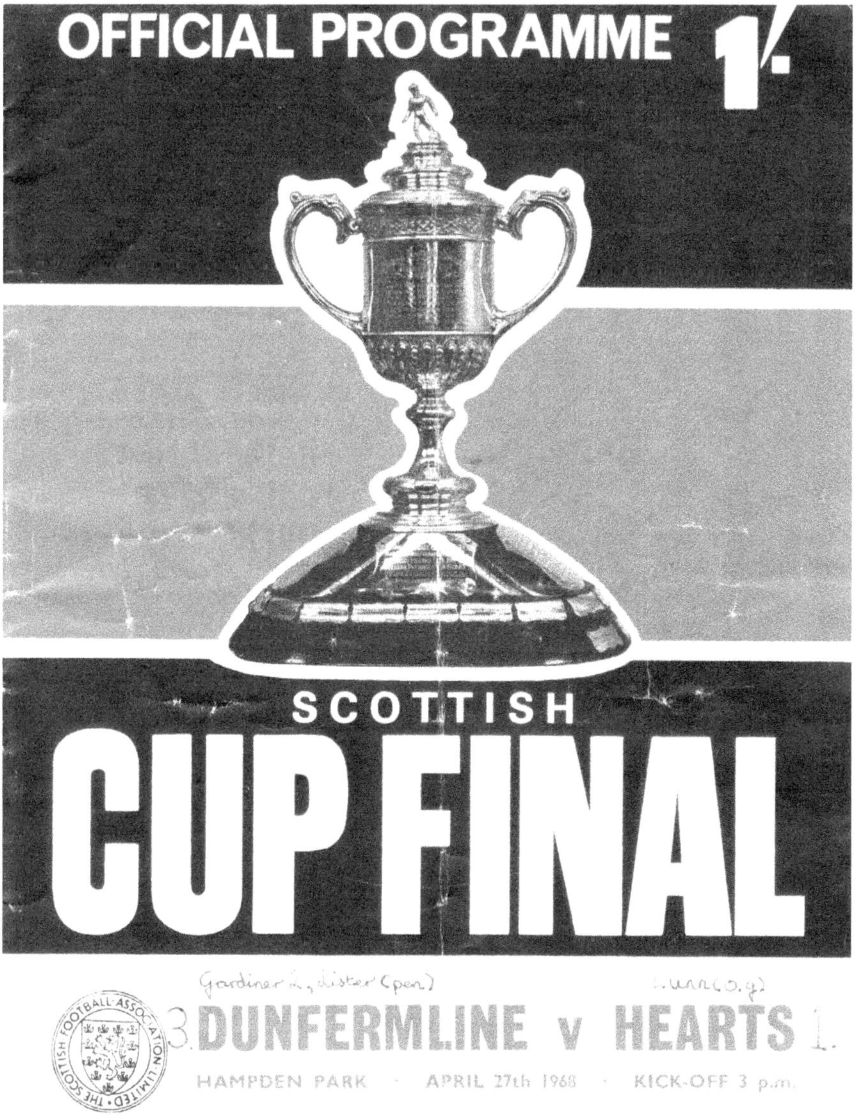

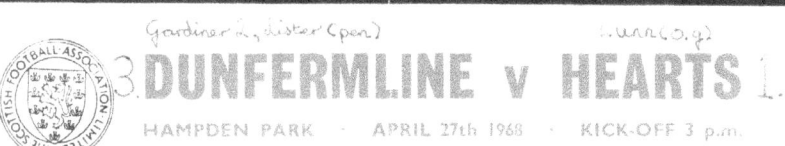

OFFICIAL PROGRAMME 1/-

SCOTTISH CUP FINAL

3. DUNFERMLINE v HEARTS 1.

(Gardiner 2, Lister (pen)) (Lunn (o.g.))

HAMPDEN PARK · APRIL 27th 1968 · KICK-OFF 3 p.m.

Glasgow Evening Times reports on two milestones

George Farm congratulates his players after winning the Scottish Cup in 1968

ATHLETIC BRING CUP HOME AGAIN

CENTRE TWICE ON TARGET

DUNFERMLINE ATHLETIC 3, HEARTS 1.

SNAPSHOTS FROM HAMPDEN

Triumphant Athletic In Jubilant Mood

TIME-TABLE OF PLAY

CUP GOALS

SKIPPER BARRY'S DELIGHT

PARK TRANSFORMATION IN SIX YEARS

NO FEARS

ATHLETIC CUP-WINNING SIDE

TOTAL GATES

A. STEVENSON
Trainer

J. METHVEN
Assistant Trainer

DUNFERMLINE WELCOMES CUP HEROES

Provost Leads Celebrations At Civic Reception

ATHLETIC CUP-WINNERS - 1968

The Dunfermline Press, May 11, 1968

Back row (left to right) — J. Thomson, J. Lunn, R. Paton, B. Martin, J. McGarty, T. Callaghan, P. Gardner; front row (left to right) — I. Lister, W. Callaghan, R. Barry (captain), H. Robertson and A. Edwards.

Paton Was Top Scorer

In the season just ended Dunfermline Athletic played 56 games in the League, League Cup and Scottish Cup—and conceded only three penalties. This is a remarkable achievement by the defence on any count but judged against the background of pivot Barry's two recent suspensions it is an amazing figure, matched only by the fact that Bent Martin saved two of them.

Though conceding only three penalties the Athletic were awarded 13. Robertson took all eight in League games and missed only one. Edwards scored from two and missed the third in the League Cup, and Robertson netted one and missed one in the Scottish Cup while Lister netted the third in the Final.

The main statistics of the season run as follows:—Played 56, won 24, lost 15 and drew seven. 66 goals scored and 57 lost. In the League 64 goals were netted and 41 conceded. In the Scottish Cup the tally was 11 4 and 13 in the League Cup 11-12.

In the League matches Dunfermline competed five doubles against Raith Rovers, Partick Thistle, Aberdeen, St Johnstone and Morton. They had 14 shutouts and failed to score themselves on five occasions—against Hibs (home and away), Rangers (away), Dundee (away) and Airdrie (home). In the six League Cup matches they had a double over Airdrie. The only teams to get League doubles over the Pars were Celtic and Hibs.

Paton was the season's top scorer with 18 goals including 15 in the League, two in the Scottish Cup and three in the League Cup. Gardner and Robertson each had 16. Other scorers were — Edwards 9, T. Callaghan 7; Fraser 6, Lister and Delaney (now with Clyde) 3 each, Lunn and Mitchell 2 each, Thomson, W. Callaghan, Kerrigan and Hunter one each, Muir (own goal).

Partick Thistle put through his own goal.

Paton had two hat-tricks and one brace, Robertson netted one hat-trick and had two braces. Fraser had a brace against Motherwell and Gardner, of course, had the best "double" when he scored twice in the Cup Final.

FINAL PLACINGS

	P	W	D	L	F	A	Pts
Celtic	34	30	3	1	106	24	63
Rangers	34	28	5	1	93	34	61
Hibs	34	20	5	9	67	49	45
Dunfermline	34	17	5	12	64	41	39
Aberdeen	34	16	5	13	63	48	37
Morton	34	15	6	13	57	53	36
Kilmarnock	34	13	8	13	59	57	34
Dundee	34	13	7	14	62	59	33
Clyde	34	15	4	15	55	55	33
Partick T.	34	12	7	15	51	67	31
Dundee U.	34	10	11	13	53	72	31
Hearts	34	13	4	17	56	61	30
Airdrie	34	10	9	15	45	58	29
St Johnstone	34	10	7	17	43	52	27
Falkirk	34	7	12	15	36	50	26
Raith R.	34	9	7	18	58	86	25
Motherwell	34	6	7	21	40	66	19
Stirling A	34	4	4	26	29	105	12

Do Athletic Need P.R.O.?

(To Editor Dunfermline Press)

The Cup Final victory confirms that Dunfermline Athletic are a team worthy of support. My Forms problem is to convey to the thousands who cheered them home into regular attenders at East End Park. I note Mr Stein has a public relations officer at Parkhead to assist him to boost his team. Celtic knows it pays to advertise. The bus stewards who week in and out organise buses from the outlying areas do a grand job. Now the Pars need a P.R.O. to cash in on their success.

J. W. ARMSTRONG
42 Middlelane Street,
Rosyth.

30th April 1968.

Boys' League

Placings in Dunfermline and District Boys League are as follows —

	P	W	D	L	Pts
Abbey View	8	8	0	0	16
Townhill	6	5	1	2	11
Blairhall Villa	6	3	2	1	8
Inverkeithing	6	3	1	2	7
Valleyfield	4	2	0	2	4
Pittencrieff	8	1	0	7	2
St Ninians	4	1	0	3	2
Halbeath	4	0	0	4	0

Wrestling

David Bell, Kelty, a member of the Rosyth Club, Dunfermline, won the silver medal in the bantamweight division at the British Championships held in London on Saturday. He won his first three bouts in clear falls and was beaten in the final by one point.

Cycling

Dunfermline & District Cycling Club's 10-mile time trial was won by Gerry Eadie in 25 minutes 7 seconds. Other times were —W. Gray, 26 min. 19 secs, and J. Marshall, 28 min 8 secs.

THOMAS C. GRAY LTD
151 High St., Dunfermline
Head Office: Edinburgh
Dunfermline 21925

DEBT Trade and Status Inquiries
RECOVERY

Pigeon Racing

LONGTOWN RACE

(Crossgates R. L. Flying Club):—
R. Watson 1191 and 1185, R. Ferguson & Son 1190.4, W. McAndres 1142, B. Gibson 1141, Kent & Gibson 1133, A. Knox 1123, W. Dewar & Son 1053, L. Mitchell 1051, T. James 1028, A. McFadyen 1014.

(Glencraig and Lochore Flying Club):—Mitchell Brothers 1307 and 1301, E. Morrison 1269, A. Hodges 1233, J. & D. Day 1240, W. Morrison 1231, A. Hamilton 1214, J. Morrison 1191, G. Stewart & Son 1149, Brown Son & King 1131, J. Finnie 1124, A. A. Stewart 1097, Comiskey 1079, A. Graham 1077, R. Brookie 1061, J. Bell 1037, F. Mitchell 1014, G. Morrison 948, Henderson Brothers 889, W. New 891.

Dunfermline Local R.P.S.:—
Knox 1244, J. & J. Forker 1222, Reid & Son 1210, Kennedy & Clark 1209, A. Williamson 1200, Barnes & Rexton 1197, W. McTair 1165, G. Dobbie 1199, J. Barclay 1167, A. Pearces 1156, R. Hutt 1154, Kilpatrick & Son 1121, G. C. Hunter 1115, Barclay & Henderson 1105, D. Dobbie 1061, Major Lock 1079, J. Frail 1061, J. Bogue 1069, B. Moodie 1051, S. Adamson 1039, H. Gozier 1003, J. Stratton 990, A. Gillon 981, Lister & Skelton 946, Watson 909, G. Hunter 901, D. Watson 897, Ferguson & Son 892, J. Philp 877, C. Seaman 836, McArthur Brothers 671.

Under-Age League

A League play-off will take place today between Railway Club and Wellwood B.C. Next Friday in the W.R.B. Cup Final, Wellwood B.C. and Oakley B.C. meet.

All clubs wishing to enter the League should apply to Mr D. Correll, 48 Izatt Avenue, Dunfermline.

April 28 2018

5,506 fans at East End Park today were beginning to nurse a few hopes that happy days were on the way back again, as the Pars clinched their place in the play-off for next year's Premiership.

Some more realistic supporters felt that the Premiership might just be a step too far too soon, but others were carried away in the excitement of it all.

Dunfermline beat Dumbarton 4-0, Dumbarton being a team who would also be involved in a play-off – but at the other end of the table.

Today, a bright pleasant sunny day, saw the Pars being given a free gift when the captain of the Sons of the Rock, Craig Barr, was sent off as early as the ninth minute for pole-axing Andy Ryan.

In days gone by, it might not have been an automatic sending off, but this was 2018 and referee Colin Steven had no hesitation.

From then on it was virtual one-way traffic with the Sons doing well to hold Dunfermline to four. Kallum Higginbotham scored twice in a seven-minute spell, the first a volley from an Aird cross and the second a curling shot which looked as if it were going past the post.

Before half time, DA were 3-0 up through Fraser Aird, and then in the second half in a game that was rapidly losing any interest for the spectators, Ryan Williamson made it four with his first goal for the club.

There was more media interest in this than might normally be expected, but it had little to do with the two teams – former player Alex Ferguson was making a return as a guest of the club.

April 29 1957

Football can be a cruel, cruel business sometimes.

Dunfermline discovered the truth of this aphorism this Monday night at East End Park.

Ayr United were already relegated, and either Queen of the South or Dunfermline Athletic could join them, depending on how they did against the Old Firm.

Queens and Pars had equal points, but the Pars had a better goal average.

In addition, Pars were at home to Rangers (already Champions, albeit in a way that had failed to impress their supporters) whereas Queens travelled to Celtic Park to play a Celtic team which had fizzled out badly after having won the Scottish League Cup last October.

Neither ground was choc-a-bloc. Celtic's attendance was pitiful, reflecting their supporters' disillusion with their team, while Rangers fans, although a few were there to see George Young's last game before retirement, had given up for the season as well.

The Celtic game kicked off earlier, and at half-time at East End Park, when the news was given that it was still 0-0 there, a cheer went up because Dunfermline were leading 1-0.

All seemed fine, but Alec Scott then scored two second-half goals for Rangers. Alex Anderson made it 2-2, but Johnny Hubbard put Rangers back ahead before Charlie Dickson made it 3-3.

The crowd knew that Celtic and Queen of the South had finished 0-0.

It was now the final minute; all Dunfermline had to do was hold out.

Then, as if Providence did not like Dunfermline or as if Nemesis was visiting them for some past misdeed, Hubbard crossed to Scott.

The ball seemed to have crossed the by-line and the Dunfermline defence stood still, but Scott managed to hook it back for Ulsterman Billy Simpson to run in and score, thus condemning the Pars to the Second Division.

This was cruel!

April 30 1887

Today at Crawford's Park Cowdenbeath, Dunfermline Athletic won their first ever Fife Cup by beating Burntisland Thistle 3-1.

This was in fact the third attempt to finish the final.

The first attempt had to be abandoned because of disorderly scenes, and the second attempt, although a better behaved occasion, had seen a 1-1 draw.

Both these games had been played at Lady's Mill Park, but on this occasion, the Fife authorities decided that the game should be played at Crawford's Park, Cowdenbeath to the distress of *The Dunfermline Press* who said "A worse choice could not have been made. A rough, uneven piece of ground, the bottom resembling a quagmire…"

It also made it a little more difficult for Dunfermline supporters to get there, but about 3,000 attended regardless, having travelled by train, horse drawn brake, dog carts; some intrepid supporters even walked the eleven miles or so!

Some were able to dodge the admission charges by watching the game from an adjacent hill.

Dunfermline won the toss and decided to play downhill. They might have been disappointed to be only 1-0 up at half time after a "scrimmage" following a Dewar throw-in.

In the second half Sandilands passed to Bathgate to make it 2-0, then Toddie made it 3-0 before Burntisland pulled one back.

The Cup was duly presented, and the players arrived home by special train to be chaired on the shoulders of supporters to the Commercial Hotel and the Old Inn.

During the week that followed the Cup was filled, emptied and refilled again many times by the "generous vintners of the town".

May

May 1 1968

May 1 1968

This morning East End Park resembled a battlefield.

Last night had seen major problems of overcrowding with some serious injuries sustained. One man was reported to be "critically ill" in Edinburgh Royal Infirmary after falling from an enclosure roof. Sadly, he would subsequently die.

Extensive damage had been done to crush barriers, turnstiles and exit gates. There was no problem of hooliganism or violence for everyone was in celebratory mode.

Dunfermline had won the Scottish Cup on Saturday, and last night Celtic confirmed that they had won the League! The gates had been locked some 15 minutes before the start with 30,000 inside and another 25,000 locked outside!

49 people were taken to hospital with injuries (mainly slight ones, fortunately) and twice the game had to be stopped as Managers Stein and Farm tried to persuade the fans to come down from the floodlight pylons and the enclosure roof!

Eventually the crowd was settled round the touch line and in the Halbeath end of the ground where the crowding was less severe. At half time, George Farm came out with the Scottish Cup, and the crowd roared as Jock Stein tried to take it from him!

The game itself was almost an irrelevance after all that but Celtic won 2-1 with two goals from Bobby Lennox as distinct from one by Pat Gardner.

Both teams received a great ovation from both sets of fans at the end, but everyone was glad to get home in one piece.

Still, it was all the price of success, as one fan put it, and totally different from the old days of the Second Division days when only a few hundred were there to see Forfar or Stranraer!

May 2 2009

Dunfermline must have been regretting their loss of form in the early spring when they lost four games in a row and won only twice between the New Year and the spring equinox.

They would also have regretted that there were as yet no play-offs for the Premier League, for they would certainly have been involved.

They would end up third in the First Division, so it was not a bad season for Jim McIntyre, although there was still a great deal of disappointment around East End Park.

Today they travelled to Palmerston Park to play Queen of the South, a team who were only two places below them.

St Johnstone had won the League by some distance, so that there was not very much at stake. This meant that both teams could play football in a relaxed manner, and this was what Dunfermline did today, beating the home team 3-0, causing the travelling fans to wonder why they hadn't done this sort of thing earlier in the season.

All the goals came before half-time. Andy Kirk headed the first one. Calum Woods then headed another, and after the much travelled and experienced Steve Tosh missed a chance to pull one back for Queen of the South, Nick Phinn powered home a very powerful drive from outside the penalty box.

3-0 was maybe a bit tough on the home side but there was no come back for them in the second half as the Pars defence held out for a good win, and gave the fans something to be happy about on the long journey home.

May 3 1998

Craig Faulconbridge will not feature highly in any list of all-time Pars greats, but if there is any truth in the old adage that "ilka doggie had his day", this was certainly true of Craig today, after his famous looping header was shown on TV again and again.

The weather was fine and sunny, and the ground was packed – but mainly with those who were wearing the green and white.

The game meant very little to Dunfermline, but it was the day that Celtic could win the Scottish League and prevent Rangers winning their ten-in-a-row.

Dunfermline supporters were offered silly money outside the ground for their tickets and in many cases took it with the result that the whole ground had a sprinkling of green and white – even at the Dunfermline end.

Rangers had lost yesterday to Kilmarnock – a Fife man called Ally Mitchell scoring a late goal for them – and a win for Celtic would guarantee them the League.

For a while all looked good for the green and white brigade after Simon Donnelly scored a fine crisp goal, and Celtic were well on top, but crucially failed to put the game to bed with another goal.

Still, their fans thought they were home and dry.

Just after the tannoy told them not to invade the park at the end came the moment that immortalised Craig Faulconbridge.

Seven minutes remained, and frantic Celtic efforts to get a winner came to nothing. Celtic would win the title the following week, but for many with the Pars at heart there were mixed emotions.

Joy at preventing another club winning a title at East End Park, but some sadness at seeing the end of terracing in the ground. Progress said some, bastardisation of a great ground said others.

Whatever your view, the game certainly marked the end of an era.

Stampede As Cup Winners And Celtic Clash

DUNFERMLINE ATHLETIC, 1; CELTIC, 2

It was almost a tragic occasion on Tuesday evening when the match of the season—the Cup holders against the League champions—took place at East End Park. After only eight minutes the players were taken off, because hundreds of teenagers had taken up a position on the roof of the enclosure. The players returned and the game resumed, but seven minutes later a crush-barrier collapsed at the north-east corner of the ground...

It Was Bound To Happen

Juvenile Cup Final Under-Sixteen

SIXTEEN ON U.S. TOUR

JAMES WOODROW
Aerated Water Manufacturer

THE CRESTA BAR
DUNFERMLINE

THE PARK TAVERN
APPIN CRESCENT
DUNFERMLINE

EAST PORT BAR
EAST PORT
DUNFERMLINE

ENGINEERING AGENCIES
HALBEATH ROAD
DUNFERMLINE

SCOTLAND'S WINNER
at the
INTERNATIONAL BREWERS' EXHIBITION, 1968

MACLAY'S EXPORT

CONGRATULATES
SCOTLAND'S CUP WINNERS

THE PARS

Maclay & Co. Ltd. and Independent Brewers; Phone Alloa 3387-8

You get VALUE from the 'PARS'
Now Try

G. & M. Supplies
(FIFE) LTD.

for VALUES

G. & M. Supplies
(FIFE) LTD.
25 KIRKGATE (opp. Abbey), DUNFERMLINE
Telephone 21706

DON'T PASS - BUY

Congratulations to the 'PARS' on a 90 minute job well done

For a DRY CLEANING job well done in 60 minutes you can't beat

Hills of Fife
CLEANING CENTRES

SUITS, COATS, COSTUMES, DRESSES
from 7/11

Man Dies After Football Crowd Disorder

Work Of The Red Cross

Honour For Mr A. B. Romanes

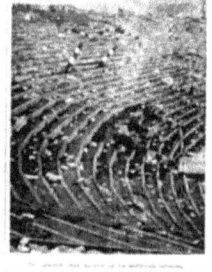

Post Office Stoppage

Havoc Wreaked In Park Tavern

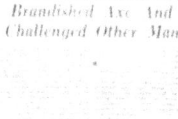

Brandished Axe And Challenged Other Man

May 4 1996

This most dramatic of seasons had, almost inevitably, gone to the last day.

For much of the season this had been a genuine five-way battle for promotion, but a loss of form had seen Dundee fall out of it long before the last day, leaving Dunfermline, Dundee Utd, Morton and St Johnstone all still in with a chance.

In reality the chances of a Perth promotion were slim; they needed to win by a big margin and hope for help elsewhere, leaving top spot (with its automatic promotion place) and second place (which meant a play-off) realistically going to East End Park, Tannadice or Cappielow.

While today's setting was dramatic, tensions a week ago had been every bit as high.

In a crucial game, Dunfermline had headed to Tannadice a point behind their opponents, knowing that a home win would almost guarantee Dundee United the title.

Given little chance by most in the media, an early opportunist goal by Stewart Petrie and some inspired goalkeeping from Ian Westwater were enough to put the Pars back top of the table going into today's last match of the season, at home to Airdrieonians.

Unfortunately, Petrie was not in the side today, having later been sent off.

Any win would be good enough to take the title, but with a two-point lead over both Dundee Utd and Morton, a slip could let either of them in; Dundee Utd also had a better goal difference.

In a quirk of the fixture list, those two clubs met at Cappielow. That game kicked off on time in front of a huge crowd of 12,523, while at East End Park there was a 13-minute delay to let in an even bigger crowd of 13,183.

Airdrie were ending a poor season in which they were about to finish just one place and two points ahead of relegated Hamilton, but the bitter rivalry between the clubs that had been a feature of recent years had not gone away.

As well as acrimony between the fans, Bert Paton and Dick Campbell had been through many battles with Alex Macdonald and John McVeigh in recent seasons, some of which had ended up in front of the SFA.

Peter Wilson, manager of Dunfermline in 1938 and 1939

With the game finally underway, there was a nervousness about the team, who were not at all convincing. However, they did manage to get a lead half an hour in, with Andy Smith heading in Marc Millar's free kick. Maybe that would settle the side, and they'd go on to win comfortably? Of course not!

If a poll had been taken as to the opposing player of that era most disliked by Dunfermline fans, Peter Hetherston would surely feature highly, and it was he who struck the equaliser.

With radios all round the ground keeping track of events at Cappielow, it looked disastrous as Dundee Utd led 2-1.

18 minutes to go, and an iconic moment. Allan Moore broke through and was taken down by former Pars keeper Andy Rhodes.

The tension as Marc Millar stepped up to take the penalty at the town end – incredible. The emotion around the ground as it went in – also incredible.

The delayed kick-off meant the result from Cappielow came through shortly afterwards – it had finished 2-2 and the Pars were champions, whatever happened at East End, but they held on for a 2-1 win anyway. It had been nervy and certainly not pretty, but that was irrelevant.

As the helicopter flew over the ground with the trophy, thoughts turned back to other things that had happened during the season, most notably the tragic death of skipper Norrie McCathie in January. The widespread feeling was 'we did it against the odds, and we did it for Norrie'.

To recover from a setback as severe as losing your captain halfway through the season was incredible – what an effort from the players and management. This was the most remarkable of seasons – Pars fans who saw it are unlikely to see anything quite like it again.

May 5 1938

Today *The Courier* announced that Dunfermline Athletic had appointed 33 year old Peter Wilson to be their player-manager in an attempt to get back up to the First Division.

Times were desperate for Dunfermline.

1937/38 had seen a season of depressing mediocrity in the Second Division. That was not in itself all that unusual for there had been many other poor seasons before then. This time there was the complicating factor that the other Fife teams had done well.

Raith Rovers had won the Second Division with a degree of comfort, and East Fife had actually won the Scottish Cup, the only team to have done so from the Second Division, and the only Fife club ever to have done so.

Such successes for one's rivals often leads to statements of breathtakingly awful cant and hypocrisy like "It is good to see local teams doing well" – all for the benefit of the naïve, but the real emotion experienced by the fans is one of jealousy.

The Board appointed Peter Wilson because he had been a great player with Celtic and latterly with Hibs, and he certainly knew the game of football.

He was still young enough to be able to play, but in practice a bad ankle injury curtailed his appearances for the Pars. An Ayrshireman from the village of Beith, Peter was a great admirer of Robert Burns, but he was also looked upon as one of the best passers of a ball that Scottish football had ever seen.

Sometimes called "Celtic's country bumpkin" because of his rustic demeanour and the famous occasion where he got lost in Woolworth's department store in Glasgow, Peter was nevertheless looked upon as a great asset to Dunfermline in their quest to return to the top division.

May 6 1989

Dunfermline today took a faltering and uncertain step towards winning Division One of the Scottish League and gaining promotion to the Premier League.

10,000 were at East End Park looking for the win that might have seen the Pars do the needful, but all they saw was a painful 1-1 draw against Clyde.

A goal by John Watson was balanced by a bizarre equaliser when goalkeeper Ian Westwater clutched a header from Jim Rooney and then stepped back over his own line with the ball in his hands.

Hugh McKinlay of *The Glasgow Herald* was puzzled by two things about Jim Leishman – one was his almost monastic vow of silence, and the other was his strange team selection which contained three centre backs and two full backs, something that was odd in a team going for promotion and needing to win a game against relegation threatened Clyde.

The really depressing news for the 10,000 Pars fans was Falkirk's 7-1 thrashing of already relegated Queen of the South.

Falkirk were the only team that could catch Dunfermline, but a point next week against Meadowbank would do the trick for the Pars.

Falkirk were two points behind but had a better goal difference. Only two points for a win in 1989, but if they beat Forfar at Station Park next Saturday and Dunfermline lost to Meadowbank, they would triumph.

Nervous times indeed at East End Park!

The Glasgow Herald then gets carried away by its own rhetoric when it talks about there being more nervous wrecks among the Dunfermline support than there were under the volcanic ash at Pompeii in 79 AD.

May 7 1988

Defeated and relegated, Dunfermline fans nevertheless revealed a touch of class in their sporting demeanour at Celtic Park today.

Celtic had won the Premier Division of the Scottish League a few weeks ago, and the Pars had been relegated about the same time.

This game at Celtic Park therefore meant nothing, but it became a celebration party for Celtic, and Dunfermline were invited.

They came in large numbers and two banners caught the attention. One said *Happy Birthday Celtic. PS Jim, We'll be back.*

It was Celtic's centenary season, hence the reason for the Happy Birthday wishes, and the other was a reassurance to Jim Leishman that they would return to the top tier!

The other said *Auf Weidersehen, Premier Division. PS Congratulations, Celtic* – the *Auf Weidersehen* being a reference to the long running "Auf Weidersehen, Pet" TV soap opera of the day.

Such chivalrous behaviour earned Dunfermline a round of applause from the Parkhead crowd, who had a soft spot for the Pars in any case, because of the Jock Stein connection and also because Dunfermline had put Rangers out of the Scottish Cup this season!

After all that, it was a shame that the game was a poor one. Chris Morris scored for Celtic early on and after that the game fizzled out, with Celtic not exerting themselves over much as they had the Scottish Cup final next Saturday against Dundee United.

Neither did they have any great desire to humiliate the Dunfermline side who were described as "workmanlike but uninspired".

Jim Leishman was carried to his fans by stewards (incredibly!) for congratulations, and given a round of applause by the Celtic fans as well.

The prediction did indeed come true. Twelve months later, the Pars were back in the top tier, having won the First Division.

May 8 1912

Clear signs of ambition are emanating from East End Park these days.

Two important decisions were made at a meeting tonight chaired by Mr James Farrell, the president. One was the decision to buy the playing park from its owners.

This would not be easy but Mr Alexander Haxton was convinced that he could find subscriptions of £1 each from 250 people, and that the committee could then be empowered to enter into negotiations to purchase the playing field.

This was good news, but of even more interest to the football fan was the letter from Mr Thomas Gray of St Bernard's, currently Chairman of the Scottish League.

The decision had been taken to increase the Second Division from 12 teams to 14 teams; he wondered if Dunfermline Athletic would be interested in applying for one of the extra places.

With one dissenting voice, it was decided that the club should apply for membership. It was clear from this that the club felt that it had to make progress, and that the Scottish League was the place to go.

Although Dunfermline Athletic represented quite a large geographical area, there had also been the feeling that Dunfermline was in danger of becoming a footballing back water.

There were quite a few other more successful clubs in their area with Raith Rovers to the east, Falkirk to the west and Cowdenbeath on their very doorstep.

Raith Rovers and Falkirk in particular were from towns of comparable size and were now in the First Division, with well attended fixtures from the large clubs from Glasgow and Edinburgh.

May 9 1998

An eventful season came to an end today with a 0-2 defeat by Hearts at Tynecastle in the sun.

There was not a great deal at stake for the Pars today.

They had guaranteed their Premier League status a few weeks ago with a series of tense draws and then a win over Motherwell, meaning that Hibs were the club to be relegated, a matter of no little pleasure to the Hearts fans in the 13,886 crowd in the Edinburgh sunshine.

This was not yet the end of the season for Hearts, however, because they had a Cup final date with Rangers at Celtic Park next week.

Dunfermline had started the year well with a rare win at Celtic Park then home wins over Hearts in both league and League Cup.

There had been a midwinter sag which included five defeats in a row. That looked like relegation form, but Bertie Paton had rallied the team and relegation had been avoided.

Andy Smith had scored 16 League goals and 26 in all; a feature of the season had been the goalkeeping of Ian Westwater who had been a consistent but seldom flamboyant character who had saved the team from quite a few hammerings.

Today Hearts were well on top with goals from Adam and Holmes as they geared themselves up for their big date next week, but for Dunfermline, survival was good enough.

Staying up meant that the club would be founder members of the new SPL starting in August, a move that saw the top division break away from the 108-year-old Scottish Football League.

It may have been inevitable after the success of the English equivalent since its formation in 1992, but many considered it a sad moment for Scottish football.

May 10 2003

A crowd of 5411 were at Dens Park, Dundee to see a good game between Dundee and Dunfermline which ended in a 2-2 draw.

There is always something nostalgic about a trip to Dens with its strange obtuse angled grandstand and the recollection that they had once taken the league title, in 1962.

Although today was a "top six" game in the Scottish Premier League with not really a great deal at stake, there was an unusual buzz about Dens Park.

Dundee had, for the first time since 1964, reached the final of the Scottish Cup, having beaten Inverness a few weeks ago, and were due to meet Rangers in three weeks' time.

Dundee went ahead in this game from the penalty spot. It was a soft award according to the Pars supporters, when Scott Wilson was adjudged to have fouled Mark Burchill. Steve Lovell scored for Dundee.

It was well into the second half before Steve Crawford levelled matters after a fine pass from Barry Nicholson. The Pars' joy did not last long, however, for almost immediately after that, Lovell scored again and for most of the rest of the game Dundee looked worthy winners.

They made, however, the fatal mistake of not scoring again to settle the game, and the Pars who had looked a beaten team for much of the second half were able to equalise when Lee Bullen snatched a goal from close range.

The trip home was all the happier because of that.

Late comebacks had been a feature of recent trips to Dens – the previous visit in November had seen a 3-2 win from 2-0 down and the time before that brought a last minute equaliser, also from 2-0 down.

May 11 1921

Today the Scottish League made its momentous decision to reform a Second Division of 20 teams with automatic promotion and relegation to the First Division, eventually two up and two down each year.

Dunfermline Athletic, then playing in the Central League, were naturally invited to rejoin and accepted the invitation for it would give them the opportunity of one day playing among the elite of Scottish football, something that a team from a town the size of Dunfermline should naturally aspire to, it was felt.

Although this was good news for the club, there was going to be one major drawback and it concerned the talismanic Scotland International Andrew Wilson.

He was technically a Middlesbrough player, but Dunfermline had been able to use his services illegally as long as they played in the unofficial Central League.

The Scottish League was of course official, so Wilson would not be able to play there. In any case there had been a certain dubiety as to Wilson's own feelings on the subject, so Dunfermline probably decided that there was no future for him in any case.

Putting the Wilson issue aside, there was little choice about returning to the Scottish League, for everyone else seemed to be moving there and the club would have no opponents otherwise.

Twenty teams would mean 38 games, and there would be little time for very much else in the season. On the other hand, the Scottish League did have a certain prestige about it, and it did offer a tremendous opportunity.

May 12 2007

Anyone who regularly follows their team away from home knows the crushing feeling experienced on the way home from a painful loss, but the phrase 'a long trip home' was meant for this day.

The Pars had been bottom of the league since November and had a terrible run of league results, but now somehow looked to have hope of survival after wins against relegation rivals Motherwell and St Mirren in the last two weeks.

In this away fixture at Inverness, things looked good at half-time as the Pars led through Jim McIntyre's goal, while St Mirren were a goal down at Fir Park.

St Mirren went 2-0 down early in the second half, and there was real excitement as everyone knew that if things stayed this way, Dunfermline would come off the bottom for the first time in six months.

It wasn't to be. St Mirren came back to win 3-2 while Dunfermline conceded the most awful of equalisers.

Goalkeeper Dorus De Vries, a real standout in a struggling team for most of the season whose saves had kept his side in many games, allowed a simple shot to slip through his hands.

Why did it have to rain and make that ball slippery?

With news coming through that St Mirren had won, a draw at Inverness was of little use, but a minute from time a Rory McAllister strike gave the home side the points and guaranteed relegation for Dunfermline on the day.

Although there was still a Hampden cup final to come, this was a painful loss. The trip back down the A9 was in near-silence for many.

May 13 1989

This was a classic last-day-of-the-season situation.

Going into the game, Dunfermline were top of the First Division, two points ahead of Falkirk.

In early December such a finish looked unlikely as Athletic sat in the middle of a very tight league before an incredible 3-month run of 11 wins in 12 league games pushed them to the top.

Dunfermline would be champions if they could take two points from the last two league games, but after letting a lead slip against Clyde in the first of these, the last day saw Falkirk still in with a chance if they could beat Forfar at Station Park.

Jim Leishman's side were at home to Meadowbank, a team who had won at East End Park in October, but with the Pars needing only a point there was great expectation of a title win as Saturday approached.

As is so often the case, it was a nervy experience, made all the worse as the visitors went a goal in front.

However, if there was to be one Pars player from the 80s you'd want in your side when you desperately need a goal, John Watson would surely be that man.

Attacking the goal at the Cowdenbeath end, Watson would run onto a through ball and hit it past the keeper for the equaliser, to great relief around the ground.

1-1 would be the final score, though in any case Falkirk had only managed a point at Forfar.

It was enough to send Dunfermline back to the Premier Division, and to confirm the near legendary status that Manager Leishman was enjoying, continuing the job he started in 1983 with the club stuck in the bottom division.

May 14 1983

Dunfermline have changed divisions more than most clubs in Scotland but, despite all the practice, relegation on the last day of the season never gets any easier.

Going into the last day fixtures, there was still a slight chance of escaping, with the Pars sitting a point behind both Ayr and Clyde who met at Shawfield.

It had been a tough season with a particularly sore point being a 6-0 loss to Raith Rovers on New Year's Day. Partly as a result of that, goal difference favoured the other teams.

Only a win would do and, even then, a draw in the other game would see both Ayr and Clyde safe, putting survival at long odds against.

When you have to win on the last day, you'd probably prefer to play a side in the middle of the league with nothing to play for; instead it was a short trip to Muirton Park, Perth, to take on a St Johnstone side needing a win to take the first division title.

The Perth side had enjoyed a good season and were certain of promotion along with Hearts, but with only a point between them, this was an important game for the Saints also.

The game went very much to form, with the title going to Perth after a comfortable 2-0 win.

Athletic's loss made conspiracy theories irrelevant — Clyde and Ayr might have agreed a draw — and Clyde won 3-2 in any case.

Speaking to *The Dunfermline Press* in the days after the game, club Chairman Jimmy Watters noted that relegation had been particularly disappointing.

Costly changes had been made at the start of the season in an attempt to set the club up for promotion back to the top tier. Instead, it was going to be another spell in the bottom division.

May 15 1993

For a spell in the early/mid 90s, Dunfermline were often referred to as a team of bottlers.

This was largely unfair, but in 1992/93 it was very much a valid criticism.

A good Raith Rovers team, easily their best since the 1950s, won the First Division comfortably, but the second promotion place had been there for the taking.

In the end it came down to a fight between the Pars and Kilmarnock. As Killie stuttered towards the season's end, the Pars completely fell apart.

Two weeks ago Cowdenbeath, long since relegated, had won 2-0 at East End, while last week a visit to Boghead had brought only a point.

The result was that Kilmarnock, five points adrift not too long ago (two points for a win still applied), went into the last day with a one-point advantage and better goal difference.

A home win over Morton was therefore essential with some help also needed elsewhere.

After dominating the early play a goal for Jocky Scott's Dunfermline side looked likely, but, as had been the case so often of late, it did not come.

As Morton came back into it, they inevitably went ahead, even though it was an own goal. Heads down, game over.

A second goal followed before a late consolation gave a final score of 2-1. The match report in *The Courier* noted that "the game, having started in a downpour, ended in a torrent of abuse for the home bosses."

With the loss of this game and promotion missed, it was only a matter of time for manager Scott and assistant Gordon Wallace.

Both were sacked four days later – Scott expressed disappointment at the decision and claimed to have done well given the resources given to him. Many wondered if he'd been watching a different game.

May 16 1979

Tonight, Dunfermline clinched promotion from Division Two with a high-pressure draw in front of a 6,000 crowd at East End Park.

Dunfermline were two points ahead of third-placed Falkirk while Berwick Rangers had already won Division Two.

Normally the Leagues would have been settled by now, but 1979 had been a terrible winter and the Pars had gone from December 9 until February 24 without playing a League game.

The games had been caught up, and the end of the season was an exciting one.

Dunfermline suffered an early set back when captain John Salton was taken off with a leg injury, and half-time was reached with the game goalless, something that would have suited the Pars.

But then Perry scored for Falkirk with a header from a free-kick and the tension visibly rose around East End Park.

In the 65th minute, a net bound shot from substitute Jim Scott was punched away by a defender and Alex McGunnigle of Glasgow correctly pointed to the spot.

In an unbearable atmosphere with many supporters looking away, up stepped the calmest man on the field, right back Andy Rolland, now in the veteran stage of a lengthy career with Dundee United, Cowdenbeath and Dunfermline to slot the ball home.

There was still a considerable amount of the game to go, but Rolland now took charge, calming everyone.

Eventually the referee eased the pressure on the bladder and the bowels of everyone by blowing for full-time and First Division football next year.

Ecstasy swept the ground, and the police were unable to prevent a police invasion.

It was enough to make everyone forget that two weeks ago Mrs Thatcher had won the 1979 General Election!

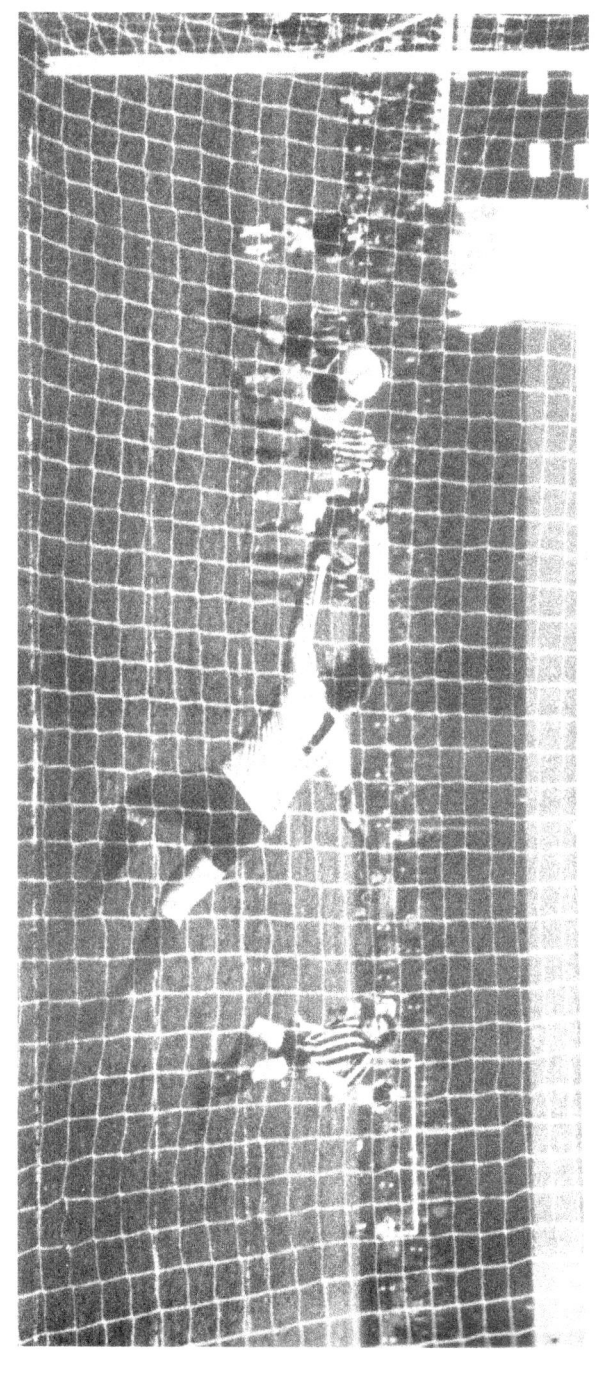
Andy Rolland scores with a penalty against Falkirk in 1979

May 17 1926

Heady and unusual, not to say confusing, times in Dunfermline!

The dust seemed now to be settling after The General Strike which had fizzled out towards the end of last week.

This Monday morning, with everyone — apart from the miners — now apparently back working, Dunfermline Athletic's Manager Sandy Paterson was able to announce that the club had managed to re-engage all their players from last season's triumphant capture of the Scottish League Second Division, apart from Gibbs, the goalkeeper.

This was good news, particularly the fact that Bobby Skinner had been re-engaged. He was the man, with his prolific goal scoring, who had lit up the town, brought the crowds to East End Park and guaranteed that for the first time ever, the Pars would be playing in the top tier of Scottish football.

The football season was now well and truly over, although junior and juvenile games would continue for some time yet.

It was now time to bask in the triumph, made all the sweeter in the minds of some supporters, although not the club officials, by the knowledge that Raith Rovers had been relegated.

It was perhaps something to gloat about, but the reality was that it meant that Dunfermline Athletic would miss out on two derby games and bumper gates.

The task that lay ahead next season would be a difficult one, but all that Dunfermline had to do was to finish third bottom!

The fact that the miners were still on strike was ominous, however, for it looked as if this particular strike was going to be a long one, and it meant that many Dunfermline supporters would not have the money to go to football matches.

May 18 2014

With long-standing financial issues finally catching up with the club in 2012/13, Dunfermline had been relegated to the third tier for the first time since 1986.

With a youthful side, 2013/14 had been an exciting season with many high-scoring games, finishing the league season second behind Rangers.

So to the play-offs, where the Pars eventually got past a good Stranraer team after extra time in the semi-final, giving them a final against Cowdenbeath who had finished 9th in the division above.

The original play-off schedule had the first leg at East End Park in midweek but with a Central Park stock-car meeting already arranged for the weekend, the two games were reversed.

The midweek leg at Central Park was not thrilling – one that looked like 0-0 all the way until two near-identical late goals from long throws meant that it finished 1-1.

A crowd of 8,000 were inside East End Park for the decisive return leg and were lively as the referee's whistle blew to start the game.

It was Cowdenbeath who would start the better. Winning a free kick inside the centre circle straight from the kick-off, the kick was lofted into the box where it would break for Hemmings to score inside 30 seconds.

From there on, Cowden were comfortably the better side and deservedly won 3-0.

For those with Dunfermline connections it was a particularly painful loss, as they were left to contemplate another season in what was now called League One, the new name for the third tier of Scottish football.

May 19 2013

Shorn of experienced players after redundancies due to entering administration, the Dunfermline team that completed the league season was a young one.

In the six games played, their record was a very reasonable 2 wins, 2 draws and 2 losses.

With a 15-point deduction to contend with, however, it was not quite enough and after losing at home to already-relegated Airdrie on the last day, combined with a surprise Cowdenbeath win at Hamilton, Dunfermline were forced into the relegation play-off position.

After the semi-final first leg, relegation seemed inevitable when Forfar played superbly to go 3-0 up at Station Park in what was an absolute hammering.

The second leg reversed the situation; the Pars won 6-1 after extra time, Forfar finishing the game with only eight men.

So to the final against Alloa, the side who had finished second in the league below. Alloa had a strong, experienced side including Calum Elliot and less-than-popular ex-Pars player Stephen Simmons.

In the first game they were simply too strong, running out 3-0 winners at Recreation Park after the kick-off had been delayed to let the crowd in. So to today's second leg at East End Park.

There was still that memory of last week's great comeback, but a repeat was heavy odds against as Alloa were a better side than Forfar. And so it proved.

On the day it was a 1-0 home win, but in truth Alloa were rarely in danger and were comfortably the better side over the two games.

Despite being relegated, the team were applauded off the park, recognition of the efforts of that young side who had really been dropped in at the deep end.

Back in January, a win at Dumbarton put the club top of the league, yet the season had now ended in relegation and a summer of uncertainty awaited.

Would the Pars survive until the start of the next season?

May 20 1937

There seemed to be no end to the woes of Dunfermline Athletic.

Season 1936/37 had brought relegation from the First Division with two losses out of 38.

As if this was not bad enough, the club announced today ahead of next week's AGM that a loss of £1416 had been sustained, thanks mainly to the drop in gate income, which was £2097 down on last year.

It was clear that a situation like this could not go on. Amid renewed speculation about the future of the football club, a motion was to be brought before next week's AGM that in order the safeguard the maintenance of professional football in the town, any future Directors would be required to be guarantors to the bank for the liabilities of the club.

This was an ill-disguised attack on some perceived corruption and pocket lining which was suspected to be going on at the top level of the club.

Whether it was true or not, this motion did mean that any future Director would have to make a financial commitment to the club, £200 as it turned out.

All this was a lot of money in 1937, but it was a grave situation for the club.

In the meantime the beleaguered Manager David Taylor, whose job was now in serious danger, made an appeal to the fans to get behind the club for the new season.

The worst of the economic recession had now passed, and unemployment was now fast disappearing, so there was no reason why this might be no more than a temporary dip in the fortunes of the club.

May 21 1995

Promotion/relegation play-offs were a new thing in 1994/95, and after finishing second in the First Division, one point behind Raith Rovers, Dunfermline took part in them.

Opponents were Aberdeen – having had a terrible season in the top division, a late run of form had seen them overtake Dundee United and finish second-bottom.

Unlike the present-day format, this was a straight home and away battle between second-bottom and second-top, and today the first leg took place at Pittodrie.

Pars fans had queued from the early hours of Wednesday morning for the 2,500 tickets.

Their team missed two chances to take an early lead. As Aberdeen got on top, future Par Stephen Glass scored the first goal with a free kick shortly before half-time, but Craig Robertson's early second half header from Allan Moore's cross had the Pars level.

Not for long though, as Duncan Shearer scored seven minutes later and again near the finish to give the home side a 3-1 first leg lead.

The moment many Pars fans remember came at 2-1. Running onto Robertson's ball over the top, Moore seemed to be blatantly taken down by Stewart McKimmie – a stonewaller penalty, surely!

Play on, said referee Les Mottram.

Mottram is more famous for a howler at Firhill where he missed both the ball going into the goal and rebounding from the stanchion, and a defender subsequently picking it up with both hands to boot up to the halfway line for the restart; the penalty decision at Pittodrie was not as bad as that, but it infuriated the Pars fans in the ground.

Having survived a scare in the first game, Aberdeen were comfortably the better side in the East End return leg, winning 3-1 again.

Crowds of 21,000 and 15,500 showed that play-offs could be popular, but for Bert Paton's Dunfermline, it was the second good season in a row to finish in tough circumstances.

May 22 2004

It was like old times again as Dunfermline supporters headed to Hampden this fine day.

Hampden had of course changed totally since Dunfermline's last Scottish Cup final in 1968.

The ground was now all-seated and Dunfermline fans filled the West end of the ground and part of the main stand.

For a while, it looked as if a major shock was to be on the cards in this, Dunfermline's fourth Scottish Cup final, but after being 1-0 up at half time, favourites Celtic took over and came back to win 3-1.

The half-time lead came from a looping header by Andrius Skerla from a Gary Dempsey corner. Celtic claimed unconvincingly that their goalkeeper David Marshall had been fouled, but the truth is that he just took his eye off the ball.

Hopes were high but then, crucially, referee Stuart Dougal failed to spot a Bobo Balde handball from another corner.

Blatant though it was in the TV replays, many in the crowd also missed it, including Pars fans at that end of the ground.

Being denied a penalty for the chance to go 2-0 up was bad enough, but it got worse straight away as Celtic broke straight up the park for the inevitable Henrik Larsson goal to equalise.

He scored again, and then Stilian Petrov finished the job for Celtic.

Manager Jimmy Calderwood was happy with his team's efforts and said it was a great occasion just to have been in the Scottish Cup final.

It was in fact Henrik Larsson's last game for Celtic before moving to Barcelona.

May 23 1935

Today at Dunfermline Police Court, two young men were fined for what was commonly known as "swicking in" or in more polite terms, entering East End Park without paying for admission at a game against Cowdenbeath.

The actual date of the game is not mentioned but it must have been a Fife Cup game played at the end of the season, for the two clubs were in different Divisions in 1935.

They had done so by climbing a wall, and claiming unconvincingly that there were only five minutes left of the game.

That cannot have been true, because the normal practice in any case had been to open the exit gates with 15 minutes to go to let the crowd out, so they could have simply walked in.

In any case, when apprehended, one of them, Thomas Beattie — a labourer of 41 Whirlbut Street — had asked to talk to Mr Knight, the Dunfermline Manager, on the grounds that he paid 30 shillings per week here, meaning that he had a bookmaking stand at the greyhound racing!

The other accused, Alexander Murray — a fishmonger, of 109 Brucefield Avenue — had nothing to say.

Mr JH Wright, the Procurator Fiscal, said that the club had been put to a great deal of expense and trouble with people who entered the ground illegally (and he might also have added that the club needed every shilling they could get!)

Baillie Miss Frew imposed a fine of 15 shillings on Beattie, who was something of a serial offender with a previous admitted conviction, but she was a little more lenient on Murray who was fined 2 shillings and 6 pence.

The admission money would have been a lot cheaper.

May 24 2018

Tonight in the Purvis Suite at East End Park, the Dunfermline Athletic Supporters Council, under the Chairmanship of John Russell, had the opportunity to ask questions of various members of the club's establishment — like Chairman Ross McArthur and Manager Allan Johnston.

In addition Dave Dawson talked about the Schools Engagement Programme, and in particular the victory in the "Best Community Project" of the SPFL Trust.

The Chairman said that 2018 had been not a bad season although there had been disappointments.

Fourth position indicated that things were moving in the right direction and certainly the improvement since a few years ago had been significant.

The fans were thanked for their support, as indeed were the volunteers who did all the jobs that were necessary on match day.

There had been hard luck in the play-off against Dundee United, and also the winter had seen a number of postponements. The average home attendance had been 5,318.

Although the team had been hammered at Ibrox in the Scottish League Cup, the game had been watched by a crowd of over 35,000, which had been significant for Dunfermline's financial position.

For his part, Manager Allan Johnston was asked questions about various players, and impressed everyone by his candid answers, particular on the issue of players being offered contracts.

Next year was going to be difficult because there were to be at least three clubs in the Championship – Ross County, Dundee United and Partick Thistle who had bigger budgets than Dunfermline.

It was a very informative evening and good public relations for the club.

May 25 2003

A controversial day as Dunfermline, safe in the top half of the SPL and with nothing to play for, headed for the last game of the season at Ibrox.

The game was far from meaningless for their opponents however, with Rangers and Celtic level on both points and goal difference going into the game.

Things looked ominous as the home side took an early lead, but a great strike from Jason Dair had the Pars level soon after.

Parity would sadly last for only five minutes, but at 2-1 Stefan Klos made a fantastic save from a Craig Brewster shot to prevent a second equalizer.

Although competitive for much of the game, things fell apart in the last half hour with the game finishing 6-1.

Rangers took the title on goal difference by a single goal, Celtic having won 4-0 at Kilmarnock.

Speaking immediately after his game finished, Celtic striker Chris Sutton, referring to Dunfermline, said "we knew they'd lie down and they have done" causing a fair amount of anger in Fife.

No doubt the comments was coloured by intense disappointment at missing out on a league title so narrowly, but many felt it was way out of order.

The SFA agreed, and suspended him for one match for the comments; more than 15 years on, it's a game that still causes arguments.

Football fans can have long memories, as Sutton himself was reminded when he walked past the away fans on his way to the camera gantry at a Dundee-Dunfermline league cup game in 2018!

May 26 2007

No-one would exactly say that 2007 was a vintage year for Dunfermline Athletic Football Club.

They were relegated from the Premier League after some absolutely dreadful League performances, but there was a sting in the tail when they reached the Scottish Cup final.

This is always a great occasion for the town with everyone benefiting through television exposure and the town in general getting a bit of a lift that the local team has reached a national Cup final.

The path to the final had included a defeat of Rangers which caused serious ructions at already troubled Ibrox, and the Pars had earned their place in the final at Hampden with a last minute penalty, taken cheekily by Jim McIntyre, in the replay against Hibs.

And so to the final where Celtic awaited.

Celtic had beaten Dunfermline in the Scottish Cup finals of 1965 and 2004, but had famously lost in 1961, an event much discussed that week by all who were old enough to have any memories of that day.

This particular Cup final, although well attended by Pars fans and played on a very pleasant day, is often ranked as being one of the worst Cup finals of all time.

Celtic, League Champions though they were, did not function very well that day, and Dunfermline, as even their most diehard fans would admit, were not really Cup final class.

Mark Burchill might have scored in the first half, but most opportunities came for Celtic. As long as they did not put them away, the Pars still had some sort of a chance, whether in a breakaway or in that great leveller – the penalty shoot-out.

However Celtic did grab a scrappy late goal through the unlikely source of Cameroon full back John-Joel Perrier Doumbe, who was on hand to prod home, a fitting end to a rather scrappy Cup final.

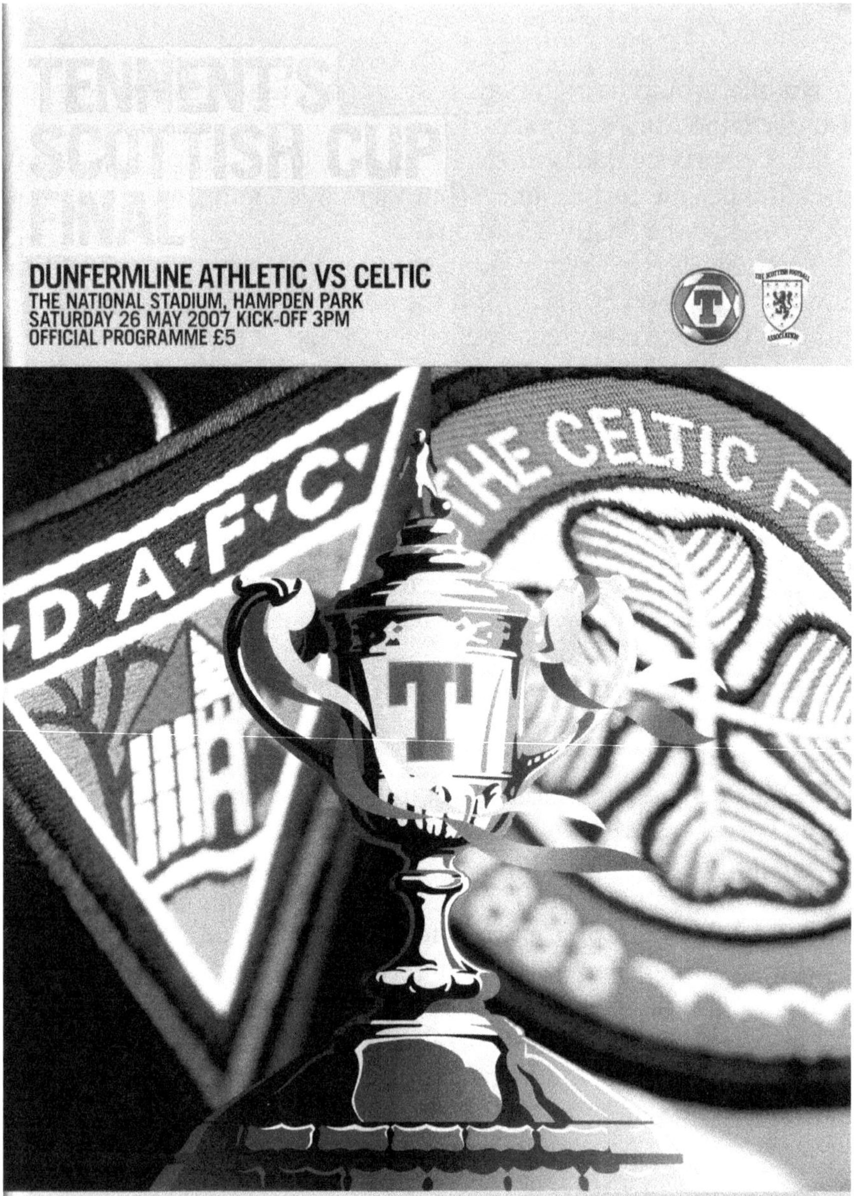
TENNENT'S SCOTTISH CUP FINAL
DUNFERMLINE ATHLETIC VS CELTIC
THE NATIONAL STADIUM, HAMPDEN PARK
SATURDAY 26 MAY 2007 KICK-OFF 3PM
OFFICIAL PROGRAMME £5
D·A·F·C
THE CELTIC FO

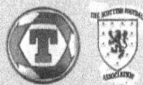

May 27 1929

These were grim times for Dunfermline Athletic and indeed for Scottish football in general.

Economic circumstances were hard, and two teams, Arthurlie and Bathgate, had been compelled to resign from the League.

This was not good news for anyone in football; the loss of Bathgate in particular, a team fairly close to Dunfermline, was a sore knock as the cold winds of recession blew ever nearer.

Tonight at St Leonard's Lecture Hall, the shareholders of the club had a chance to see the accounts of the club at the AGM under the chairmanship of Mr J Fraser.

A depressing picture was reported with a loss of £655, a considerable amount of money in 1929. It would have been a lot more but for the transfer of some players, notably Jimmy Stein who was now doing well along with fellow Scotsman Alec Troup at Everton.

Dunfermline were now struggling in the Second Division to which they had been relegated in 1928. *The Courier* puts things tactfully, one feels, when it says that "considerable discussion took place" before the balance sheet was reluctantly accepted. It was not that they really had much choice in the matter!

The position was grim, and there was no real solution to the problem other than for the team to play better and to challenge for promotion sometime soon.

It was all the sadder because only three years previously the town had been filled with optimism when the League was won in 1926.

There was a General Election to be held in three days' time, and there was a chance that Ramsay MacDonald's Labour Party could win. Could that make any difference?

May 28 1955

This morning's *Courier* contained a vivid account of yesterday's AGM of the Scottish League, a meeting that broke up in a little disarray.

Dunfermline's position was probably safe, but it would have been nice to see it all cut and dried.

Dunfermline had won promotion to the 16 team First Division a month ago, and even when Berwick Rangers carried a motion to increase the First Division to 18 teams, this did not seem to be any kind of threat.

All that would happen would be that the two relegated teams (Motherwell and Stirling Albion) would stay in the First Division.

The problem arose when Secretary Fred Donovan announced that a number of "reserve" teams would be withdrawing from the "C" or Third Division, leaving a very small Third Division from which two teams would be promoted.

A number of Second Division teams now saw a threat to their position in all this, and the decision was reversed and left open until another meeting was to be held on June 17.

Dunfermline's promotion did not seem to be under any threat, but it was always possible that the meeting on June 17 could decide on a smaller First Division from which the Pars could be excluded.

It would be unfair, but stranger things had happened, so the position was much talked about among Dunfermline supporters this morning.

At the same meeting, Dunfermline had brought forward a motion to the effect that any official accused of a breach of rules should be entitled to be present at his hearing.

It did not seem to be all that unreasonable, but it was thrown out.

May 29 1920

Saturday night is not a usual time for any meeting of football clubs to discuss their future, but there was an air of conspiracy about this one.

The meeting was held in Edinburgh and consisted of 12 clubs, all frustrated with the failure of the Scottish League to resurrect its Second Division. This had been functioning until 1915 but had failed to reappear after the war, and there were no apparent plans to bring it back for season 1920/1921.

There had of course been a Central League in 1919/20 in which Dunfermline participated, and the likelihood was that the Central League would continue, but it was felt that the League was much diminished in the eyes of the public by the inclusion of reserve or "A" teams from Dundee, Hearts and Falkirk.

This meeting was all about excluding "A" teams, and Dunfermline were joined by Cowdenbeath, Lochgelly United, St Bernard's, East Fife, Dundee Hibs, St Johnstone, King's Park, East Stirlingshire, Armadale, Bathgate and Alloa Athletic with a view to forming a "new" Central League.

Mr A Latto of St Johnstone was in the chair, and the decision was taken to meet again next week after further consultation. It is clear that there was a great deal of political shenanigans here, and arguably the real reason for this meeting was to put pressure on the Scottish League to re-form the Second Division.

The continuation of an unofficial Central League did have certain attractions for Dunfermline, for as long as they played in an unofficial League, they would still have the great Scotland Internationalist Andy Wilson.

May 30 1939

It was no secret that war was approaching.

Indeed it was virtually inevitable after Hitler had seized all of Czechoslovakia in March, and the guarantees then given to Poland by the British and the French Governments.

But it had to be assumed that football would continue in season 1939/40, and in the meantime the business of preparation for the new season had to continue with Manager Peter Wilson looking for new players.

The AGM was scheduled for June 8, and, ahead of that, the financial statement was issued today. It contained the news that everyone suspected, namely that Dunfermline had made a loss of £973.

They had enjoyed a reasonable season in 1939, finishing fifth in the Second Division, with a few good wins in the Scottish Cup, but the team had departed in a replay to Alloa in the round before the quarter final.

Sadly however, attendances had not been great, and even loyal die-hard DA fans were now reluctantly agreeing with the sneers of the supporters of other teams that East End Park was not the greatest stadium in the world.

Although there had been a slight increase in gate revenue, it was not enough and there had been no income from transfers this season. Players' wages were higher than last year as well.

It was clear that although the club was in no immediate danger of bankruptcy or liquidation, there was also no easy way out of the situation, and the seriousness of the international situation in Europe added to the concern for the future.

May 31 1967

There were mixed feelings tonight in Dunfermline as everyone clustered round black-and-white televisions to watch events in Germany where Rangers lost the European Cup Winners' Cup final (narrowly and after extra time) to Bayern Munich.

The mixed feelings centred round Alex Smith, a local boy who had played for Dunfermline until 1966 when he had disappointed his fans by accepting a transfer to Rangers.

The club itself had benefited to the tune of £55,000 (then a Scottish record), but Smith had never controlled things at Ibrox in the way that he did at East End Park.

It was a difficult season for Rangers, featuring their infamous Scottish Cup defeat at Berwick and having to live under the permanent shadow of Jock Stein's Celtic while more and more people were beginning to question their religious policy.

Alex had not let himself down, however, but he must have wondered whether he would not have been better staying with those who loved him in Dunfermline.

Tonight, playing out of position in the forward line, he did well enough, but it was a strange team selection, and matters were not helped by their Chairman publicly questioning the value of some of his players.

However, even those to whom supporting Rangers does not come naturally were a little disappointed, for Alex who had played eight seasons for Dunfermline, and it would have been nice to see both the European Cup and the European Cup Winners' Cup in Scotland at the same time.

However, it was not to be, and Smith's agony must have been intense.

June

June 1 1993

The town is in a ferment today wondering who the new Manager will be following the sacking of Jocky Scott.

It was generally agreed that season 1992/93 had been a massive disappointment, particularly the last few games, and something more energetic was required.

Last night the Directors met to discuss the "postbag of applications" but Chairman Ray Woodrow refused to go further than that.

Clearly, a shortlist is being drawn up, and a decision is promised soon. Indeed there will have to be a speedy decision because the new season will soon be upon us.

In the absence of any hard news, *The Dunfermline Press* has been speculating as to the possibilities and has conducting a readers' survey. The fans' favourite is quite clearly the ever-popular Jim Leishman who, many supporters believe, should never have been dispensed with in the first place.

Close to him come two ex-players in Bertie Paton and Alex Totten, but *The Dunfermline Press* also, it being an era of player-managers, mentions a few men now either at the end of their careers or approaching that milestone.

Names include Roy Aitken, Gordon Strachan, Charlie Nicholas, Davie Cooper and Murdo MacLeod. Those who are in favour of Jim Leishman are however aware that it may not happen, for there are those in power who might find it difficult to work with the ebullient Jim.

Indeed, it is no secret that Boardroom instability and internal squabbling have played no small part in the current distressing position of Dunfermline Athletic FC.

The new Manager, whoever he may be, will have to be good, both at football management and keeping Directors and, of course, supporters happy!

June 2 1885

This is the day traditionally given for the founding of Dunfermline Athletic Football Club.

A meeting was held at the Old Inn and a committee was quickly elected and plans put in hand to lease a ground at East End Park (not quite the same site as the ground is on today but slightly to the west).

This was the time when football clubs were being founded all over Scotland, the game being given a boost by Scotland's obvious success against England and the fact that more and more factories and workplaces were beginning to give their workers a half day on a Saturday.

Even the Church came round to seeing that football was a better idea for young men on a Saturday afternoon rather than the ale houses and whorehouses which were all too willing to take away all the hard earned wages at 12.00 noon on a Saturday when the "hooter" went.

Football teams were being created all over the country, as we have said, but there was no guarantee that they were going to last. There was a requirement for a group of committed players, and for people who were prepared to put in a lot of hours to keep the club running.

There certainly seemed to be no lack of people interested in this game, which of course has been played for centuries in an unofficial sort of way.

The difference now was that the rules of the game had been codified and written down. Anyway, the good ship Dunfermline Athletic had been launched and hopes were expressed for her future well-being.

There was no guarantee, however, of longevity.

June 3 1912

Tonight in Glasgow at the AGM of the Scottish League, Dunfermline Athletic were elected to the Scottish League.

This was a significant step in the development of the club for the word "Scottish" was significant, albeit Dunfermline had made it only to the Second Division.

It also meant considerably more travelling, with away fixtures against clubs in the West of Scotland such as Ayr and Vale of Leven.

It had been decided a couple of months ago that the Second Division should be expanded to 14 teams, and Dunfermline had been formally invited to apply.

Five teams had applied viz. Dunfermline, Johnstone, Peebles Rovers, Bathgate and Galston, and the issue had been decided on a vote by the existing members.

Clearly Dunfermline had "knocked on a few doors" and they had in their favour a good ground (by no means perfect, but better than some at the time) and geography with close proximity to a railway line.

In the event, it was Dunfermline and Johnstone who were elected, Peebles Rovers being perhaps a little too remote, and Bathgate and Galston possibly lacking some facilities.

The other issue of the meeting, chaired by William Ward of Partick Thistle, was whether there would be automatic promotion and relegation.

It was decided that it would not apply this year for the bottom two teams in the First Division were St Mirren and Queen's Park.

Queen's Park still had a lot of influence and support, and St Mirren had already committed themselves to a heavy wage bill on the basis that they would be in the First Division.

Automatic promotion and relegation was deferred.

June 4 1959

Dunfermline's European adventures in the 1960s are well known, but a lesser known trip abroad took place at the end of season 1958/59.

Having won on the last day of the league season to stay up by a single point, management and players headed for an 8-day holiday in Switzerland in early June.

The centrepiece of the trip was a friendly against Young Boys of Berne in the wonderfully named Wankdorf Stadium; the Pars would lose a high-scoring game 5-3.

Chairman David Thomson said afterwards that the Swiss side were very quick off the mark while Dunfermline were not at match fitness and suffered in the summer heat.

After the match, there was some puzzlement at many refereeing decisions: "Pushing seemed to be quite in order, but a hard but fair tackle inevitably resulted in the whistle being blown".

It is perhaps an indication of the differences in interpretation of the laws of the game between Britain and mainland Europe that can still be seen today; these have their roots a long time in the past.

An interesting aside is that part of the match was played under floodlights. Floodlighting had gradually been introduced in Scottish grounds during the 1950s with the first game under small lights at Ochilview in 1951 and the first 'real floodlights' on pylons used at Easter Road in 1954.

Four months after this game in Berne, lights would be used at East End Park for the first time in a friendly against Sheffield United.

Scotland learned that it was late in adapting this technology – floodlights had been widely used in Switzerland since the mid-1930s.

June 5 1961

It is often said that you can tell from the demeanour of a town's inhabitants just exactly how their team is doing.

If this is so, it would be very easy for visitors to the town – to play in bowling tournaments, for example, or to watch Fifeshire play cricket at McKane Park – to judge from all the smiling faces that 1961 was a very special year for Dunfermline.

The object of attention, the Scottish Cup, was frequently absent from East End Park being shown off at various functions or being taken to a local hospital so that an ill fan could see the trophy and have his picture taken with it.

It was something that Jock Stein would insist that his players did from time to time, and something that he was very good at doing himself, always insisting that "football, without fans, is nothing".

Youngsters, even those who had not yet started school, were being taught how to say "Connachan, Fraser and Cunningham; Mailer, Sweeney and Miller; Peebles, Smith, Dickson, Thomson and Melrose".

The eleven gentlemen themselves were now local celebrities and far more important to the auld grey toun than Robert the Bruce, Malcolm Canmore or Andrew Carnegie ever were!

And yet on this June holiday morning, there was still an air of unreality about it all.

For older supporters who were still coming to terms with the fact that the Pars had now been an established First Division team for several years, there was the additional thought that there was this fairly new European Cup Winners' Cup to think about as well.

June 6 1997

Manager Bert Paton was quite happy with his squad after last season in which they had finished 5th out of 10 in the Scottish League Premier Division.

They had not really come close to a European place, but they had comfortably avoided relegation and that was an important thing.

It was particularly important, he said, now that Raith Rovers had been relegated, to keep at least one Fife team in the top tier.

When asked if he was in the market for a new signing, he admitted that he had made a bid for someone but had refused to say who it would be, even whether it was a defender or an attacker, although he rather gave it away by saying that those who had seen the Pars last season would be aware that "we have still not got the ideal set up at the back". Midfielder Brian Rice was considering the terms offered for next season.

But team spirit was good. The players had just got back from the club post season holiday in Megaluf, and training would resume on July 7 for the August 2 start to the season.

Less happily the club had been forced to announce an increase in prices for next season. It would be £11 (£5 for a Junior) for the ground, £12 for the wing stand and £14 for the centre stand for next season.

This was more or less in line with prices in other Premier League grounds, but the club was offering a very good deal in a season ticket for £183, for which the supporter could either opt to stand on the West Terracing or have a seat in the newly built North Stand.

tions of style used to secure effect, it would be difficult to question the truthfulness of his instances of persecution. One of these is the nocturnal search of a suspected house, the inmates of which are rudely awakened and ordered to allow their house to be searched. Everything is turned upside-down, and the contents of drawers, &c., emptied on the floor. The young lady of the house living there is suspected of having sympathy with the Nihilists, and as she darts forward to seize a piece of manuscript, she is immediately seized, bound, and hurried off to prison. There she is kept in solitary confinement—on bare suspicion. She is periodically examined, and at last, after months of imprisonment, is released—with, perhaps, her health broken, and her reason gone. Those who are "suspected," and sent off to Siberia, are as severely dealt with as though they were criminals. Few of them ever return; barbarity of the most inconceivable description does its work in due time. In St Petersburg, the treatment of prisoners and suspects is no better, and, as a rule, when prisoners turn ill, they are allowed no difference of treatment. Without care of any kind, they quickly lose the use of their limbs, the warders refuse to change the straw of their beds, and they are left to perish in their own corruption. This is the Russian Bastille for political prisoners, which, by the way, has its position opposite the palace of the Czar himself. As might be expected, in all the departments of social life—in the Press, and in all agencies for culture and progress—the same tyrannical despotism is exercised. With such a Reign of Terror over the whole country, the power of officials must be terrible; no man will care to predicate what will

Local Intelligence.

Masons' Trip.—The operative masons of Dunfermline, to the number of about 70, had a trip to Alloa last Saturday. The early part of the day was spent in the vicinity of Dollar, and in the afternoon the band contest at Alloa was the source of attraction.

Malicious Mischief.—*James Barclay*, a boy residing in Music Hall Lane, was convicted, at the Burgh Court on Saturday, of breaking several panes of glass in Bruce Street. Bailie Lamond, the presiding Magistrate, imposed a fine of 7s. 6d., or five days' imprisonment.

Parochial Affairs.—A meeting of Dunfermline Parochial Board was held on Tuesday—ex-Bailie Fisher presiding. From a minute of the Poorhouse Committee, it appeared that the number of inmates in the Poorhouse was 103, and that the expenditure for May had been £47, 10s.

Assault with a Felt Hat.—On Thursday, at the Burgh Court, *George Arglie*, miner, Townhill, was accused of creating a disturbance in East Port Street, and assaulting a woman by striking her in the face with a hard felt hat. Accused, with a smile, admitted his guilt; and Bailie Burt imposed a fine of £1, or ten days' imprisonment.

Disturbance at Hill of Beath.—A labourer on tramp named *James Kilau* was brought before Sheriff Gillespie at the Sheriff Court on Tuesday, on a

Begging.—At the Burgh Court, on Saturday,—Bailie Lamond on the bench—*James M'Kenzie*, a tramp, was found guilty of begging in Maygate, and was sent to jail for ten days.

Breaking the Peace on Carnegie Street.—*Joseph M'Kenzie*, a cattle dealer, was convicted at the Burgh Court on Wednesday of so conducting himself in Carnegie Street, the previous night, as to cause a breach of the peace. Bailie Burt imposed a fine of £1 or ten days' imprisonment.

Edward Meechan Once More.—*Edward Meechan* again made his appearance at the Burgh Court on Wednesday, on a charge of breach of the peace, with eleven previous convictions for similar offences recorded against him. He had gone into the Police Office on Tuesday night demanding that lodgings be provided for him. He refused to leave, and ultimately lay down on the floor and created a great disturbance. A fine of 10s. or seven days' imprisonment was imposed.

The New Football Club.—The first general meeting of what is to be known as the Dunfermline Athletic Football Club, was held in the Old Inn on Tuesday night. The interim committee reported that they had taken the East End Park, and that there were already 60 members on the roll. The election of office-bearers was then gone on with, as follows:—Mr E. Lennox, Captain; Mr A. Ramsay, Captain 2nd Eleven; Mr D. Knight, Treasurer; Mr A. Westwood, Secretary; Messrs D. Johnston, D. Scotland, J. Brown, A. Hynd, W. Robertson, Members of Committee.

DUNFERMLINE CRICKET CLUB.

A GENERAL MEETING of the above Club will be held in the PAVILION, on WEDNESDAY Evening first, 10th inst., at 8.30.

Business:—Football Constitution.

June 7 1933

The AGM of Dunfermline Athletic FC was held tonight.

Mr William Whyte, the Chairman, had indicated that, although he wanted to stay on as a Director, he wished to be relieved of the office of Chairman, and so for this reason, Mr Martin Porter chaired the meeting and was duly confirmed in the post as Chairman at the AGM.

The balance sheet showed a loss of £226 over the year, something that was blamed on poor attendances at home games and the general economic situation in the country with high unemployment etc.

It was disappointing and raised the prospect that senior part-time professional football might have a struggle to survive in the town.

It was in this context that questions were asked about why promotion was not achieved, in particular about the apparently unexplained loss of form towards the end of the season which manifested itself in a loss to King's Park on the last day.

As this had also happened in the recent past on another occasion, questions were asked as to whether Dunfermline Athletic really wanted promotion. (Such questions are by no means unknown today and with many clubs!) The answer was that it was a "fallacy" to believe that the club did not want promotion.

On a more positive note, a suggestion was made that a Supporters Club should be formed for the purpose of raising funds for the club, and the Directors and the shareholders were all in agreement with this.

In the meantime, plans were being put in place by Manager Willie Knight on the playing side of the club for the new season.

June 8 1944

The news from Europe, both in Normandy and Italy, was good.

Two days ago had been what now turns out to have been the largest amphibious landing of all time; it was already clear that a bridgehead had been established with troops now pouring into France in further landings and advances being made into France.

But back home there remained anxiety in the hearts of many people. Behind all the rhetoric of "What a plan!" "The morning has come" and "Advance, Britannia", and the absurd rumours that the Germans would soon surrender, there lay the knowledge that there are many worried mothers and wives, in Dunfermline and everywhere else, dreading the arrival of a man on a Post Office motor bike with a telegram.

Other things were going on – people were being given honours for things unconnected with the war effort, and an unofficial miners' strike in Fife was called off.

There was still a little football going on with East End Park still open and indeed being used for football games, mainly at juvenile or junior level. Last Saturday for example saw a draw in the Brown Cup semi-final between Blairhall Star and the Old Boys Club, and the replay was scheduled for next Wednesday.

These games were remarkably well attended in the circumstances, for football as always was a great comfort to people, even in the extreme times of summer 1944.

But when the game finished, it was back home to listen to the BBC News on the wireless. Things had definitely taken a turn for the better, but there was still a long way to go.

June 9 1926

"It was the best of times; it was the worst of times". So says Charles Dickens in his *A Tale of Two Cities* about the French Revolution.

It is strange that this aphorism could also apply to Dunfermline in summer 1926.

On the one hand, there was still the opportunity to bask in the glory of the winning of the Second Division Championship in April and to recall the 53 League goals that Bobby Skinner scored.

It had been a great season, but then hard on the heels of it came the General Strike. The General Strike itself lasted less than two weeks and was probably only of symbolic importance to both sides, but the miners were still carrying on with their strike.

This would clearly have its effect on the town of Dunfermline and the Fife coalfield. Hardship was already making its presence felt.

Today came the news that Bobby Skinner would be suspended from August 13 to August 27, effectively missing the first three games in the First Division.

This had followed the game against Queen of the South at the end of last season in which Skinner had been ordered off after the Dumfries veteran defender and player-coach Joe Dodds was "laid low".

Dodds, an excellent defender for Celtic in his time and who had even played a season at Cowdenbeath, was now quite old, and Skinner had done himself few favours with this action.

It was clear that the Pars were going to need Skinner in the First Division, and he was no use whatever sitting in the stand. Discipline was very important!

Bert Paton, Manager of the Month

June 10 1993

After a difficult season that had seen Athletic fail to return to the top flight, Bert Paton was today appointed as manager, with Dick Campbell as assistant.

Towards the end of the 1992/93 season the Pars looked likely to take the second promotion spot behind Raith Rovers.

A terrible run of form at the end of the season saw Kilmarnock take that spot instead, leading to the sacking of Jocky Scott and another season in the First Division for the club.

It was a difficult time for any new manager – after the controversial departure of Jim Leishman in 1990 there had been unsuccessful spells for both Scott and before him, Iain Munro.

Paton was an interesting choice having played for the club with distinction in the late 1960s, most notably being the club's leading goal scorer in European matches and playing in the famous 1968 Scottish Cup final win against Hearts.

With a playing career ended by injury, Paton became involved in management, initially at junior level with Lochgelly before spells at Cowdenbeath and Raith Rovers as manager and a remarkable period as assistant to Alex Totten at Dumbarton, then St Johnstone before returning to junior football at Rosyth.

When the Dunfermline job came up this time, Bert applied, saying afterwards that he felt it was time for a manager who identified with and had some feeling for the club.

The season would start with a poor set of results, but things would improve and the feeling of excitement would gradually return.

Gary Riddell

June 11 1989

April 1989 saw the horrific, unforgettable scenes of Hillsborough, where 96 lives were ended.

Lives of football fans who had gone to watch their team, just as many thousands of us do in grounds across the country every week.

The Hillsborough Disaster Appeal was set up shortly afterwards, and to aid the fundraising efforts players from DAFC took part in the Dunfermline Half Marathon.

In extremely sad circumstances, this too ended in tragedy with the death of one of the runners – Pars defender Gary Riddell – who collapsed close to the 10-mile mark and could not be revived despite the best efforts of a nearby doctor and ambulance crew.

Aged only 22, and dying in the act of doing something to help others, it is certainly one of the most tragic events in the club's history.

A native of Ellon, Gary signed for Aberdeen on S-forms, but with the club at the height of its powers and with a central defensive partnership of Alex McLeish and Willie Miller, breaking into the first team at a young age was asking a lot.

Looking to get first team experience, a move to East End Park in September 1987 to join Jim Leishman's newly promoted side was an ideal move – he saw plenty of first team action in the Premier Division that season and, although the Pars went straight back down, 1988/89 was a much more successful year.

A memorable First Division championship was won on the last day, with a big contribution from the young defender who made more than 20 appearances.

To everyone's great sadness, he was not there for flag-day in August.

June 12 1921

Today's *Sunday Post* contained an interesting new comment on the Andy Wilson saga.

The reformation of the Scottish League Second Division (and Dunfemline's admission to it) had brought the issue to a head.

Scotland International Wilson had played for Dunfermline with a great deal of success in the two official seasons since the Great War, even though he was retained by Middlesbrough.

Middlesbrough had not been able to do anything about it because the Central League was unofficial but the new Second Division of the Scottish League was official, and Wilson would not be allowed to play for Dunfermline next season.

Dunfermline were disputing this, of course, even to the extent of considering to refuse entrance to the Scottish League Second Division and to try to reform the Central League.

Now it appeared that Wilson himself, currently in Canada with an unofficial Scottish team, said that he would prefer to stay in Montreal and play there next year.

This was a surprising statement, to put it mildly, and was greeted with a certain amount of incredulity in Scotland, but it did show how reluctant he was to return to Middlesbrough.

The special correspondent of *The Sunday Post* added a note which stated "You can accept that statement with absolute authority. Wilson is in deadly earnest about this, and it may be that he will be footing it (sic) permanently before long in the leading team in this city (Montreal)".

In fact, with the benefit of hindsight, it looks as if Wilson was using his popularity in Montreal as a tool to up the ante in his struggle for more wages with Middlesbrough and Dunfermline.

June 13 1885

Today Dunfermline Athletic played their first ever game, beating Edinburgh University 2-1.

There had been a Dunfermline Football Club before that, but they also played cricket.

Cricket is of course an older game than football, but football had made great strides in Scotland in the past few years, helped by Scotland beating England five years in a row from 1880 to 1884 inclusive.

The cricketers of the original Dunfermline Club had tried to get "heavy" with the Dunfermline footballers, so the footballers decided to break away and founded their own club specifically for football.

They looked around the town for a piece of land, and by sheer chance, the North British Railway Company had a perfect spot in the east end of the town available, so what better name to call the ground than East End Park?

The game kicked off in sweltering heat with admission set as 3 pennies and ladies were admitted free.

It would have been difficult however, as the ground wasn't totally enclosed, to stop people watching the game for nothing.

Dunfermline played in maroon jerseys and blue pants or knickerbockers for their first game and beat the students 2-1.

Little is known about the game but we know that the Dunfermline team was Niven, Reynolds, Smith, Westwood, Ross, T Lyon, Sandison, Toddie, Stewart, D Lyon and Lennox.

It would be some time before the infant club started thinking about Leagues etc. and any idea of professionalism or paying a player would not come around for several years.

Mind you, although technically illegal to pay players, one did hear rumours....

June 14 1890

In the early days of Scottish football, there were many local cup competitions.

Today, the final of the Dunfermline and District Charity Cup took place at East End Park between Dunfermline Athletic and Lassodie.

The early play was described as 'fast, but far from scientific' with the Lassodie players being accused of much unnecessary charging. They were 'far too clumsy ... to play the short passing game with much success'.

Despite being pulled back to 1-1 then 2-2, a winner from Bruce put Dunfermline 3-2 up. The game was then delayed by two pitch invasions, but the game did eventually finish with no further goals.

It appeared that the cup had been won, but Lassodie lodged a protest at a meeting of the Charity Association the following Thursday. Protests were common in this era and often succeeded. In this case, the grounds for protest were:

- Encroachment of spectators over the touchline
- Playing an unqualified man
- Inefficiency of the referee
- Time lost during the match was unchecked

On the first point, the protest was upheld and the game ordered to be replayed on a neutral ground – the cup had not been won after all.

The village of Lassodie once housed 2000 people but has now completely disappeared.

A mining village sited to the North-East of Dunfermline, close to Kingseat and Loch Fitty, its first houses were built in the 1860s as coal mining began. It survived until the 1940s, or for as long as the pits stayed open.

It seems incredible that an entire village can be completely removed with almost no trace of it ever existing, but this can be paralleled in Ayrshire at Glenbuck, the home of Bill and Bob Shankly.

All that remains at Lassodie is a war memorial.

Dunfermline Athletic in the 1890s.

June 15 1910

The Dundee Evening Telegraph is impressed by the efforts of Dunfermline Athletic to build up a strong team of mainly local lads for next season.

Today they signed a man from Charlestown called James Thomson, who last season played with distinction for Kirkcaldy United. He is "of splendid ability".

This is in addition to the signing of John Croall from Alloa Athletic and the re-signing of their captain Jim Brown.

Dunfermline have taken on a new lease of life with the formation of the Central League.

They lost out to Bo'ness last year, but they were clearly gearing themselves up to make an assault on the Central League, although the ultimate goal would have to be entrance into the Scottish League.

There was a certain frustration about all this, for the Second Division currently stood at 10 teams, something which would seem to allow for a certain amount of expansion and the incorporation of ambitious teams. In the absence of any system of qualification or promotion, the Scottish League remained a self-perpetuating oligarchy of those whose faces fitted.

And there did not seem to be much that Dunfermline could do about it, other than to do well in the Central League and to keep asking the question. However the signing of new players did seem to give some sort of indication that ambition was present.

As everyone knew however, signing on players (at high fees sometimes) did not guarantee a good team, but the supporters were delighted that one of the signings at least was a local boy who knew how much football meant to everyone in the area.

June 16 1933

For some time, greyhound racing had been held at East End Park in the evenings and on Saturdays when there was no football.

This had turned out to be a tidy little earner for the club in these hard economic times. A few kennels had been brought into the ground as well and leased to a few owners.

This helped ease Dunfermline Athletic's financial worries but problems arose when some neighbours complained about the dogs being a nuisance, a matter that today ended up in court.

There does not seem to have been any suggestion or allegation of cruelty. There was a lot of gambling in the 1930s as people behaved recklessly in a desperate attempt to win a fortune and escape poverty. Possibly the complaint was motivated on religious grounds by people who did not like gambling.

Perhaps the dogs did indeed make a nuisance by barking in the middle of the night.

Or perhaps the complainers did not like football and the crowds that hung about their houses before a game.

However that may be, Baillie Allan dismissed the case on the technicality that the case had been brought to the wrong court. Mr A Shearer, the Town Clerk, suggested that the plaintiffs should proceed by petition on section 17 of the Summary Jurisdiction Act.

Dunfermline Athletic were safe from prosecution for the meantime.

In the world outside, there still seemed to be no remedy for unemployment with the National Government no more successful than the Labour one, and there was this rather funny little man with a moustache in Germany who kept saying things about wanting to abolish the Treaty of Versailles.

There was something ominous about him.

June 17 1955

Although Dunfermline had known for about six weeks that they were second in the Second Division and therefore eligible for promotion to the First Division along with the winners Airdrie, it was only today at the EGM of the Scottish League that this was confirmed.

Indeed the Leagues had been reconstructed.

Division "C" was abolished and Division One, as it would now be called, would now consist of 18 clubs while Division Two would have 19.

This was on the motion of Berwick Rangers and was passed by 25 votes to 7.

Thus the two teams who would have been relegated, namely Motherwell and Stirling Albion, would in fact remain in the top Division, and Dunfermline would now join a Division of 18 rather than 16.

There were disadvantages in all this, especially in Division Two where in a 19 team League, there would be one team having no game every week.

The advantage for Dunfermline, who were believed to have voted in favour of the new set up, would be that it would be more difficult to be relegated, a particular peril in this, their first year after winning promotion.

The new League season would start on September 10. The draw for the Scottish League Cup was also made at this meeting, and Dunfermline found themselves in the same section as Aberdeen, Clyde and Hibs – no-one's idea of an easy section consisting as it did of last season's League winners Aberdeen, Scottish Cup winners Clyde and Hibs, who were often considered to be the best footballing team of this era.

But then again, the Pars were now back among the big boys!

June 18 1892

Dunfermline Athletic were again invited to join the Midland League today.

There had been a Midland League last season in which Dunfermline had participated, but there had been no strong administration or organisation, and some teams like Raith Rovers, for example, had left to try their luck elsewhere.

At a meeting in Stirling today, the League was reformed. 13 teams were invited including Dunfermline. East Stirlingshire failed to turn up, but the remaining 12 decided to form a League of 10 teams which they hoped would be more viable that the previous Midland League.

Dunfermline failed to gain admission on the first vote which elected Dunblane, Falkirk, King's Park, Camelon, Bridge of Allan and Alloa Athletic. These six then retired into another room and came back with invitations to Alva, Grangemouth and Dunfermline Athletic to join them.

That made nine, and the Secretary was then instructed to send an invitation to East Stirlingshire to join them. Failing that, the remaining place would be offered to either Fair City or Clackmannan.

Dunfermline's representatives professed themselves to be happy with what had happened, but it did not escape the notice of anyone that Dunfermline were the furthest east of all the teams, and that some of the clubs did not necessarily have very direct rail connections.

Travelling might be a problem as might also be the expense. But at least for the moment it seemed that the moribund Midland League had been given a boost.

The problem for Dunfermline was that there were not enough teams in Fife of an appropriate standard to form a viable Fife League.

June 19 1954

Very few people in Dunfermline (or indeed Scotland) had this new phenomenon called Television.

It had been launched in 1936, had been shelved for the duration of World War II and had only reached Scotland in 1952.

The Coronation in 1953 had seen a boost in sales, and now a further boost came with the Switzerland World Cup of 1954.

This was also the first time that Scotland had deigned to enter the World Cup, having refused an invitation in 1950.

It was probably true to say that there was still a strong body of opinion of the persuasion that the World Cup was "not real football", and that "continentals" and South Americans knew nothing about the game.

However, those who did have a friend rich enough to possess a television set and who were thus able to watch this strange new contrivance were soon disabused of this notion of Scottish supremacy.

Scotland, whose Manager Andy Beattie resigned in the middle of the tournament before this game was played — you couldn't make that one up, could you? — went down 0-7 to Uruguay, a country that quite a lot of Scottish people had never heard of.

For some youngsters, it was a devastating and permanently scarring experience. Those who missed this game did themselves a good turn.

For Dunfermline at least, there was at least some consolation in that of the eleven who played for Scotland, none had even the most tenuous connection with Dunfermline.

Many people felt however that Billy Liddell, once of Townhill and now of Liverpool might have made a difference.

The whole exercise, however, was the prototype of Scottish self-destruction and would be a feature of most future World Cups!

June 20 1951

It was generally agreed that season 1950/51 was a poor season for the Pars.

This was reflected in the financial statement, released today, which saw a loss of £2061, a sharp change from a profit of £1831 made last season.

The reason was not hard to find, for it lay on the poor performances on the field.

This year team finished up in the lower half of the "B" Division, failed to qualify for the quarter finals of the Scottish League Cup and departed the Scottish Cup without a whimper at the first time of asking to Clyde.

This was in contrast to the previous year when Dunfermline had narrowly missed promotion to Division "A" and had reached the final of the Scottish League Cup.

It was hardly surprising that there was a great deal of comings and goings at Board and management level throughout the summer with Manager Webber Lees eventually being asked to resign and the club once again being run by the Directors, in particular Tom Younger.

The one straw of consolation in season 1950/51 was that they were marginally better than Cowdenbeath, but that was hardly something to boast about.

When the supporters looked at the other Fife neighbours, East Fife and Raith Rovers, they were seen to be comfortably placed in Division "A".

The financial position did not exactly encourage optimism.

Everyone knew that it was a chicken and an egg situation, in that a little success on the field would bring in more money to spend on new players and some much-needed ground repairs.

June 21 2002

Midsummer 2002 saw Dunfermline embroiled in a rather strange dispute with St Mirren concerning a player called Scott Walker.

The player was clearly unhappy at St Mirren and was desperate for a move to the more successful Dunfermline Athletic who had finished in the top six of the Scottish Premier League.

The trouble was that, although Walker was prepared to buy himself out of his contract which still had a year to run, the cash strapped St Mirren were not prepared to allow this to happen and in any case were looking for a fee of £30,000 for him.

The case seemed to be deadlocked, and there was the general impression that we were not getting to hear the whole truth, but Walker did eventually find his way to East End Park.

In another (apparently) separate case between the same two clubs, it was now generally agreed that Junior Mendes' move to the Pars had not been a success and he returned to St Mirren.

In addition, this week's *Dunfermline Press* contained an interview with John Ritchie, who was working with the youngsters.

He delivered an upbeat report on the youth set up which would soon yield big dividends.

The 2002/03 season would open at Celtic Park on August 3.

In the meantime, the Pars were off to play a few games in New Zealand before returning to Europe to take part in a tournament in The Netherlands.

Manager Jimmy Calderwood was very confident about his young team continuing to develop and to prosper in the SPL.

June 22 1948

Newspapers of the time often make mention of the fact that Dunfermline supporters are none too hopeful of their team's prospects.

For the past two official seasons since the end of the war, the team had held its own and more in the Scottish League Second Division.

The trouble is that this was not considered good enough for a town of Dunfermline's size, and their record did contrast rather badly with that of Raith Rovers and East Fife.

East Fife in particular had won both promotion and the Scottish League Cup last season.

Dunfermline have also not had the best of luck with their Managers, but a lot of people in the town are now asking the question of the Directors, one of whom, Sandy Terris the Vice-Chairman, seems to be running the team.

Today however, the announcement was made of a signing, a young lad called Thomas Hood from Blantyre Victoria.

Reports of him are good, but he is of course untried at senior level, and he is not really the sort of signing that the fans want to hear about.

What they really want is a tried and tested player with loads of experience but, of course, this sort of player costs money – something that the Pars do not really have a lot of.

But this is 1948. In other respects, optimism is in the air, the war is well and truly over and very soon the National Health Service will be unveiled. It is indeed a brave new world, but where will the Pars fit into it?

June 23 1938

It is not very often that the first sight that fans get of their new Manager is as a referee, but this is exactly what happened tonight at East End Park.

Sadly rain reduced the attendance, but even so, a fair number of people turned up to see Paton and Baldwin Ladies beat Fife Ladies 2-0 in a Charity game for the Dunfermline and West Fife Hospital.

The Dunfermline City Pipers appeared as well, and Dr Alan Tuke from the hospital turned up to kick off.

There was a problem about a referee however, because it was impossible to get a "real" referee, for the SFA for a long time had a ridiculous rule that their referees were not allowed to perform at a women's football match.

What the thinking behind this was no-one can say, other than sheer Scottish awkwardness and prejudice.

The recently appointed Manager of Dunfermline Athletic, Peter Wilson, had no such inhibitions and appeared to do the needful.

He had been appointed about a month ago, and it was the first chance that many fans had of seeing him. He had been a good player for both Celtic and Hibs, had been capped four times by Scotland, and he had not cancelled his playing registration so that he could play next season if he wanted to.

He was 33 and certainly still looked quite athletic as he ran about the field. At half time and full time he joked with the crowd about how he did not realise what a difficult job it was to referee a game and that he would never criticise the likes of Peter Craigmyle, the famous referee of the 1930s, again.

June 24 1962

It was the close season, but this did not in any way dampen the enthusiasm for the new season among Pars fans.

There were several reasons for this. One was that the team had finished fourth in the First Division in 1962, and they had enjoyed a successful tour of Norway.

The most obvious sign of a better future was the building of the new stand; would it be ready for the new season?

Manager Jock Stein showed the other side of his undoubted talent, by being seen at the ground almost every day, talking to the workers and passing supporters, calling them by their first names and discoursing at length about the Chile World Cup and other footballing matters.

This being the silly season for newspapers when there was very little real football news, the journalists appreciated Stein talking to them, and giving them copy about his own lengthy and wide career as a player and a coach, and throwing in the names of a few youngsters that Dunfermline might be interested in.

A story was being circulated that Aberdeen were about to make a bid for Charlie Dickson, Dunfermline's talented goal scorer, although now arguably past his best.

Jock denied any approach and Aberdeen denied it as well. There was possibly nothing in it all, but it did serve its purpose of filling a column or two in the newspapers and getting the fans to talk about the game.

Nobody wanted to wish away the summer and the marvellous weather, but it would be nice when the football season started again!

June 25 1993

The Dunfermline Press wonders today whether new Manager Bertie Paton and his Assistant Dick Campbell realise just exactly what they have let themselves in for.

Their appointment was met with a certain degree of enthusiasm, even from those who would have preferred Jim Leishman, and there was little doubt that the two men concerned had the interests of the club at heart.

But they had now been told about the enormity of the debt that the club was immersed in, and quite simply there would be very little, if any, money available for buying players.

Paton however remained upbeat, saying the usual things that new Managers say about what a wonderful club this was, but then went even further saying "If I die tomorrow, I will die happy, for it is a job I have always wanted."

The season to come will be a particularly difficult one. Because of League reconstruction, five teams will be relegated into what will be the third tier and only one will be promoted, and the Pars will be up against it.

Still, they will have the backing of a poet called John Murphy, a Dunfermline man now working for Marathon Oil UK who says

> A long and painful time it's been
> Since Big Jim went away
> We've been through hell and back again
> But noo we're pleased to say
> Aye oor Bert "This is it,
> Tak us frae the dark,
> Again we'll see some fitba' players
> Oot on East End Park"

Not exactly Poet Laureate stuff that, but it does at least show some sort of enthusiasm!

June 26 1939

Dunfermline Athletic were certainly in the doldrums.

Their ground was widely criticised in the local press as being "no credit to the town", their financial situation was dire with a loss of £800.

They had suffered two recent failures to get themselves out of the Second Division.

It was a classic chicken and egg situation. The club needed money. The only way to make money was to earn promotion to the First Division, but that needed money to supplement the rather threadbare squad that Manager Peter Wilson had at his disposal.

But one of their strongest assets was a vigorous Supporters Club who were doing their best to raise money for the club. Perhaps an indication of the perilous times in which the country was living, they also turned to "propaganda", a word much used these days in the context of the events in Germany.

Today they announced in *The Courier* that they were going to patrol the streets and housing areas with pamphlets urging people to buy a season ticket for next season, doing so in weekly instalments if necessary.

The pamphlet argued that a successful football team would be in everybody's best interests in that games against the big Edinburgh and Glasgow teams would bring money to the town, and that money would be spent in shops and pubs.

It was a brave effort to raise the profile of the club at a time when it was much needed. It would have been nice to know if their efforts had any success, but this was 1939, and soon things would change utterly for reasons that had nothing to do with football.

June 27 1949

The appointment of Webber Lees a few days ago is clearly being greeted with enthusiasm in the town.

He was seen at the Dunfermline Week Five-A-Side tournament at East End Park on Saturday, but this Monday is the first day of him taking up his duties.

He certainly inherited a team in a bit of a mess. The club had not had a Manager for some time, the team being run by the Director Sandy Terris who, despite genuine enthusiasm, was short on real knowledge of the game.

The team had suffered a serious blow in the last game of last season when a 0-4 defeat to Raith Rovers had cost them promotion.

Webber Lees had been associated with Albion Rovers for 23 years with varying degrees of success, but he had taken them to the First Division on three separate occasions and had a good eye for talent, particularly a centre half whom he had unearthed during the war called Jock Stein.

His departure from Coatbridge had caused a few ructions in the Albion Rovers support, some of whom felt that he had been the victim of internal politics at that club.

Lees was a well-known man in the town, owning a sports equipment shop, and it must have been a wrench for him to leave and travel east to Fife.

On the other hand, there was no better example of a "sleeping giant" than Dunfermline Athletic, a club in a fairly large town and with a reasonable although increasingly disillusioned support, the older ones perpetually reminiscing about Andy Wilson and Bobby Skinner.

June 28 1919

A momentous event happened in the world today.

This was the signing of the Treaty of Versailles which meant that Great War was now officially at an end.

Coincidentally, it had all started some five years earlier to the day with the assassination of Archduke Ferdinand on June 28 1914.

Soldiers could now be officially demobilised and a flood of ex-servicemen was expected soon, although since the armistice last November a number had already returned.

All this meant good news for Dunfermline Athletic who could now expect to be at virtually full strength for the start of the season.

The decision had been made to leave the Eastern League which had served its purpose during the war years and to move to the Central League, which was a bigger organisation and had a wider geographical area, but now that travel was getting a lot easier, distance was less of a problem.

There had been no sign as yet of the Scottish League wishing to form a Second Division of teams like Dunfermline.

Until such time as that happened, the Central League would continue to be the home of Dunfermline Athletic, who could expect to be one of the stronger teams there.

In the meantime, there was some wonderful summer weather to enjoy, particularly at McKane Park where cricket had now made its re-appearance. Today Dunfermline were playing Forfarshire.

The attendance was huge but the sheer amount of disabled and blinded ex-Servicemen was striking.

June 29 1973

It may be midsummer, but training had already started for the new season.

By winning promotion last season Dunfermline had also won a place in the pre-season Dryburgh Cup, which begins in late July, with a difficult game at Celtic Park.

For this reason, Manager George Miller had been sure to get his side together before the end of June.

Some of his squad were full-timers while others trained only part-time, but Miller assured supporters that the part-timers would be doing extra work to ensure that they were ready for the start of the season.

Miller also announced that Graham Shaw had been offered full time terms and had accepted them, having decided to give up his job in an Edinburgh bank.

The fixture list had now been issued, and the Pars not only had to go to Celtic Park in the Dryburgh Cup, but the first game in the "real" season after the League Cup was the visit of Celtic to East End Park.

Other highlights of the season would seem to be the visit of Rangers on November 3 and the New Year's Day fixture against local rivals East Fife.

Pessimists were already describing this game as a "relegation derby" but perhaps they were just being realistic! Even the most optimistic of fans, however, realised that this was not going to be an easy season.

It was good to be back in the First Division and the enthusiasm for the new season was impressive, but the glory years of only five years ago now seemed to be a long way away.

June 30 1955

It was generally agreed that the new enclosure on the North side of the ground had been a success.

It had been built last year to replace the old one which was small, in danger of falling down, had holes in the roof, and was a grizzly mixture of rusty corrugated iron and rotting wood.

Its replacement was a lot healthier but not much bigger than its predecessor. It was often said that one of the reasons why Dunfermline failed to attract the crowds that they would have liked to was because the facilities at East End Park were far from adequate.

Aware of this, the energetic Dunfermline Athletic Supporters Club, under enthusiastic Chairman Harold Phillips, at their AGM decided to extend the enclosure on both sides to allow covered accommodation for up to another 3,000 spectators.

This was perhaps a little on the optimistic side, it was felt, but on the other hand, the Pars were now in the First Division and it might mean that everyone who came to a game would be able to watch it standing out of the rain.

One of the side effects of the increasing prosperity so obvious in the 1950s was that people were now beginning to get choosy and were no longer prepared, unquestioningly and uncomplainingly, to stand in the wet as pre-war spectators had done.

A football club now had to care for its spectators! It was hoped, according to Mr Phillips, that work could start soon before the beginning of the new season.

Illustration Credits

Cover – East End Park – Peter Miles
Page ii – East End Park – Peter Miles
Page x – Norrie McCathie portrait in Norrie McCathie stand – Peter Miles
Page 2 – Early East End Park – Dunfermline Athletic Heritage Trust
Page 4 – 1907/08 team photograph
Page 9 – Jock Stein – Celtic Star
Page 29 – Bobby Skinner – Dunfermline Athletic Heritage Trust
Page 38 – Fixture list for 1939/40 season – Dunfermline Press
Page 46/47 – Past players at centenary game in 1985 – Dunfermline Press
Page 65 – Andy Geggan against East Stirlingshire in 2013 – Craig Brown
Page 67 – Alex Edwards – Dunfermline Athletic Heritage Trust
Page 76 – Jim Leishman as a Pars player – Dunfermline Press
Page 83 – Charlie Dickson – Dunfermline Athletic Heritage Trust
Page 87 – Programme cover, Fife Select Vs. Sunderland – Gordon McKenzie
Page 94 – League Cup fixture against Rangers in 1951 – Dunfermline A H Trust
Page 96 – 1951/52 team photograph – Dunfermline Press
Page 101 – 1949/50 team photograph – Dunfermline Athletic Heritage Trust
Page 103 – Kyle Turner celebrates scoring at Firhill in 2019 – Craig Brown
Page 106 – Sol Bamba, September 2006 – Neil Farrell / DAFC.net
Page 119 – 1981/82 team photograph – Dunfermline Press
Page 122 – George Peebles – Dunfermline Athletic Heritage Trust
Page 127 – 1949 League Cup semi-final programme – Duncan Simpson
Page 144 – Willie Callaghan – Dunfermline Athletic Heritage Trust
Page 151 – 1949 League Cup final programme – Duncan Simpson
Page 153 – 1949 League Cup final action – East Fife FC
Page 163 – Bert Paton as a player – Dunfermline Athletic Heritage Trust
Page 170 – John Lunn – Dunfermline Athletic Heritage Trust
Page 185 – 1911 Scottish Qualifying Cup winners – Dunfermline Athletic H Tt
Page 203 – Jenkins / McCathie /Watson in 1984 – Dunfermline Press
Page 208 – Moffat scores at Ayr – Craig Brown
Page 216 – DAFC Vs Valencia programme cover – Gordon McKenzie
Page 246 – DAFC Vs West Bromwich Albion programme cover – Gordon McKenzie
Page 259 – DAFC Vs Wigtown and Bladnoch - Dunfermline Press
Page 269 – Scott Wilson scores the winner against Hearts – Neil Farrell / DAFC.net
Page 274 – Noel Hunt – Neil Farrell / DAFC.net
Page 276 – Broadwood snow – Neil Farrell / DAFC.net
Page 288 – Roy Barry – Dunfermline Athletic Heritage Trust
Page 313 – Last game before lockdown – Craig Brown
Page 317 – Andy Wilson – Dunfermline Athletic Heritage Trust
Page 324 – 2006 CIS Insurance Cup final programme – Gordon McKenzie

Lasting memories ... Harry Melrose with the Scottish Cup

Page 328 – team photograph at end of Great War – Dunfermline Athletic H Tt
Page 335 – 1965 Scottish Cup semi-final – Dunfermline Press
Page 338 – 1968 Scottish Cup semi-final programme – Gordon McKenzie
Page 342 – 1961 Scottish Cup semi-final programme – Gordon McKenzie
Page 351 – DAFC Vs Slovan Bratislava – Dunfermline Press
Page 353 – 1925/26 team photograph – Dunfermline Athletic Heritage Trust
Page 260 – Gary Riddell in action against St Mirren in 1988 – Dunfermline A H T
Page 365 – Harry Melrose – Dunfermline Athletic Heritage Trust
Page 368 – 2004 Scottish Cup semi-final – Neil Farrell / DAFC.net
Page 371 – 1961 Scottish Cup final programme – Gordon McKenzie
Page 374 – Martin Hardie celebration against Raith Rovers in 2011 – Craig Brown
Page 376 – 1965 Scottish Cup final programme – Gordon McKenzie
Page 379 – Thomson scores the first goal with a diving header - Dunfermline Press
Page 382 - That year they also won the Fife Cup and the Penman Cup - Dunf. Press
Page 386 – 1968 Scottish cup final programme – Gordon McKenzie
Page 388 – 1968 Scottish Cup final report – Dunfermline Press
Page 389 – 1968 Scottish Cup, George Farm – Dunfermline Press
Page 391 – 1968 Scottish Cup final report (1) – Dunfermline Press
Page 392 – 1968 Scottish Cup final report (2) – Dunfermline Press
Page 393 – 1968 Scottish Cup final report (3) – Dunfermline Press
Page 394 – 1968 Scottish Cup final report (4) – Dunfermline Press
Page 398 – Damage to East End Park in 1968 – Celtic Star
Page 402 – DAFC Vs Celtic, 1968 report (1) – Dunfermline Press
Page 403 – DAFC Vs Celtic, 1968 report (2) – Dunfermline Press
Page 405 – Peter Wilson – Celtic Wiki
Page 419 – DAFC Vs Falkirk 1979 – Dunfermline Press
Page 431 – 2004 Scottish Cup final programme – Gordon McKenzie
Page 446 – Early news and implications of the breakaway – Dunfermline Press
Page 449 – Bert Paton – Dunfermline Athletic Heritage Trust
Page 451 – Gary Riddell – Dunfermline Athletic Heritage Trust
Page 456 – Team photograph from the 1890s – Dunfermline Athletic Heritage Trust
Page 476 – East End Park from above – Peter Miles
Page 476 – Harry Melrose with the Scottish Cup – Dunfermline Press

Lasting memories ... East End Park in more normal times.

Index

A

Abercorn 130
Abercromby 71
Aberdeen 5, 34, 44, 45, 56, 71, 107, 111, 118, 125, 136, 144, 159, 177, 190, 192, 195, 200, 240, 251, 253, 261, 280, 281, 295, 297, 341, 345, 361, 362, 363, 383, 384, 422, 449, 456, 463
Adam (Hearts) 409
Ainslie Park 21
Aird, Fraser 392
Airdrie , 50, 54, 68, 69, 100, 107, 138, 149, 165, 181, 195, 198, 212, 238, 252, 262, 271, 281, 306, 310, 347, 348, 354, 402, 420, 456
Aitken (East Fife) 152
Aitken (Celtic) 436
Albion Rovers 21, 173, 181, 218, 279, 294, 316, 318, 354, 466
Allan (1905) 178
Allan (Cowdenbeath) 231
Alloa 13, 14, 18, 60, 69, 72, 81, 137, 141, 235, 237, 240, 250, 354, 420, 431, 432, 454, 457
Alva 457
Ancell, Bobby 14, 32, 48, 58, 136, 306
Anderlecht 213
Andersen, Veltle 290
Anderson, Alex 117, 136, 306, 393
Anderson, George 4, 59, 147, 169, 185
Anderson, Willie (referee) 383
Andrews (Cowdenbeath) 39
Annan Athletic 35, 40
Annfield 117, 162
Arbroath 7, 14, 20, 25, 27, 36, 48, 56, 60, 136, 138, 219, 251, 279, 280, 318, 363
Archibald, Sandy 25, 293

Armadale 60, 235, 315, 431
Arsenal 125
Arthurlie 199, 239, 309, 429
Ashcroft, Lee 27, 250
Astle (West Bromwich Albion) 245
Athletic Bilbao 297, 307, 319
Auchterderran School 81
Auld (Celtic) 179, 258, 372
Ayr United 58, 73, 113, 136, 154, 175, 207, 208, 252, 308, 323, 331, 350, 393, 414, 438, 474
Ayr Academicals 113

B

Baillie (Rangers) 146
Bain (1920s) 257, 353
Baird, Jack 7, 370
Baird (Raith Rovers) 224
Balde (Celtic) 423
Balfour (Hibs) 268
Ball (Queen of the South) 273
Ballantyne (1911) 185
Bamba, Sol 106, 357
Banks (Hearts) 270
Bannister, Ernest 277
Barrowman, Andy 30, 35
Barry, Roy 45, 86, 89, 124, 179, 191, 275, 288, 289, 351, 364, 366, 383, 384, 410
Bathgate 60, 257, 278, 350, 394, 429, 431, 438
Bauld (Hearts) 348
Baxter, Jim 86, 146, 183, 212, 333
Bayern Munich 433
Beadling, Tom 18
Beattie, (Scotland) 458
Beattie (Kilmarnock) 247, 267
Beattie, William, 424
Beecham (Stirling Albion) 53
Beith 113, 405

475

Berwick Rangers 228, 260, 267, 280, 308, 341, 358, 416, 430, 433, 456
Beveridge (1902) 121
Bewick (1911) 185
Bilney (referee) 180
Black (1930s) 78
Black (East Fife) 152
Black (Hibs) 375
Blackburn Park 70, 80, 108
Blackie (1981) 119
Blackpool 16
Blairhall 95, 444
Blantyre Victoria 461
Blue Brazil *see Cowdenbeath*
Boghead 184, 348, 415
Bolt, Bob 24, 356
Bolton Wanderers 16
Bo'ness 23, 60, 221, 244, 454
Boruc (Celtic) 188
Bowhill Rovers 81
Bowie, Jim 119, 195
Bowman (Dundee United) 68
Boyle, (referee) 298
Bradford City 24
Bradley (Hibs) 304
Brand (Rangers) 212, 302
Brechin 22, 26, 33, 53, 58, 73, 78, 136, 154, 280, 294, 331
Brewster, Craig 89, 240, 364, 426
Bridge of Allan 457
Briggs (Dundee United) 129
Brittle (referee) 286
Broadwood 275, 276
Brockville 34, 72, 79, 86, 200, 243, 248, 262, 361, 362
Brogan (Celtic) 123, 255
Broomfield 50, 100, 252, 347
Brown (1900s) 70
Brown James 185, 186, 309, 454
Brown (1981) 119
Brown (East Fife) 152
Brown (Morton) 285

Brown, Bobby (Rangers) 93, 99,
Brown, John (Rangers) 290
Brown Cup 444
Broxburn 23, 60, 224
Bruce (1890) 452
Buceli (referee) 319
Buchanan, Gregor 40, 191
Buchanan, Liam 142
Buckley (Aberdeen) 136
Bullen, Lee 364, 410
Burchill, Mark 161, 410, 427
Burley (Celtic) 135
Burnley 24, 152
Burns, Mandy 238
Burns, Robert (poet) 257, 405
Burns, Thomas (director) 7, 353
Burns (referee) 59
Busby (Manchester United) 284, 318
Butcher (Motherwell and Inverness) 89, 142
Byrne, Shaun 39

C

Cairney (Partick Thistle) 174
Cairns (Rangers) 293, 296
Calder, Bobby 283
Calderwood, Jimmy 45, 275, 334, 364, 423, 460
Caldwell (Partick Thistle) 102
Callaghan, Tommy 79, 164, 247, 258, 293, 346, 383, 384
Callaghan, Willie 54, 86, 129, 145, 146, 164, 213, 234, 297, 343, 384
Camelon 457
Cameron (1914) 199
Campbell, Dick 20, 402, 447, 464
Campbell, Iain 188
Campbell, Ian 262, 363
Campbell (1935) 168
Cannon, Jim 98, 101, 152, 305
Cappielow 61, 285, 402, 404
Carabine (Third Lanark) 326

Cardle, Joe 19, 35, 36, 104, 206, 207, 334
Carnegie, Andrew 51, 440
Carroll (Celtic) 150
Cathkin 50, 54, 136, 166, 273, 326
Cattenach (Celtic) 258
Celtic 7, 8, 17, 44, 45, 49, 59, 62, 66, 71, 77, 81, 88, 91, 97, 107, 111, 112, 118, 123, 135, 141, 146, 148, 150, 168, 171, 177, 179, 180, 186, 188, 189, 199, 210, 211, 214, 218, 220, 227, 244, 245, 247, 254, 255, 258, 271, 272, 280, 289, 290, 296, 297, 299, 302, 303, 304, 307, 315, 316, 321, 322, 332, 341, 345, 347, 348, 356, 357, 362, 364, 368, 372, 376, 378, 384, 393, 397, 399, 405, 407, 409, 423, 426, 427, 433, 445, 460, 462, 468
Central League 5, 23, 63, 72, 143, 182, 200, 205, 224, 237, 296, 309, 315, 411, 431, 450, 454, 467
Central Park 27, 98, 221, 232, 263, 419
Challenge Cup 39, 43, 186, 334
Chalmers, Jim 281
Chalmers, Willie 166
Chalmers (Celtic) 214
Clackmannan 60, 457
Clark, Jimmy 109, 353
Clark, John 298
Clark, Nicky 19
Clark (1903) 59
Clark (1950) 348
Clark (Aberdeen) 253
Clarke, Pat 226
Clarkson, Jimmy 93, 95, 99, 100, 101, 152, 153, 231
Clepington Park 56
Cliftonhill 181, 331
Clyde 109, 112, 164, 195, 239, 254, 275, 287, 341, 361, 406, 413, 414, 456, 459

Clydebank 223, 238, 304
Coatbridge 181, 218, 466
Collins (Hibs) 71
Colville, Harry 73, 131, 169
Comrie, Aaron 21
Connachan, Eddie 212, 243, 286, 376, 378, 440
Connolly, James 148
Cook (referee) 212
Cooke (Dundee) 144
Cooke (St Mirren) 18
Cooper (Motherwell) 167, 436
Cooper (1911) 186, 309
Copland (Morton) 52
Courier 14, 32, 56, 58, 99, 100, 109, 110, 121, 143, 152, 159, 166, 168, 172, 178, 186, 187, 190, 224, 251, 268, 281, 296, 309, 344, 378, 405, 415, 429, 430, 465
Cousin (Dundee) 141, 314
Cowdenbeath , 5, 7, 10, 13, 20, 23, 27, 36, 39, 42, 56, 57, 60, 73, 86, 93, 98, 100, 121, 136, 138, 177, 180, 181, 221, 226, 231, 232, 263, 272, 280, 291, 325, 331, 363, 394, 408, 413, 415, 416, 419, 420, 424, 431, 445, 447, 459
Cox (Annan) 35
Coyle (Airdrie) 107
Coyle (Hibs) 147
Craib (Dundee) 223
Craig (Livingston) 161
Craig (Aberdeen) 192
Craigie (1931) 344
Craigmyle (referee) 462
Crampsey (journalist) , 215
Crawford (Steve) 18, 21, 102, 105, 161, 240, 250, 394, 410
Cree (1889) 147
Crerand (Celtic) 316, 368
Crichton, William 185, 199
Croall John 454
Crockett (referee) 247

477

Cruickshank (Hearts) 92, 383
Cruickshanks (1921) 205
Cullis, (Wolverhampton Wanderers) 283
Cunningham, Willie 16, 66, 124, 133, 144, 155, 162, 214, 220, 273, 297, 332, 336, 372, 378, 440
Cunningham (Rangers) 315, 349
Cunnington, Eddie 22
Cusack (Motherwell) 167
Cushley, John 118, 214, 220, 330
Cuthbert (Raith Rovers) 43

D

Dair, Jason 34, 426
Dall, Brian 119
Dand (1929) 278
Dargo, Craig 41
Davidson (Hearts) 92
Davidson (referee) 262
Davis (Hibs) 346
Dawson, Dave 425
Dawson (Hearts) 277
Deans (Celtic) 171
Delaney, Pat 66, 179, 292
Dempsey, Gary 423
Dempster (Bathgate) 278
Denholm (Beath) 143
Dens Park 26, 33, 155, 159, 168, 271, 304, 311, 341, 354, 410
Deuchars (Alloa) 137
De Vries (Dorus) 270, 412
Devrindt (Anderlecht) 213
Dewar (1890s)
Dewar (East Fife) 86
Dick (Third Lanark) 136
Dick (Queen of the South) 139
Dickson, Andy 32, 117 248, 280, 284, 318
Dickson, Charlie 53, 82, 83, 85, 90, 162, 183, 211, 248, 249, 260, 273, 284, 295, 306, 314, 318, 321, 358, 376, 378, 393, 340, 463
Dickson, Jimmy 138 180, 271, 352, 353
Dinamo Zagreb 164
Division One 24, 30, 32, 117, 140, 181, 184, 226, 250, 287, 306, 358, 363, 406, 456
Division Two 6, 132, 137, 204, 219, 237, 261, 287, 291, 306, 308, 337, 342, 350, 416, 456
Dobson (1934) 279
Dodds (Queen of the South) 445
Doig (East Stirlingshire) 202
Donaldson (1911) 185
Donnelly (Paul) 111, 119
Donnelly (Celtic) 399
Dossing (Dundee United) 129, 312
Dougal (referee) 34, 423
Doumbe (Celtic) 427
Dow (Ryan) 18, 102
Dow (1919) 63
Dowie, Eddie 328, 353
Downie (referee) 195
Drizic. Milos 327
Dryburgh Cup 468
Dublin (Celtic) 322
Duff, Willie 213
Duffield (Raith Rovers) 176
Duffy (King's Park) 344
Duffy (1954) 58
Duggan (Raith Rovers) 250
Dumbarton 13, 48, 154, 184, 186, 232, 237, 279, 287, 318, 348, 358, 392, 420, 447
Dunblane 457
Duncan (East Fife) 152
Duncan (Hibs) 165
Duncan (1911) 185
Dundee 8, 20, 23, 25, 26, 27, 32, 33, 36, 42, 45, 50, 54, 56, 58, 59, 60, 68, 89, 92, 99, 104, 111, 129, 133, 135, 141, 142, 155, 159, 168, 173, 175, 176, 178, 183, 184, 190, 195,

196, 205, 212, 223, 225, 226, 227, 233, 236, 240, 241, 247, 249, 250, 254, 268, 271, 272, 274, 280, 291, 292, 296, 297, 298, 304, 306, 312, 314, 329, 333, 341, 344, 347, 354, 367, 402, 404, 407, 410, 416, 422, 425, 426, 431, 454

Dundee Evening Telegraph 23, 59, 454

Dundee United 20, 27, 33, 45, 56, 58, 60, 68, 89, 104, 111, 129, 133, 135, 142, 173, 175, 176, 184, 195, 196, 225, 227, 236, 240, 249, 250, 274, 291, 292, 298, 306, 312, 341, 344, 367, 402, 407, 416, 422, 425

Dunfermline and District Charity Cup 452

Dunfermline and West Fife Hospital 462

Dunfermline Athletic Football Club *passim*

Dunfermline Athletic Supporters Council 425

Dunfermline City Pipers 462

Dunfermline Press 17, 82, 175, 237, 394, 414, 436, 460, 464

Dunlop (1982) 119

Dunn (Hibs) 304

Duns 84, 280

Dunterlie Park 199, 239

Durkin (Cowdenbeath) 231

Duthie (1955) 73, 281

E

East End Park ii, 2, 5, 11, 13, 14, 17, 19, 20, 21, 24, 32, 33, 34, 39, 40, 42, 43, 44, 45, 48, 49, 51, 54, 55, 56, 59, 61, 62, 66, 70, 73, 78, 80, 82, 85, 86, 90, 91, 92, 93, 95, 97, 99, 108, 110, 111, 124, 129, 130, 132, 133, 134, 141, 143, 144, 154, 155, 161, 164, 169, 171, 172, 173, 174, 175, 176, 178, 179, 180, 182, 184, 191, 192, 195, 197, 198, 201, 202, 209, 210, 211, 212, 213, 214, 215, 218, 219, 222, 223, 224, 225, 228, 231, 233, 234, 236, 237, 238, 240, 245, 247, 248, 253, 254, 255, 257, 260, 261, 262, 267, 270, 277, 278, 281, 282, 283, 286, 289, 290, 292, 293, 298, 302, 304, 306, 307, 308, 312, 316, 318, 322, 323, 326, 327, 329, 330, 331, 333, 334, 336, 341, 344, 346, 352, 358, 362, 363, 367, 370, 371, 375, 392, 393, 397, 398, 399, 402, 406, 408, 413, 416, 418, 419, 420, 424, 425, 432, 433, 437, 439, 440, 444, 449, 451, 452, 455, 460, 462, 464, 466, 468, 469, 472

Eastern League 23, 70, 80, 108, 196, 268, 467

Easter Road 43, 71, 91, 147, 165, 233, 307, 322, 439

East Fife 14, 19, 23, 53, 60, 86, 95, 100, 126, 128, 152, 204, 232, 240, 305, 306, 345, 378, 405, 431, 459, 461, 468

East Stirlingshire , 41, 60, 63, 65, 139, 202, 363, 431, 457

Edinburgh City 21

Edmiston (Dundee United) 58, 173

Edinburgh Evening News 91

Edwards, Alex 66, 67, 85, 86, 112, 123, 164, 171, 192, 197, 210, 225, 249, 267, 284, 289, 307, 341, 372, 384, 474

El Bakhtaoui, Faissal 39, 40, 104, 331

Elgin xiv, 19, 143

Elliot (Alloa) 420

European Cup Winners' Cup 71, 90, 245, 289, 433, 440

Evans (Wales) 296

Everton , 111, 155, 245, 429

Ewing (Partick Thistle) 217

479

F

Fair City 457
Fairs Cities' Cup 346
Falkirk 7, 23, 34, 41, 68, 70, 72, 79, 80, 86, 108, 131, 138, 139, 154, 198, 200, 204, 210, 226, 243, 248, 250, 252, 262, 307, 350, 352, 356, 361, 362, 406, 408, 413, 416, 417, 431, 457
Fallon (Celtic) 123, 372
Farm, George 16, 52, 86, 125, 165, 192, 210, 213, 220, 255, 256, 258, 383, 387, 397
Farningham, Ray 111, 252
Farquharson, Hugh 24, 166
Farrell, James 185, 187, 353, 408
Faulconbridge, Craig 399
Ferguson, Alex 66, 144, 164, 179, 197, 267, 292, 307, 332, 336, 346, 359, 392
Ferguson, Eric 62
Ferguson (referee) 290
Ferguson (1906) 251
Ferguson (1947) 354
Fernie (Celtic) 211
Ferranti Thistle 132
Ferrier (Motherwell) 356
Fife Ladies 462
Fife League 342, 457
Fife Select 86
Findlay (Rangers) 99
Finlay (East Fife) 152
Firhill 79, 102, 140, 217, 267, 292, 311, 422
Firs Park 41, 139
First Division 7, 12, 13, 14, 16, 23, 28, 34, 41, 53, 61, 85, 90, 117, 120, 123, 126, 138, 139, 154, 168, 169, 177, 195, 198, 200, 218, 222, 226, 236, 242, 243, 251, 252, 257, 271, 273, 284, 285, 287, 291, 299, 302, 306, 308, 318, 323, 344, 350, 352, 356, 361, 362, 364, 375, 398, 405, 407, 408, 411, 413, 415, 416, 421, 422, 430, 438, 440, 445, 447, 449, 456, 463, 465, 466, 468, 469
Fisher, Willie 268
Fitzpatrick (referee) 281
Flannigan (Hibs) 147
Fleming, Derek 298
Fleming, George 79, 164, 272
Fleming, Jim 297
Fleming (East Fife) 152
Fleming (Rangers) 95, 128, 293
Foote (referee) 66
Ford (Hearts) 171, 233
Forfar 5, 20, 48, 56, 60, 100, 111, 143, 173, 177, 205, 318, 358, 397, 406, 413, 420
Forrest, Bobby 119, 160, 198
Forrest, (Rangers, Aberdeen) 183, 333, 192, 197
Forsyth, Tam 111, 198
Forthbank Park 69
Forthbank Stadium 69
Frame (1930) 110
Fraser, Cammie 112, 162, 378, 440
Fraser, Jim 210, 220
Fraser, John 7
Fraser Provost 323
Fraser (1908) 4
Fraser (1926) 353
Fraser (Clyde) 109
Fraser (Dundee United) 36, 104
French, Hamish 18, 135, 176, 220, 432, 445

G

Galabank 35
Gallacher, Hughie 28, 305
Gallacher, Jackie 305
Gallacher, Paul 30, 44
Galston 438
Gardiner (Rangers) 99

Gardner, Pat 125, 192, 210, 225, 256, 258, 289, 343, 383, 384, 397
Garland (1926) 279
Gayfield 14, 25, 39, 363
Geggan, Andy 20, 27, 64, 65, 181, 191
Gemmill (Scotland) 364
Geoghegan (Aberdeen) 253
Gibb (1926) 353, 418
Gibson, Fred 185, 186
Gibson, Tom 283
Gibson, Willie 174, 206
Gibson (Clyde) 254
Gillespie, Jim 165, 253, 255, 330
Gilmour (1921) 205, 221
Glass, Stephen 161, 320, 422
Glasgow Herald 71, 90, 146, 262, 292, 378, 406
Glavin (Partick Thistle) 242
Glebe Park 22, 58, 154, 294
Glenbuck 452
Goldthorpe (Motherwell) 160
Goodwin (St Mirren) 18
Gordon, Jimmy 205, 221, 296
Gordon (Hearts) 270
Gough (England) 349
Gould (Celtic) 135
Gourlay (Kirkcaldy United) 325
Graham, David 206
Graham (Partick Thistle) 311
Grangemouth 457
Grant, Roddy 22, 298
Gray (1921) 205, 251
Gray (St Bernard's) 408
Gray (Third Lanark) 326
Greenock Morton 61
Greer (1905) 178
Greig (Rangers) 171
Gretna 322
Groves (Hibs) 148
Gymnasium 186

H

Hadky (St Mirren) 18
Haffey (Celtic) 123, 368
Hafnarfjordur 89
Halbeath end 40, 45, 281, 397
Hall, Alex 57, 130, 277, 309
Halligan (Hibs) 304
Halliwell, Bryn 322
Hamill (1981) 119
Hamilton Academical 61, 73, 161, 184, 305, 306, 308, 402, 420
Hamilton, Jim 105
Hamilton, Rowan 363
Hamilton (Cowdenbeath) 98
Hamilton (Hearts) 92
Hamilton (Hibs) 124
Hamilton (Kilmarnock) 247
Hamilton (1930) 278
Hammill, Adam 270
Hampden 13, 81, 128, 149, 150, 152, 184, 195, 256, 275, 322, 333, 337, 341, 343, 345, 347, 349, 356, 357, 358, 363, 364, 368, 376, 384, 412, 423, 427
Hannigan (Morton) 52
Hardie, Martin 44, 334, 371, 374
Hardie (1913) 309
Harkness (journalist) 99
Harper (Albion Rovers) 21
Harper (Aberdeen) 118, 261
Harris (1927) 97
Harris (1981) 119
Harrison (1936) 24
Hartford (West Bromwich Albion) 245
Hartson (Celtic) 188
Harvey (1909) 143
Harvey (1953) 53
Hawkshaw (St Johnstone) 299, 359
Haxton, Alexander 408
Hay, Davie 45, 89, 120
Hay (1908) 143, 190
Hayes (Inverness) 44

Hearts 33, 63, 71, 91, 92, 97, 118, 124, 140, 141, 143, 149, 150, 171, 212, 233, 240, 247, 249, 269, 270, 272, 275, 277, 297, 302, 343, 357, 359, 362, 363, 383, 409, 414, 431, 447
Hearts of Beath 143
Heddle, Ian 201
Hegarty (1981) 119
Hemmings (Cowdenbeath) 419
Henderson, George 48,95, 101, 152, 232
Henderson (Rangers) 183, 333
Henderson (referee) 233
Henderson (1981)
Herd (1908) 4
Herd (1926) 239, 293, 323, 353
Herrera (Inter Milan) 234
Herriot, Jim 54, 133, 140, 177, 183, 260, 273, 295, 359
Hetherston (Airdrie) 404
Hiernian 8, 21, 42, 49, 58, 60, 71, 91, 100, 107, 120, 124, 126, 127,128, 147, 148, 149, 165, 171, 175, 178, 184, 198, 233, 240, 244, 247, 268, 271, 280, 291, 297, 304, 306, 307, 308, 320, 322, 326, 330, 332, 335, 346, 357, 375, 405, 409, 427, 431, 456, 462
Higginbotham, Kallum 20, 392
Hillsborough 315, 449
Hippolyte, Myles 26, 33
Hogg (Aberdeen) 144
Holmes (Hearts) 409
Hood, Thomas 461
Hood (Celtic) 255
Hopkirk, David 207
Houston (Forfar) 111
Howitt (Motherwell) 66
Hughes (Alloa) 137
Hughes (Celtic) 255
Hunt, Noel 188, 274, 27
Hunter, Ian 66
Hunter, Jackie 196
Hunter (Motherwell) 356
Hunter (MP) 336
Hunter (1976) 287,
Hutt (1981) 119

I

Ibrox 49, 52, 61, 81, 93, 99, 135, 146, 254, 302, 333, 341, 347, 361, 362, 425, 426, 427, 433
Innes (Falkirk 243
Inter Cities Fairs Cup 155, 215, 216, 297, 319, 336
Inter Cities Fairs' Cup 329
Inverness 20, 36, 44, 142, 320, 364, 366, 371, 410, 412
Inverness Caledonian Thistle 20, 44, 320, 364
Irvine, Willie 241
Irvine (Dundee United) 236
Isasi (Zaragoza) 336
Izatt, David 3, 57, 185

J

Jack, Ross 71, 167, 227, 252, 290, 327
Jackson. Darren 132
Jackson (referee)
Jansen (Celtic) 135
Jefferies, Jim 40, 43, 191
Jenkins, Grant 119, 120, 132, 139, 203, 363
Johansen (Rangers) 146
Johnson (1981) 119
Johnston, Allan 19, 33, 104, 207, 240, 425
Johnston (1939) 78
Johnstone, George 100, 101, 152,153
Johnstone (Celtic) 179, 322

K

Karlsen, Geir 262
Keith (1947) 209
Kelly, Willie 100
Kelly (Celtic) 378
Kemp (St Johnstone) 299
Kennedy (Berwick) 260
Kennedy (Celtic) 368, 376
Kennedy (Clyde) 254
Kennedy (Livingston) 161
Kennedy (US President) 183
Kennedy (1919) 182
Kenny, Stephen 270, 320, 357
Kerr (Dundee United) 129, 249, 312
Kerr (Hamilton) 305
Kerray, Jim 50, 123, 234, 249, 299
Kilgannon, John 297, 307
Kilgannon (Stirling Albion) 162
Kilmarnock 14, 64, 66, 84, 85, 105, 120, 131, 234, 247, 248, 249, 267, 283, 297, 320, 322, 329, 333, 359, 399, 415, 426, 447
King's Park 60, 69, 117, 182, 344, 431, 443, 457
Kinnear, Davie 12, 241
Kinnell, Bert 209, 241, 354
Kinnell, George 86
Kinninmonth, Alex 242
Kirk, Andy 35, 44, 101, 152, 174, 226, 310, 370, 398
Kirkcaldy 90, 98, 139, 176, 189, 209, 256, 278, 342
Kirkcaldy United 70, 113, 251, 309, 325, 454
Kirkland (referee) 311
Klos (Rangers) 426
Knight, Willie 7, 13, 24, 84, 110, 134, 138, 168, 279, 294, 424, 443
Kozma, Istvan 223, 327

L

Lady's Mill Park 394
Laidlaw (Brechin City) 294
Laing, Derek 154
Laird (East Fife) 152
Langlands (Forfar) 205
Larsson (Celtic) 135, 423
Lassodie 452
Latto (St Johnstone) 431
Law (Scotland) 125, 171
Lawlor (Stirling Albion) 162
Lawrie (1900s) 159, 178
Lawson (Raith Rovers) 241
League Cup 14, 18, 19, 20, 21, 26, 27, 32, 33, 35, 36, 45, 48, 50, 53, 54, 58, 66, 71, 73, 77, 79, 85, 91, 93, 94, 95, 98, 99, 100, 104, 105, 107, 118, 123, 124, 126, 127, 128, 135, 146, 149, 150, 151, 152, 153, 171, 173, 184, 189, 195, 212, 232, 238, 240, 261, 302, 305, 320, 322, 357, 384, 393, 409, 425, 456, 459, 461, 468
League One 419
Leeds United 86, 336
Lees, Webber 126, 459, 466
Leggat (1930) 110
Leigh (Raith Rovers) 85
Leishman, Jim 31, 49, 76, 77, 105, 111, 119, 167, 202, 223, 227, 252, 262, 290, 310, 327, 357, 363, 406, 407, 413, 436, 447, 449, 464
Leitch, Scott 22
Leith 80, 304
Leith Amateurs 271
Lennox (Celtic) 397, 451
Leonard, Mike 204
Liddell (Liverpool) 196, 348, 458
Liddell (1911) 185
Liddle (Forfar) 111
Liney (Dundee) 314
Linton (Cowdenbeath) 226

Lister, Ian 210, 343, 383, 384
Livingston 4, 45, 132, 161, 322
Lochee 56, 178
Lochgelly 23, 56, 60, 70, 190, 235, 251, 254, 431, 447
Logan (entertainer) 220
Logie Green 134
Longridge, Jackson 26
Lovell (Dundee) 410
Love Street 184, 238, 284
Low (1908) 251
Low (1926) 109
Lowland League 41
Lunn, John 170, 171, 210, 213, 332, 336, 383, 384
Lyon (1885) 451

Mac/Mc

McAndrew (1930) 12, 110, 354
McArthur Ross 425
McArthur (East Fife) 128
McArthur (referee) 190
MacAskill (politician) 35
McAvennie (Celtic) 303
McBride, Joe 118, 131, 179, 223
McCabe, Rhys 36
McCall Ian 327
McCall, Jackie 101, 152, 348
McCallum Willie 242, 262
McCallum (Brechin) 294
McCallum (Motherwell) 66
McCarry (St Johnstone) 299
McCathie, Norrie 71, 105, 107, 154, 191, 201, 203, 227, 238, 252, 290, 327, 404
McCleary (1926) 7
McCormick (Third Lanark, Aberdeen) 54, 144
McCrae (Kilmarnock) 247
McCunnie, Jamie 357
McCurry (referee) 270
McDiarmid Park 364

MacDonald, Pat 283
MacDonald (Airdrie) 402
MacDonald (Prime Minister) 81, 138, 429
McDonald, Tommy 90, 150, 236, 243, 260, 280, 282, 286, 295, 368, 376
McDonald (Hibs) 126
McDonald (Motherwell) 89
McDougall (1908) 4
McDougall, Steven 174
McGairy, Tom 152
McGarr, Ernie 118
McGarrity (East Fife) 152
McGarty, John 383, 384
McGhee (Hibs) 147
McGillivray (Third Lanark) 54
McGinley (referee) 223
McGovern (1981) 119
McGovern (Ross County) 334
McGowan, Bob 24, 84, 166, 168, 218
McGregor, Allan 322
McGrogan, Felix 24
McGrory (Celtic) 97, 150, 180, 218, 244, 247
McGunnigle (referee) 416
McIlroy (Kilmarnock) 234
McInally, Arthur 6
McInally (Celtic) 28, 97, 180
McIntyre, Jim 45, 142, 174, 320, 370, 371, 398, 412, 427
McIntyre (Hibs) 149
McKane Park 70, 278, 440, 467
McKendrick (referee) 36
McKenzie 1925 55
McKenzie (referee) 178
Mackie, Ken 77, 262, 287, 330
Mackie (1923) 219
McKimmie (Aberdeen) 422
McKinlay (1950s) 58
McKinlay (journalist) 406
McLauchlan (Ayr United) 207
McLaughlan (1911) 4, 185

McLaughlin, John 133, 144, 273, 372
McLean, Adam 101, 152
McLean, Jim 66, 112, 214, 215, 333
McLean (Celtic) 97, 180
McLean (Raith Rovers) 176
McLeod (1903) 59
McLeod (Hibs) 147
MacLeod (Scotland) 136, 261
MacLeod (Celtic) 436
McLindon, Dan 260, 368, 376
McMahon (Hibs) 147, 148
McManus, Tam 320, 367
McManus (Dundee United) 249
McMenemy (Celtic) 315
McMillan, (Airdrie, Rangers) 212, 281
McMillan, (Prime Minster) 50, 92
McMorran (Third Lanark) 54
McNair (Celtic) 296, 315
McNamara, Jackie 104
McNaughton, Sandy 119, 120, 308
McNeil (Raith Rovers) 370
McNeill (Celtic) 62, 123, 171, 220, 255, 316, 372
McRae (Brechin City) 73
McRae (soldier)199
McSeveney, Willie 48, 232
McVeigh (Airdrie) 402
McWilliam, Gerry 73 302,349
McWilliam (Tottenham Hotspur) 318
McWilliams, Derek 107

M

Madden (referee) 26, 250
Mailer, Ron 141, 378, 440
Main (referee) 99,
Main (St Johnstone) 298
Maley (Celtic) 59, 180
Maloney (Celtic) 188, 322
Manchester United 53, 125, 172, 284, 318
Marcelino (Zaragoza) 336

Marshall (Celtic) 423
Marshall (Middlesbrough) 6
Marshall (Motherwell) 89,
Marshall (1924) 138
Martin, Bent 146, 210, 267, 336, 341, 384
Martin, Lewis 40
Martin (referee) 268, 323
Mason (Third Lanark) 326
Masterton, Gavin 310
Masterton (1926) 353
Maule (Raith Rovers) 209
Maxwell (Dundee United) 68
Mayes, Gerry 93, 99, 101, 126, 128, 152, 348
Meadowbank 132, 204, 406, 413
Mehmet, Billy 89
Meiklejohn (Partick Thistle) 283
Melrose, Harry 53, 90, 123, 124, 144, 155, 184, 204, 212, 217, 228, 236, 248, 259, 263, 280, 286, 295, 314, 321, 326, 329, 332, 335, 361, 365, 372, 378, 440, 473
Mendes, Junior 460
Mercer, Bob 172, 221
Mercer, Bonar 119, 204
Mercer, Wallace 149
Merchiston Park 63
Methil 95, 128, 204, 293
Methven (East Fife) 204
Michael Colliery 86
Middlesbrough 6, 23, 72, 172, 232, 315, 411, 450
Midland League 457
Millar, Marc , 91, 404
Millen, Ross 43
Miller, Eddie 185, 353
Miller, George 54, 92 118, 144, 155, 160, 242, 243, 295, 378, 440. 468
Miller, Jimmy 117, 173
Miller (1930) 278
Miller (Aberdeen) 449
Milne, Alexander 130

485

Mitchell, Barrie 210, 213, 330
Mitchell (Dundee United) 225
Mitchell (Kilmarnock) 399
Mitchell (1926) 353
Moffat, Michael 20, 40, 207, 208
Moffat (Airdrie) 181
Moffat (1903) 59
Moffat (1926) 61
Moir (Scotland) 348
Montrose 56, 178, 263, 280
Moodie, John 93, 98, 99
Moore, Allan 68, 91, 404, 422
Moore, Jordan 64
Moran (Falkirk) 248
Morris (Celtic) 407
Morris (Dundee United) 104
Morris (East Fife) 152
Morris (Raith Rovers) 352
Morrison Steve 119, 360
Morrison Stuart 132, 139
Morrison (1930s) 218,
Mortensen (Aberdeen) 297
Morton 52, 61, 143, 174, 175, 195, 222, 285, 298, 305, 343, 348, 402, 415
Morton (Rangers) 293, 296, 315, 349
Motherwell 32, 45, 52, 66, 79, 89, 97, 117, 120, 141, 160, 167, 177, 190, 195, 197, 232, 252, 280, 307, 332, 356, 409, 412, 430, 456
Mottram (referee) 422
Mowat (referee) 263
Moyes, David 327
Muir (1926) 109
Muir (1953) 231
Muir (Kilmarnock) 131
Muirton Park 299, 354, 414
Mullen (St Mirren) 18
Mullin (Albion Rovers) 181
Munro, Iain 31, 149, 176, 447
Murdoch (Celtic) 123, 179
Murphy, Danny 161

Murphy, John 464
Murray, Euan 311
Murray (Aberdeen) 118, 253
Murray (Airdrie) 100
Murray (Dundee United) 36
Murray (Hearts) 233
Murray (Queen of the South) 177
Murray (Rangers) 302, 347
Murray (Third Lanark) 54
Murray (1911) 185
Mutch (Arbroath) 20

N

Nakamura (Celtic) 188
Neilson (referee) 113
Neilson (Hearts) 240
Nelson (1981) 119
Nep Stadium 282
Newcastle United 84, 152, 186, 349
Newlands-Robertson (1911) 185
New Zealand 249, 460
Nicholas (Celtic) 436
Nicholl, Jimmy 176
Nicholson, Barry 45, 89, 275, 364, 366, 410
Nicol (1903) 59
Ninian Park 88, 296
Nisbet, Kevin 21, 102
Nithsdale Wanderers 55
Niven (Rangers) 140
Niven (1885) 451
Northern League 5, 56, 59, 121, 159, 178, 190, 251, 342

O

O'Boyle, George 22, 71, 167, 298
O'Brien, George 48, 136, 169, 173, 211, 231, 281
O'Brien, Colin 184, 308
Ochilview 41, 64, 286, 439
Ogston (Aberdeen) 144

Old Boys Club 444
Olympiakos 192
O'Neill (Celtic) 376
Orgryte 133
Orion 56
O'Rourke (St Patrick's Athletic) 90
O'Rourke (Hibs) 165
P

Palmerston Park 273, 398
Parkhead 177, 188, 220, 244, 255, 258, 271, 376, 407
Pars United 41
Partick Thistle 79, 102, 103, 140, 174, 217, 242, 267, 272, 283, 287, 292, 311, 313, 357, 361, 362, 384, 425, 438
Paterson, Sandy 55, 353, 418
Paterson (1920s) 7, 235
Paterson (1930s) 110, 294
Paterson (referee) 273
Paton, Bertie 19, 68, 91, 104, 124, 135, 154, 163, 164, 176, 179, 192, 225, 231, 247, 256, 272, 273, 289, 298, 323, 329, 343, 346, 383, 384, 402, 409, 422, 436, 441, 446, 447, 462, 464
Paton and Baldwin Ladies 462
Peacock (Celtic) 376
Pearson (1914) 199
Pearson (Clyde) 254
Pearson (Aberdeen) 297
Pearson (St Johnstone) 330
Peebles, George 85, 90, 92, 112, 117, 122, 123, 131, 140, 141, 169, 183, 212, 215, 217, 234, 236, 243, 284, 286, 295, 299, 314, 321, 326, 329, 333, 368, 378, 440
Peebles Rovers 280, 438
Penman (Raith Rovers) 98
Penman (Rangers) 146
Persson (Dundee United) 129, 133
Pertwee, Jon 220

Peterhead 26, 33, 331
Petrie, Stewart 68, 91, 402
Petrie (Arbroath) 280
Petrov (Celtic) 423
Phillips Harold, 469
Phillips (referee) 302
Philp (1911) 185
Philp (East Fife) 152
Phinn, Nick 226, 398
Pitblado (1900s) 4, 59, 113, 121, 178
Pittodrie 118, 125, 190, 295, 297, 364, 422
Porter, Martin 443
Porterfield (Raith Rovers) 86
Puis (Anderlecht) 213

Q

Queen (bookmaker) 8
Queen of the South 16, 132, 139, 169, 177, 206, 262, 273, 341, 361, 371, 393, 398, 406, 445
Queen's Park 13, 80, 198, 201, 296, 304, 315, 337, 363, 438
Quigley (Hibs) 147
Quinn (Celtic) 59

R

Rae (1900s) 199
Rafferty, Stuart 227
Raith Rovers 5, 7, 13, 14, 16, 23, 40, 43, 68, 70, 73, 82, 85, 86, 90, 98, 125, 135, 138, 139, 174, 176, 186, 189, 201, 209, 226, 233, 240, 241, 244, 250, 252, 256, 258, 278, 279, 305, 306, 308, 325, 334, 342, 345, 350, 352, 361, 362, 370, 371, 374, 405, 408, 414, 415, 418, 422, 441, 447, 457, 459, 461, 466
Ramsay (Armadale) 235
Rangers 7, 12, 21, 24, 43, 49, 52, 61, 66, 73, 93, 94, 99, 100, 107, 111,

118, 123, 126, 141, 146, 149, 150, 155, 167, 171, 183, 186, 197, 205, 212, 221, 227, 228, 244, 245, 247, 254, 267, 270, 272, 273, 280, 284, 290, 293, 296, 297, 302, 303, 304, 307, 308, 315, 319, 329, 333, 341, 347, 348, 349, 355, 357, 361, 362, 383, 384, 393, 399, 407, 409, 410, 416, 419, 426, 427, 430, 433, 456, 468
Rarity (1930) 110
Rattray (Raith Rovers) 70
Ravn (Aberdeen) 297
Real Zaragoza 336
Recreation Grounds 159
Recreation Park 137, 420
Redmond (1938) 69
Reid, John 166, 281
Reilly, Felix 58, 117, 173, 306
Reilly (Hibs) 126
Rennie (East Stirlingshire) 202
Reynolds (1885) 451
Rhind (Queen's Park) 80
Rhodes, Andy 107, 404
Rice, Brian 441
Richmond (referee) 35, 275
Riddell, Gary 360, 448, 449
Ritchie, John 22, 460
Ritchie (1926) 323, 353
Ritchie (Morton) 285
Robertson, Bobby 201
Robertson, Craig 62, 238, 360, 422
Robertson, Hugh 79, 125, 129, 179, 225, 258, 292, 341, 343, 384
Robertson, Jimmy 108
Robertson, Tom 59, 185
Robertson (1938) 69
Robertson (Falkirk) 70, 80
Rolland, Andy 86, 416, 417
Rooney (Dundee United) 249
Rooney (St Johnstone) 330
Rooney (Clyde) 406
Ross, Craig 188

Ross (Stenhousemuir) 286
Ross (1885) 451
Rosyth , 10, 15, 42, 78, 447
Rough (Partick Thistle) 242
Rougvie, Doug 71, 167, 227
Roxburgh (Partick Thistle) 272
Rugby Park 84, 120, 267
Rundell (Arthurlie) 239
Russell, John 425
Rutkiewicz, Kevin 371
Ryan, Andy 18, 39, 392

S

Salmond (referee) 39
Salton, John 119, 416
St Bernard's 60, 72, 108, 134, 186, 187, 309, 408, 431
St Johnstone 7, 24, 56, 57, 60, 64, 118, 124, 126, 142, 146, 159, 298, 299, 321, 327, 330, 343, 354, 357, 359, 384, 398, 402, 414, 431, 447
St Mirren 18, 21, 30, 34, 45, 77, 105, 154, 175, 177, 210, 242, 284, 302, 321, 329, 345, 347, 360, 361, 367, 412, 438, 460
St Patrick's Athletic 90
Sandison (1885) 451
Sandison (Airdrie) 107
Savage (1908) 190
Schools Engagement Programme 425
Sclater (1930) 110
Scott, Jim 416
Scott, Jocky 146, 346, 415, 436, 447
Scott (Ireland) 315
Scott (Fakirk) 79
Scott (Hibs) 325
Scott (Rangers) 393
Scottish Cup , 5, 7, 8, 16, 17, 19, 25, 32, 81, 88, 89, 97, 108, 112, 113, 118, 125, 138, 147, 148, 150, 162, 181, 186, 191, 192, 199, 200, 201,

205, 210, 212, 226, 233, 237, 240, 243, 250, 251, 254, 255, 256, 257, 258, 260, 261, 262, 263, 267, 270, 271, 272, 273, 275, 277, 278, 279, 280, 282, 283, 284, 285, 286, 287, 290, 291, 292, 293, 295, 297, 302, 303, 304, 305, 306, 307, 312, 314, 320, 321, 326, 329, 332, 333, 335, 336, 338, 340, 341, 343, 345, 346, 356, 357, 359, 361, 364, 367, 368, 369, 372, 373, 376, 377, 378, 381, 383, 384, 385, 387, 397, 405, 407, 410, 423, 427, 428, 432, 433, 440, 447, 456, 459, 473

Scottish Football Association 28, 187, 263, 348, 364, 378, 402, 426, 462

Scottish League 5, 6, 7, 18, 19, 20, 21, 22, 23, 25, 26, 27, 28, 30, 32, 33, 35, 36, 41, 45, 48, 50, 53, 54, 57, 60, 66, 70, 71, 79, 85, 91, 93, 95, 98, 99, 100, 104, 105, 107, 108, 118, 126, 127, 134, 135, 146, 149, 150, 151, 152, 159, 171, 172, 173, 180, 184, 186, 189, 190, 192, 195, 199, 205, 210, 212, 214, 219, 233, 234, 239, 240, 242, 243, 244, 251, 254, 258, 261, 271, 272, 273, 279, 286, 291, 294, 297, 302, 303, 305, 306, 309, 314, 316, 322, 325, 329, 342, 350, 354, 357, 358, 363, 393, 399, 406, 407, 408, 411, 418, 425, 430, 431, 438, 441, 450, 454, 456, 459, 461, 467

Scottish League Cup 18, 19, 20, 21, 26, 27, 32, 33, 35, 36, 45, 48, 50, 53, 54, 71, 79, 85, 91, 93, 95, 98, 99, 100, 104, 105, 107, 118, 126, 127, 135, 146, 149, 150, 151, 152, 171, 173, 184, 189, 195, 212, 240, 261, 302, 305, 322, 357, 393, 425, 456, 459, 461

Scottish Premier League 30, 34, 44, 275, 320, 327, 409, 410, 426, 460

Scottish Qualifying Cup 5, 113, 143, 186, 187, 277

Scottish Referee 190, 251
Scott's Park 70, 113, 325
Scoular (Alloa) 137
Scullion (1981) 119
Seawright (Airdrie) 100
Second Division 5, 6, 7, 10, 13, 14, 19, 23, 25, 28, 31, 42, 60, 61, 70, 77, 90, 108, 111, 112, 126, 129, 130, 132, 134, 136, 138, 172, 175, 177, 186, 190, 195, 199, 201, 202, 205, 209, 228, 232, 239, 254, 257, 261, 271, 273, 277, 279, 280, 281, 284, 285, 287, 291, 294, 306, 309, 325, 326, 344, 348, 350, 353, 354, 363, 375, 393, 397, 405, 408, 411, 418, 429, 430, 431, 432, 438, 445, 450, 454, 456, 461, 465, 467
Shankland (Cowdenbeath) 98
Shankly, Bob 8, 141, 452
Shaw, Graham 468
Shaw, Greg, 68
Shaw (Hibs) 128
Shawfield 28, 112, 164, 254, 414
Shearer (1921) 205
Shearer (Aberdeen) 422
Shearer (Rangers) 212, 333
Sheffield United 439
Shevlane (Hearts) 92
Shields, Greg 367
Shielfield Park 260
Shortt (Stenhousemuir) 352
Simmons, Stephen 420
Simonsson (Orgryte) 133
Simpson (Celtic) 214
Simpson (Rangers) 393
Sinclair, Chris 154
Sinclair, Jackie 54, 77, 133, 215, 273, 299, 326, 333
Sinclair (1921) 60
Skerla, Andrius 423
Skinner, Bobby 28, 29, 55, 61, 97, 109, 137, 175, 180, 222, 239, 254,

257, 271, 293, 323, 350, 352, 353, 418, 445, 466
Slavin, Maurice 57, 185, 277
Slovan Bratislava 351
Smith, Alex 124, 129, 139, 140, 162, 197, 215, 236, 248, 260, 272, 282, 295, 314, 319, 326, 332, 345, 378, 409, 433, 440
Smith, Allan 64
Smith, Andy 298, 404, 409
Smith Callum 19
Smith Chris 370
Smith, Mark 154, 290
Smith Paul 71, 327
Smith, Stirton 101, 152
Smith, Trevor 139
Smith (Aberdeen) 192
Smith (Dundee) 126 141
Smith (Hibs) 147
Smith (1885) 451
Smith (1921) 221
Sneddon (Kilmarnock) 247
Somerset Park 64, 207, 308, 331
Southern League 15
Speedie (Dumbarton) 186
Spittal (1908) 4
Spittal (Dundee United) 104
Stanton, Pat 119, 120, 165, 198, 308
Stark (Celtic) 62, 303,
Station Park 111, 205, 358, 406, 413, 420
Steaua Bucharest 303
Steel (Scotland) 348
Stein, Jimmy 55, 239, 257, 293, 304, 350, 353, 429
Stein 8, 9, 32, 50, 54, 77, 85, 88, 92, 112, 123, 124, 132, 141, 150, 155, 162, 165, 171, 177, 181, 189, 214, 215, 220, 234, 243, 249, 258, 260, 280, 282, 286, 295, 299, 316, 321, 333, 345, 368, 372, 376, 381, 384, 397, 407, 433, 440, 463, 466

Stenhousemuir 10, 41, 60, 64, 110, 239, 279, 282, 286, 352
Stevenson (Hibs) 346
Stevenson (Motherwell) 356
Stevenson (1927) 293
Stewart (East Fife) 152
Stewart (Raith Rovers) 209
Stewart (St Mirren) 345
Stewart (1885) 451
Stewart (1981) 119
Stillie, Derek 364
Stirling 26, 33, 49, 53, 63, 69, 98, 117, 154, 161, 162, 182, 226, 307, 308, 314, 318, 344, 358, 361, 430, 456, 457
Stirling Albion 26, 33, 49, 53, 69, 98, 117, 154, 161, 162, 226, 307, 308, 314, 318, 358, 361, 430, 456
Strachan, Hugh 172, 219, 221, 293
Strang (1903) 59, 121
Stranraer 189, 191, 280, 397, 419
Struth (Rangers) 93, 293
Sunday Post 55, 63, 72, 78, 97, 126, 138, 196, 218, 239, 349, 450
Sunderland , 86
Sutherland, Ben 5
Sutton, Chris 49, 188, 426
Sutton, Joe 7, 109, 219, 350, 353
Sutton, John 105
Sweeney, John 376, 378, 440
Syme, Robert 24, 84, 278
Syme (referee) 107, 225

T

Tade (Raith Rovers) 142, 371
Tait (1981) 119
Tannadice 36, 56, 104, 196, 225, 236, 249, 268, 291, 306, 312, 347, 402
Tansey (Inverness) 44
Taylor, David 24, 421
Telfer (Rangers) 284, 302

Terris, Sandy 461, 466
The Hawthorns 245
Third Division 237, 430
Third Lanark 6, 50, 54, 109, 136, 144, 166, 273, 326, 344, 347
Thompson, Gary 363
Thomson, Alec 168, 244
Thomson, Dave 376, 378, 379, 440
Thomson, David 439
Thomson, James 454
Thomson Jimmy 176, 255
Thomson, Robert 331
Thomson (Celtic) 81, 97
Thomson (Dundee) 296
Thomson (1903) 59, 121
Thomson (1911) 185
Thomson (1981) 119
Tinkler (Livingston) 161
Tod, Andy 45, 91, 188, 298
Toddie (1885) 394, 451
Tosh (Queen of the South) 398
Totten, Alex 436, 447
Tottenham Hotspur 349
Townhill 196, 348, 458
Tracey (Cowdenbeath) 57
Troup (Everton) 429
Turnbull (Hibs) 125
Turner, Kyle 21, 102, 103
Turner (1926) 353
Tynecastle 107, 126, 233, 270, 277, 297, 321, 332, 343, 345, 357, 359, 363, 409

U

Ujpest Dozsa 282, 286
Ure (Arsenal) 125
Uriarte (Athletic Bilbao) 319
Urquhart (referee) 121
Uruguay 458

V

Vail (1903) 59
Valencia 111, 215
Vale of Leven 60, 237, 438
Vardar 150
Vaughan (Raith Rovers) 250
Victoria 56, 81, 159, 334, 461
Vincent, James 33
Volunteer Park 235

W

Waddell (Dundee) 314
Waddell (Kilmarnock) 146, 234, 329, 348
Walker, Scott 460
Walker (Celtic) 62, 227, 303
Walker (Hearts) 92, 277
Wallace, Gordon 415
Wallace, Ryan 39, 40, 41, 310
Wallace (Hearts, Celtic) 92, 124
Wallace (1974) 262
Wankdorf Stadium 439
Ward (Partick Thistle) 438
Watson, Jimmy 131, 318
Watson, John 107, 132, 139, 201, 202, 203, 252, 290, 363, 406, 413
Watson (MP) 138, 235
Watson (Motherwell, Rangers) 160, 183
Watson (1930s) 279, 294
Watt (referee) 100
Webb (referee) 152
Webster (referee) 307
Wedderburn, Nat 36
Weir (Hibs) 149
Wellesley Juniors 81
Welsh (Airdrie) 281
Wembley Stadium 337
Wemyss League 143
West Bromwich Albion 111, 245, 289, 474

491

Westwater, Ian 62, 135, 402, 406, 409
Westwood (1885) 451
Wharton (referee) 82, 112, 179, 267, 333
Whigham (Falkirk) 243
White (Rangers) 146
Whitelaw (Partick Thistle) 140
Whitelaw (1914) 130
Whittle, Alex 40
Whyte, Andy 101, 152
Whyte, Hugh 174, 202,
Whyte, William 443
Whyte (1980) 119, 285
Wigtown and Bladnoch 259
Wilcox (1981) 119
Wilkie (1911) 185
Williams, Owain Fon 311
Williamson, Jackie 368, 376
Williamson, Ryan 26, 392
Williamson, Willie 257, 271, 293
Wilson, Andrew 6, 10, 13, 23, 60, 63, 72, 137, 172, 182, 200, 224, 284, 296, 315, 317, 323, 349, 353, 403, 411, 431, 450,466
Wilson, Peter 24, 180, 375, 405, 432, 462, 465, 472
Wilson, Scott 89, 161, 269, 270, 410, 470
Wilson, Tommy 223
Wilson, Willie 84
Wilson (Aberdeen) 125
Wilson (Celtic) 77
Wilson (Cowdenbeath) 121
Wilson (Prime Minister)
Wilson (Rangers) 183, 212, 333, 347
Wilson (St Mirren) 284
Wing (Dundee United) 129
Wolverhampton Wanderers 144, 152, 283
Woodburn (Rangers) 93, 323
Woodrow, Ray 436
Woods, Callum 398
Woods (1903) 59

Wright, Alec 118, 165, 220, 330
Wright, Keith 149
Wright, Tommy 99, 101, 209
Wright (Procurator Fiscal) 424
Wylie, Robert 10
Wyllie (1900s) 143, 186
Wyllie (1926) 353

Y

Yacamini (referee) 173
Young, Darren 89, 105, 322, 364
Young, Derek 34, 188
Young (Kirkcaldy United) 113
Young (Raith Rovers) 85
Young (Rangers) 393
Young (1981) 119
Younger, Tom 459
Younger (Hibs) 128

Z

Zurawski (Celtic) 322

Years

1885 280, 437, 442, 451
1890 452
1902 56, 121, 159, 187
1903 59
1905 113, 178
1908 5, 190
1911 24, 185, 186, 187
1912 57, 60, 254, 364, 408, 438
1914 3, 24, 42, 130, 199, 291, 304, 325, 467
1915 11, 60, 70, 80, 108, 431
1916 3, 148, 325
1919 23, 51, 63, 72, 182, 200, 224, 431, 467
1921 6, 23, 60, 137, 172, 205, 221, 349, 411, 431, 450
1922 13, 134, 237

1924 7, 24, 137, 138, 175, 235, 304, 337
1925 29, 55, 109, 137, 352, 353
1926 28, 29, 61, 81, 180, 222, 237, 239, 254, 271, 323, 337, 350, 418, 429, 445
1927 81, 84, 97, 257, 293
1930 110
1931 24, 81, 344
1935 84, 168, 218, 424
1936 24, 166, 375, 421, 458
1938 15, 69, 378, 403, 405, 462
1939 10, 15, 78, 403, 432, 465
1940 15
1945 25, 69, 196
1947 12, 209, 241, 354
1948 98, 283, 461
1949 85, 100, 101, 126, 127, 151, 152, 153, 466
1950 32, 64, 94, 305, 348, 458, 459
1951 93, 96, 99, 439, 459
1952 14, 32, 96, 458
1953 16, 32, 48, 95, 231, 316, 458
1954 32, 58, 136, 173, 232, 316, 372, 439, 458
1955 32, 112, 117, 281, 306, 430, 456, 469
1957 73, 112, 393
1958 53, 82, 112, 131, 217, 222, 284, 302, 318, 358, 439
1961 8, 88, 90, 122, 141, 150, 162, 212, 260, 273, 280, 295, 321, 345, 365, 368, 369, 376, 377, 381, 384, 427, 440
1962 85, 112, 124, 140, 155, 177, 215, 216, 236, 243, 259, 282, 286, 329, 347, 410, 463
1963 50, 54, 92, 123, 139, 171, 183
1964 8, 41, 88, 133, 144, 234, 249, 299, 312, 333, 410
1965 66, 129, 214, 247, 273, 297, 307, 319, 326, 332, 335, 346, 359, 372, 373, 384, 427

1966 79, 164, 179, 197, 214, 247, 272, 336, 346, 433
1967 16, 86, 125, 267, 292, 312, 341, 433
1968 16, 17, 192, 210, 225, 238, 258, 338, 340, 343, 383, 384, 385, 387, 396, 397, 423, 447
1969 146, 213, 245, 246, 256, 289, 351
1970 52, 118, 233, 255
1973 77, 86, 242, 468
1975 8, 195, 204
1979 184, 195, 285, 416, 417
1981 119, 120, 308
1982 8, 198
1983 19, 111, 202, 413, 414
1984 202, 203
1985 47, 88, 132, 139, 201
1987 49, 62, 238, 449
1988 290, 303, 360, 407, 449
1989 71, 167, 223, 227, 252, 299, 310, 406, 413, 449
1990 22, 31, 447
1992 22, 49, 322, 409, 415, 436, 447
1995 68, 298, 370, 422
1996 176, 238, 298, 402
1997 91, 135, 441
2000 19, 34, 240, 452
2003 49, 410, 426
2004 45, 89, 240, 274, 275, 364, 366, 423, 427
2006 105, 106, 322, 324
2007 161, 269, 270, 320, 357, 367, 412, 427, 428
2011 30, 35, 44, 142, 226, 334, 355, 370, 374
2013 41, 64, 65, 310, 355, 419, 420
2014 40, 43, 191, 419
2015 36, 39, 104, 181, 207, 208
2016 20, 27, 36, 41, 331
2017 19
2018 26, 33, 392, 425, 426
2019 18, 21, 102, 103, 240, 250

www.ingramcontent.com/pod-product-compliance
Lightning Source LLC
Chambersburg PA
CBHW052040220426
43663CB00012B/2388